Treasurer's Guidebook

A Practitioner's Guide

Second Edition

Steven M. Bragg

For more information about AccountingTools® products, visit our Web site at www.accountingtools.com.

ISBN-13: 978-1-64221-013-2

Printed in the United States of America

Table of Contents

Preface

The treasurer is responsible for a broad range of activities, which include bank relations, cash forecasting, investments, fund raising, risk management, and even insurance. These are critical high-risk activities, so the treasurer must also have a detailed knowledge of processes, controls, and treasury management systems. The *Treasurer's Guidebook* addresses all of these topics and more, with the intent of giving a new treasurer a solid grounding in how to perform the job.

The book is divided into three sections. In Chapters 1 through 10, we focus on the core treasury activities, which begin with an overview of treasury management and then walk through all major job functions. In Chapters 11 through 13, we cover ancillary treasury functions that may not always be in included in a treasurer's job description. These functions are insurance, credit management, and working capital management. In Chapters 14 through 17, we cover the treasury back office, which deals with administrative functions.

You can find the answers to many questions about treasury activities in the following chapters, including:

- What are the differences between cash sweeping and notional pooling?
- How do I create a cash forecast?
- Which investment strategy should I follow?
- How can I reduce the risk of foreign exchange fluctuations?
- Which types of insurance does my business need?
- How do I create an internal credit rating system for customers?
- What is the proper accounting for a hedging transaction?
- What are the components of a treasury management system?
- Which controls should be applied to the various treasury transactions?

The *Treasurer's Guidebook* is designed primarily for professionals, who can use it as a reference tool for all aspects of the treasurer's job, from accounting to risk management.

Centennial, Colorado
August 2018

About the Author

Steven Bragg, CPA, has been the chief financial officer or controller of four companies, as well as a consulting manager at Ernst & Young. He received a master's degree in finance from Bentley College, an MBA from Babson College, and a Bachelor's degree in Economics from the University of Maine. He has been a two-time president of the Colorado Mountain Club, and is an avid alpine skier, mountain biker, and certified master diver. Mr. Bragg resides in Centennial, Colorado. He has written the following books and courses:

7 Habits of Effective CEOs
7 Habits of Effective CFOs
7 Habits of Effective Controllers
Accountant Ethics [for multiple states]
Accountants' Guidebook
Accounting Changes and Error Corrections
Accounting Controls Guidebook
Accounting for Casinos and Gaming
Accounting for Derivatives and Hedges
Accounting for Earnings per Share
Accounting for Income Taxes
Accounting for Intangible Assets
Accounting for Inventory
Accounting for Investments
Accounting for Leases
Accounting for Managers
Accounting for Stock-Based Compensation
Accounting for Vineyards and Wineries
Accounting Procedures Guidebook
Agricultural Accounting
Behavioral Ethics
Bookkeeping Guidebook
Budgeting
Business Combinations and Consolidations
Business Insurance Fundamentals
Business Ratios
Business Valuation
Capital Budgeting
CFO Guidebook
Change Management
Closing the Books
Coaching and Mentoring
Conflict Management
Constraint Management
Construction Accounting

Corporate Bankruptcy
Corporate Cash Management
Corporate Finance
Cost Accounting (college textbook)
Cost Accounting Fundamentals
Cost Management Guidebook
Credit & Collection Guidebook
Crowdfunding
Developing and Managing Teams
Effective Collections
Effective Employee Training
Employee Onboarding
Enterprise Risk Management
Entertainment Industry Accounting
Fair Value Accounting
Financial Analysis
Financial Forecasting and Modeling
Fixed Asset Accounting
Foreign Currency Accounting
Fraud Examination
Fraud Schemes
GAAP Guidebook
Governmental Accounting
Health Care Accounting
Hospitality Accounting
How to Audit Cash
How to Audit Equity
How to Audit Fixed Assets
How to Audit for Fraud
How to Audit Inventory
How to Audit Liabilities
How to Audit Receivables
How to Audit Revenue
How to Conduct a Compilation
How to Conduct a Review

(continued)

How to Run a Meeting
Human Resources Guidebook
IFRS Guidebook
Interpretation of Financial
Statements
Inventory Management
Investor Relations Guidebook
Law Firm Accounting
Lean Accounting Guidebook
Mergers & Acquisitions
Negotiation
New Controller Guidebook
New Manager Guidebook
Nonprofit Accounting
Oil & Gas Accounting
Optimal Accounting for Cash
Optimal Accounting for Payables
Partnership Accounting
Payables Management
Payroll Management
Performance Appraisals

Project Accounting
Project Management
Property Management
Accounting
Public Company Accounting
Purchasing Guidebook
Real Estate Accounting
Records Management
Recruiting and Hiring
Revenue Management
Revenue Recognition
Sales and Use Tax Accounting
Succession Planning
The Balance Sheet
The Income Statement
The MBA Guidebook
The Soft Close
The Statement of Cash Flows
The Year-End Close
Treasurer's Guidebook
Working Capital Management

On-Line Resources by Steven Bragg

Steven maintains the accountingtools.com web site, which contains continuing
professional education courses, the Accounting Best Practices podcast, and
thousands of articles on accounting subjects.

The *Treasurer's Guidebook* is also available as a continuing professional education
(CPE) course. You can purchase the course (and many other courses) and take an
on-line exam at:

www.accountingtools.com/cpe

Chapter 1
Treasury Management

Introduction

The treasury function administers the financial holdings and obligations of an organization. This is a major task in an organization that has millions or even billions of dollars in cash and investments, receivables, payables, and debt. Even in a smaller organization, these tasks are essential to the ability of a business to continue in operation. Consequently, though treasury is an administrative function, it is still one of the most vital parts of a business.

In this chapter, we address the responsibilities of the treasury function as a whole and the treasurer in particular, how treasury fits into the organizational structure of a business, and numerous management issues.

Treasury Responsibilities

Ultimately, the treasury function is responsible for the liquidity of a business – the entity must always be able to pay its bills on time, and have sufficient cash available to support its plans. This is the core function of the treasury department. However, this one item represents an excessively simple view of the responsibilities of the group, which can be quite broad in a larger and more complex organization. The following list provides a more detailed view of treasury responsibilities:

- *Control cash*. The department marshals the flow of cash through the organization, ensuring that there is always sufficient liquidity to meet current and future financial obligations.
- *Issue credit*. A business may loan funds to its customers via accounts receivable. Since this is essentially a financing function, the examination and granting of customer credit may be assigned to the treasurer.
- *Mitigate risk*. The department is frequently tasked with management of all insurance policies, which allows certain risks to be shifted to a third party. In addition, the treasury group may use hedging instruments to offset the variability in value of certain foreign exchange and interest rate transactions.
- *Obtain a return*. The treasury staff may be expected to earn a significant return on invested funds, though this responsibility can contravene the more important requirement to safeguard funds. The usual outcome is that a modest return is expected, while the safety of invested funds is paramount.
- *Raise funds*. The department is responsible for obtaining debt financing at reasonable rates, and for selling shares under reasonable terms.
- *Safeguard funds*. The department is responsible for investing excess funds appropriately, with an overriding objective of not suffering a capital loss.

Treasurer Job Description

The treasurer manages the treasury department. If the department is a small one, then the treasurer may be directly responsible for many tasks that would normally be assigned to specialists within the department. In order to give the broadest possible scope to the treasurer's job description, we will assume that the treasurer personally handles most activities within the department. Under this assumption, we derive the following job description for a treasurer:

Operational Requirements

- *Forecast cash flows.* This information is needed to pinpoint when extra cash is needed, and when excess cash will be available, which then drives the treasurer's planning to obtain additional financing or invest funds.
- *Manage working capital.* A key component of the cash forecast is working capital, which is the net amount of current assets and current liabilities. The treasurer is not usually responsible for the management of these items (except for the extension of credit to customers), but can model how changes in operational decisions will result in different working capital requirements.
- *Aggregate cash.* Cash may be separated into a number of bank accounts throughout an organization. The treasurer must create a system to aggregate this cash so that it can be properly deployed to meet the operational and investment needs of the business.
- *Invest funds.* Excess cash should be invested so that any investment vehicles mature in time for the cash to be available for operational needs. This can result in several tranches of investments, some of which are available on short notice, while other tranches cannot be immediately accessed.
- *Invest pension funds.* If the company has a pension plan, the treasurer is responsible for investing it within the guidelines stated in the plan.
- *Obtain debt and equity financing.* The treasurer works with the Chief Financial Officer (CFO) to raise funds as needed. This can include the sale of stock to the investing public or through private placements, as well as obtaining loans from many types of lenders or selling bonds. These activities will likely require the maintenance of ongoing relations with a number of intermediaries, such as investment bankers and brokers.
- *Hedge transactions.* The interest rates and foreign exchange rates to which a business is subjected can vary unfavorably, so the treasurer can engage in hedging activities to mitigate the risk of loss, as well as other risk mitigation strategies.
- *Issue credit.* The treasurer can control the credit policy that forms the basis for issuing credit to customers, and may make the decisions to grant or withhold credit to specific customers. This gives the treasurer a valuable control over one of the larger elements of working capital.
- *Maintain insurance policies.* Since the treasurer is already using hedging to deal with certain types of financial risk, it is logical to extend the risk man-

2

agement concept and have the treasurer oversee all insurance policies. This can include ongoing adjustments to policy coverage to ensure that changes in the business are reflected in its insurance coverage.

- *Advise management.* The treasurer must take a leading role in all financial planning activities, to ensure that a realistic assessment of the funding requirements of the business is included in budgets.

Third Party Requirements

- *Maintain bank relationships.* The treasurer is the primary point of contact between the organization and the banks with which it does business. In this role, the treasurer can consolidate banking services and negotiate for preferential pricing.
- *Oversee outsourcing relationships.* If any tasks within the treasury department have been outsourced, the treasurer oversees the outsourcing relationships, including entering into contracts and measuring performance.

Management Requirements

- *Oversee the treasury staff.* The treasurer hires and fires treasury employees, rates their performance, approves training, promotes employees when suitable, schedules activities, and engages in other actions normally associated with management.
- *Maintain a system of policies, procedures, and controls.* This is a particularly important job responsibility, since the treasury department may handle very large amounts of cash, which cannot be misplaced or stolen. This is one of the few areas in a business in which 100% process compliance is needed.

A treasurer should have a Bachelor's degree in accounting or finance, as well as 10+ years of progressively more responsible treasury experience. The individual should have a thorough understanding of forecasting, cash management, hedging activities, bank account management, and international transactions.

Treasury Organizational Structure

In a smaller organization where there is no CFO or treasurer, all treasury tasks are handled by the controller. Once treasury tasks become too overwhelming for the accounting staff, a CFO is usually hired, and the treasury tasks are transferred to this individual. Since a CFO cannot personally handle all of the treasury tasks of a growing business, they are soon transferred to a treasurer. Thus, the treasurer is usually the last person hired in the accounting and finance management troika of the CFO, controller, and treasurer.

Once a treasurer has been hired, it does not mean that the full range of treasury activities is automatically placed under this person's direct supervision. Instead, there is usually a long-term trend toward centralization of treasury activities, which tends to follow these steps:

1. *Focus on investment benefits.* The treasurer needs to prove the benefits of having a treasury, and so offers to centralize investments so that higher returns can be obtained.
2. *Focus on borrowing costs.* The treasurer takes over debt management, so that high-cost debt can be replaced. Again, the focus is on contributing to the profit of the business.
3. *Focus on netting benefits.* The treasurer offers to provide netting services to reduce the amount of foreign exchange fees being incurred by the subsidiaries.

Up to this point, the focus has been on the more obvious profit improvements. The next step is to point out to senior management that a possible cost area to eliminate is the duplicative treasury positions at the local level, replacing them with a core group of highly-qualified employees in a central treasury department. This will result in one or more of the following changes:

- The treasury group takes over all banking relationships, likely eliminating some banks entirely.
- The treasury group centralizes the management of hedging transactions.
- The treasury group takes over the credit function.
- The treasury group establishes and operates a centralized payables system.

Thus, over a period of time, the treasury organizational structure evolves into a key administrative function that centralizes numerous financial activities.

A variation on the gradual centralization concept is that larger organizations may still need to maintain local treasury staffs. This is because local expertise may be needed in certain markets, where knowledge of local regulations is essential. This is especially important when there are currency controls. There may also be a need to maintain a staff in one or more of the major currency markets, such as London, New York, and Tokyo, as well as to operate regional groups in the approximate time zones in which there are company operations. In short, absolute centralization may not occur – pockets of treasury staff may be required in select locations.

Given the overwhelmingly financial nature of the treasurer's job, this position always reports to the CFO, alongside the controller. However, the treasury function itself contains numerous activities that cannot all report to the treasurer, for control reasons. Instead, the function is split up into three areas, each of which reports to a different person. These areas are as follows:

- *Front office.* This group focuses on decision making and initiating transactions, and reports to the treasurer. Examples of its tasks include funding, investments, risk management, and bank interactions.

- *Back office*. This group executes transactions. Examples of its tasks include processing transactions, confirmations, settlements, and account reconciliations. Given the essentially accounting orientation of this group, it reports to the controller. By doing so, there is also a clear separation of duties between the front office and back office.
- *Middle office*. This group is tasked with monitoring all treasury activities and reconciling the transactions initiated by the front office with the actual transactions processed by the back office. Its activities can include risk reporting, limit monitoring, valuation, and performance evaluations. This group necessarily must operate independently from the other two groups and so usually reports to the CFO. Alternatively, this group could report to the chief risk officer (if such a position exists), or even to the internal audit director.

Treasury Organizational Chart

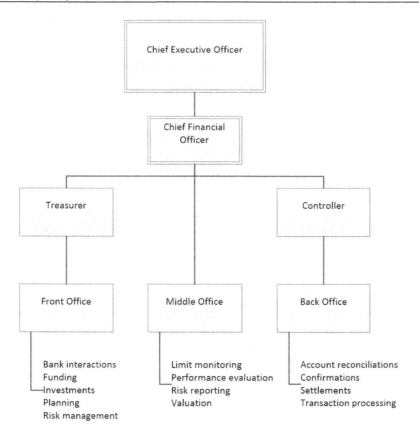

In addition to the reporting breakdown noted in the preceding organizational chart, the credit department reports to the treasurer.

Treasury Centralization

A smaller organization with a few locations likely has a decentralized treasury system, where cash is received and paid out locally. The management of cash is probably a minor side function of the accounting staff. As an entity expands in size, a number of factors will appear that make centralization of the treasury function an increasingly attractive option. These factors are:

- *Cash visibility.* There may be a large amount of cash sequestered in local bank accounts that is not earning interest at all, or which is being invested at very low rates of return.
- *Geographic boundaries.* Expansions to the business may result in operations being conducted in countries where cash flows are controlled. If so, it may be difficult to extract funds from some locations.
- *Risk of loss.* When there are large amounts of cash floating in the system with minimal oversight and controls, there is a greater risk of loss.
- *Cost effectiveness.* If individuals in each location are engaged in treasury activities, this represents a very inefficient use of staff time, since it is duplicative.
- *Service providers.* There may be an overabundance of service providers scattered among the subsidiaries, resulting in a large administrative burden to manage them.

These issues may lead management to contemplate the installation of a centralized treasury function. The following factors all argue in favor of centralization:

- *Controls.* It is much easier to maintain a strong system of controls over treasury activities when all parties engaged in those activities are located in one place. It is also easier to provide consistent training to employees, so that a consistent process flow (with integrated controls) is followed by everyone.
- *Expertise.* When treasury functions are centralized, a small number of specialists can be hired who are experts in such activities as account management, investments, and hedging. These specialists can improve the efficiency of existing processes, and are also qualified to engage in more complex transactions than would be possible at the local level.
- *System costs.* A centralized treasury unit can afford the initial cost and ongoing fees associated with the best treasury management systems, which might be a prohibitively expensive alternative if these systems were to be installed in every local facility.
- *Service providers.* The number of service providers can be reduced by concentrating services with a few providers whose services most closely align with the needs of the company. With fewer providers, it is also easier to manage these relationships. Further, concentrating the company's business with a few providers allows for the possibility of volume discounts.

However, there are also issues that can detract from the ability of a business to centralize its treasury function. Some of these issues can make centralization either impossible or quite difficult to enact. These concerns are:

- *Company culture*. Perhaps the largest issue is the presence of a "hands off" corporate culture, where local managers are encouraged to act independently from corporate oversight. In this environment, any move to centralize treasury functions may be looked upon as an infringement of local rights, and will receive a strong pushback.
- *Location*. It can be difficult to attract a qualified treasury staff if the company's headquarters is located in an area well away from urban centers. In such a location, the highly-trained people needed for treasury will be outside of their normal networks and support structures.
- *Regulations*. The corporate headquarters may itself be located in a country that has onerous cash controls or tax structures that would interfere with the proper conduct of treasury functions.
- *Technological diversity*. The different computer systems used by the subsidiaries may not easily integrate with the treasury management system that corporate management wants to install in a centralized location. This is a particular problem when a business is constantly adding subsidiaries through acquisitions, since each new acquiree must be integrated into the centralized treasury system. The issue can usually be overcome eventually by constructing custom interfaces between the various systems.

The preceding concerns can result in a hybrid solution, where only a small number of the more complex treasury transactions are centralized. For example, foreign exchange and hedging transactions could be centralized, while cash management and banking relationships could be left for local subsidiaries to handle. This approach allows for the use of a small number of specialists to handle transactions for which there is a risk of loss if handled incorrectly.

At the other extreme from a hybrid or localized solution is the in-house bank. Under this approach, a central group literally acts as a bank for the subsidiaries, offering account management, funding, investment services, netting, foreign exchange, and hedging services. An in-house bank is responsible for managing all treasury-related services for the business, with the subsidiaries funneling their treasury needs through this group. An in-house bank requires a high level of in-house treasury expertise, and so is not usually found outside of the largest entities. The main benefit of an in-house bank is the reduction in overall banking costs by aggregating a number of small transactions into a few larger ones. In addition, the use of an in-house bank results in detailed information about cash flows, which can be useful for the tax planning related to international transactions.

Treasury Outsourcing

It is possible to outsource some parts of the treasury function. This usually occurs during the growth stages of a business, when it cannot afford the services of a complete treasury staff. Instead, a business can shift one or more of the following functions to a third party, such as a bank, while retaining a treasurer to oversee activities:

- Cash flow management
- Cash pooling services
- Foreign exchange deal execution and confirmation
- Payable and receivable netting

If the business grows further, it can then afford to shift some or all of these functions back in-house. However, some functions may be outsourced again at a later date if it becomes apparent that the treasury staff is incapable of processing transactions without a high error rate.

The Performance Culture

The treasury function tends to evolve as a business increases in size and complexity, which means that it gradually becomes responsible for more activities, and has a larger impact on company profitability. In this evolving role, it is entirely possible that the treasury staff will constantly be in reactive mode, where employees work a great deal of overtime, have constant deadlines, and are continually cleaning up prior mistakes.

A better approach is to develop a performance-based culture, where the treasury staff is encouraged to automate or outsource some processes, thereby giving them more time to deal with the most critical activities, and to examine processes for improvements. Here are several ways to develop a performance culture:

- *Systems.* Invest in the best possible treasury management system, and ensure that the treasury staff is thoroughly trained in how to use it. This may require an investment in a "best of breed" system when not all of the purchased features are actually needed; by doing so, the department can grow into the system as its responsibilities gradually increase over time.
- *Processes.* Ensure that the staff is thoroughly trained in how each process within the department functions, who is responsible for each task, and why controls are being used. Also, have an error reporting system in place that brings any issues to the attention of the staff at once, coupled with a process for examining these errors and taking corrective action. Given the risk of major financial losses, there should be zero tolerance for errors.
- *Metrics.* Post all relevant metrics for the treasury department, and discuss them with the staff at regular intervals. Employees should be aware of trends in these metrics, and how their actions can improve the results.

- *Staff.* The preceding activities may uncover cases in which certain employees are unable or unwilling to learn new systems and processes. If so, these individuals should be rotated out of the department or let go, and replaced by new employees who are more willing to take the proactive approach needed to develop a performance culture.
- *Teamwork.* Foster a culture of teamwork, where the treasury staff routinely engages in cross-functional activities, both within and outside of the department, in order to improve departmental results. This triggers a better knowledge of company processes, and also cross-trains employees.
- *Service focus.* The treasury department is essentially a service function within an organization – it assists other parts of the business. Given this orientation, the treasury staff should constantly be required to communicate with their counterparts throughout the organization, to see if there are unmet needs that the treasury department can address.
- *Open books.* The treasury staff has a profound impact on a company's financial statements, especially in the areas of interest expense, interest income, and unhedged gains and losses. Accordingly, the treasurer should present the company's monthly financial statements to the staff, and discuss the reasons for the company's performance in detail. Doing so develops buy-in by the staff in regard to their role in supporting the organization.

Schedule of Activities

The treasurer should collect information about when treasury activities must be completed, reports issued, transactions initiated, and so forth, and organize them into a department-wide schedule of activities. It is quite likely that each member of the treasury department is well aware of when their work is supposed to be done, so this may not initially appear to improve the situation in the department. However, there are three good reasons for creating it:

- *Vacations.* Employees leave for vacations and forget to tell their replacements about due dates.
- *Departures.* An experienced employee leaves the company, and the rest of the department has to scramble to figure out when that person's work should be done.
- *MBWA.* This is management by wandering around. The treasurer can use the schedule of activities to chat with the staff about upcoming due dates. This may sometimes detect issues that would otherwise have been forgotten, and is also an excellent excuse to talk to the staff, which may bring up other issues worth investigating.

Process Reviews

There are a number of processes that run through the treasury department. For example, it is involved with customer credit, cash receipts, investments, and hedging. These processes change periodically to accommodate changes elsewhere in the business. Each incremental change may alter the efficiency with which transactions can be completed, usually making them slower. Over time, a series of these incremental changes can seriously impact the efficiency of the department.

To counteract the ongoing decline in process efficiency, schedule periodic process reviews that are designed to root out inefficiencies and streamline processes. A typical review involves documenting each step in a process, including an examination of all forms, reports, and controls, as well as the movement of paperwork between personnel. The process review team then documents errors created by the system, the time required to complete an average transaction, and the queue time during which a transaction sits between processing activities. Based on this information, the team configures a new process flow that may contain any of the following improvements:

- *Eliminate approvals*. A process may require multiple approvals, where only one is needed.
- *Eliminate data*. A transaction may call for the entry of more data into the treasury system than is actually needed.
- *Process moves*. A process may require the movement of paperwork between employees, so concentrate activities with fewer people. By doing so, queue times are eliminated from the process.
- *Automation*. In a few cases, it may be possible to shift manual processing to an automated solution. However, only use this approach when there is a solidly favorable cost-benefit tradeoff. In many cases, an expensive automation solution will not yield much of an overall benefit to the company as a whole.
- *Report reductions*. Are reports really needed? In many cases, a process may result in a variety of reports being issued that are not used by the recipients. Interview recipients to determine which reports can be eliminated, or which information on specific reports can be eliminated.
- *Eliminate controls*. Some controls are redundant, and so only interfere with a process without reducing risk. However, only eliminate controls after having consulted with the auditors, who may have a different opinion.

A process review is a time-consuming activity that involves a number of people both within and outside of the treasury department. For this reason, it is impossible to engage in a continual review of processes. Instead, consider scheduling reviews on a rotating basis, so that a single process is reviewed in detail perhaps every six months to a year. The exact review interval will depend upon the amount of change within a company. If little has changed in the past few years, there may be little reason to invest in a process review. However, if there have been substantial changes, such as acquisitions, it may be necessary to engage in an ongoing series of reviews.

Department Layout

If the treasury department appears to be operating at near-maximum capacity, with employees working furiously throughout the day, then it may be possible to squeeze some extra capacity out of the department by altering its layout. The goals are a combination of improving the workflow within the department and reducing the amount of employee travel time within the building. Here are several layout improvements to consider:

- *Printers*. Provide employees with decent-quality printers that are positioned adjacent to their computers. Doing so eliminates the startling amount of travel time between employee work areas and a central printer; employees may travel back and forth many times during the day. Continue to retain the central printer for higher-speed printing jobs.
- *Furniture*. If there is unused furniture or office equipment cluttering the department, then dispose of it. By doing so, it is possible to improve the traffic flow within the department and (better yet) compress the department into a smaller work area, so that total travel times within the department are reduced.
- *Clustering*. Monitor the travel patterns of employees within the department. It is likely that some people must interact with others on the far side of the department, or must access filing cabinets located well away from where they sit. Based on this information, configure the department to cluster to-gether those employees who interact most frequently. This may also result in the central document storage area being broken up and distributed closer to users.
- *Cubicles*. It is difficult to reconfigure the department into clusters when everyone uses cubicles, since they require skilled furniture movers to disas-semble and rebuild. Instead, eliminate the cubicles in favor of clusters of desks, which can more easily be moved around in the department.
- *Carts*. An enhancement on the concept of clustering is to issue mobile office carts to employees. They can then shift any documents they need from fixed storage locations into the carts, and roll the carts to where they are working. If employees switch to different workstations during the day, they can just move the carts along with them.
- *Supplies*. Stock an office supplies cabinet, and place it in the middle of the treasury area. Then forbid anyone to keep an excess "stash" of office sup-plies at their desks. By doing so, it is possible to eliminate much of the clut-ter in employee work areas.

The reconfiguring recommendations just noted do not preclude the use of offices. There is still a need for private meetings from time to time, as well as meeting rooms. However, the proportion of offices to the general work area assigned to the department should be low.

Once a realignment of the department has been completed, undertake a formal review of the situation about once a year, which may even involve the use of a consultant who specializes in office workflow. In addition, make minor reconfiguration tweaks to the office layout whenever an opportunity presents itself, possibly at the suggestion of an employee, or as the workload shifts among employees.

The improvements outlined in this section will be much less useful in situations where there is clearly excess capacity in the department, since the incremental improvement in efficiency afforded by changing the layout will only create a moderate increase in the level of available capacity.

Skills Review and Training

It is common practice to decide which treasury employees are deficient in certain skill areas, and then give them training in those areas. However, doing so can involve a considerable amount of additional (and expensive) training, much of which may never be used. If a company pays for some portion of an employee's college education, then this cost-benefit effect becomes even more glaring. In short, many training programs result in employees learning skills for which they have no use within the company.

A more prudent view of training is to use an error tracking system to determine where employees require additional training *in their current jobs*, and apply the exact amount of specific training to reduce the number of errors that they are causing. Or, consider linking training to specific upgrades that will be made to the department's systems. For example, a department's error tracking system reveals that the staff is not using the on-line ACH payments feature on a bank's website, resulting in the issuance of more expensive wire transfers. The treasurer has a trainer come to the company's offices to train the staff for a few hours in this feature, as well as to monitor their usage of it over the next few days. As another example, a treasurer has just upgraded the treasury management system to a new version of the same software. She pays the software supplier to send a consultant to the company to give users a training session on the specific changes that were made to system features, and how best to take advantage of them.

In short, avoid broad-based training, such as paying for finance degrees at the local university, or sending employees to conferences. Instead, expend funds on training that very specifically improves the operations of the department. Also, training is more effective if conducted on-site, where employees can use it immediately. It may be more expensive to bring in consultants to conduct such training, but the results easily offset the costs.

Because of the need to engage in extremely specific training, it is nearly impossible to create a long-term training plan for employees. Instead, training needs are usually uncovered and addressed in the short term. The only case where employees are involved in a longer-term training plan is when someone will be promoted to a different position, and so must engage in a course of study to learn all aspects of the new position.

Summary

We have noted that the roles and responsibilities of the treasurer and treasury department will evolve over time. This does not mean that the treasury department will inevitably be centralized into a core group of experts. It is quite possible that several factors outlined in this chapter will halt the drive toward centralization, resulting in a somewhat more dispersed treasury function. If so, the job description of the treasurer will be reduced, and may involve a large number of "dotted line" relationships with local accounting and treasury departments. If so, the skill set of the treasurer should include a much higher ability to enact change through persuasion, since this person's absolute authority over the treasury function may be reduced.

Chapter 2
Bank Relations

Introduction

The treasurer is the main point of contact between an organization and its banks. In this role, the treasurer needs to decide upon the appropriate number of banks to use, how to maintain an ongoing dialog with each one, and how to negotiate the key terms of banking arrangements. These issues and more are covered in the following pages.

> **Related Podcast Episode:** Episode 124 of the Accounting Best Practices Podcast discusses lender relations. It is available at: **accountingtools.com/podcasts** or **iTunes**

Bank Centralization

A treasurer may inherit a position that is burdened with a vast number of banking relationships. This can be a problem, since the treasury staff may have to deal with an array of loan covenants, overlapping collateral requirements, and bank accounts from which it is difficult to extract cash. The situation can also arise from an acquisition, where the acquiree has a large number of banking relationships. If so, the treasurer should certainly pursue a target of reducing the number of banks. There are several reasons for doing so:

- *Administration*. The treasury staff must keep track of a large number of relationships. Reducing the number of relationships reduces the amount of low-value administrative time.
- *Technical savvy*. Smaller banks generally have not made the investment in technology that large banks can make, so a company may find that it cannot engage in certain activities with smaller banks, such as account sweeping, zero balance accounts, or self-directed electronic payments.
- *Aggregation benefits*. When banking transactions are spread among many banks, no one bank is receiving sufficient business from the company to warrant special attention. By centralizing banking activities with just a few banks, there is more of an incentive for the remaining banks to provide more attentive service, and possibly provide volume discounts.

Ideally, there should be a small group of banks, with one *relationship bank* providing the bulk of all banking services to the company. This bank typically provides a substantial line of credit, manages most of the company's bank accounts, and handles any cash concentration requirements.

When deciding upon a strategy for reducing the number of banks, the treasurer should identify the relationship bank, and focus on shifting its bank activity primarily to that bank. This analysis will likely result in a plan to gradually shut down accounts and loans with non-critical banks. These accounts and loans are then moved to either the relationship bank or a small number of secondary banks that provide services that the relationship bank cannot handle. For example, the relationship bank may not be able to provide checking accounts in Africa, so a secondary bank based in that region is brought in to handle this specific requirement.

Banker Dialog

Banks are much more likely to enter into long-term cooperative relationships with a company when the treasurer treats them as openly as possible. This means setting up a reporting schedule and sending the required information to the bank exactly on schedule, every time. In addition, it makes sense for the treasurer to personally meet with the assigned bank representative at regular intervals; this extra "face time" is needed to discuss any additional topics with the representative, as well as to build relations that may go on for years. These meetings are also useful for educating the bank's representative in the mechanics of how the company operates, its key customers and suppliers, competitors, and so forth.

The preceding points do not mean that the treasurer should overwhelm a bank with detail. It is critical to establish the correct amount of information flow, and then to maintain it for a long time. Otherwise, the bank representative might be buried with so much detail that it is not possible to see the key issues that are really impacting a business.

The following additional points can be used to establish a reasonable slant to the information being provided to a bank:

- *Excessive optimism.* Bankers are constantly being bombarded with overly optimistic statements from their customers, claiming excessively high sales and profit levels. Bankers respond well when a modest growth rate is suggested, for which there is a reasonable expectation of success. This shows that the management team (or at least the treasurer) has sufficient experience to understand that the best possible projection is rarely achieved.

- *Surprises.* Bankers do not want to continually receive happy messages from their customers, followed suddenly by a major earnings shortfall or other disaster. Instead, if the treasurer sees issues looming in the near future, it is best to bring them up with the bank as soon as these issues become probable. That way, the bank will not be blindsided when a negative event actually happens, and so can formulate an appropriate response well in advance.

- *Expected loan drawdowns.* Bankers appreciate it when they have reasonable warning of when a customer wants to draw down a portion of its available credit. If there is no need for a portion of a line of credit (other than to act as a reserve), tell the bank. By doing so, the bank can more accurately plan for how to use its capital.

Frequency of Reporting

Though we have just noted that timely financial reporting be made to the bank, this does not necessarily mean that reports should be issued every month. A more appropriate reporting interval is quarterly. The reason is that there will be an occasional month of poor results, which might be flagged by a banker. However, these poor results tend to be averaged out over multiple months, so a quarterly financial statement might offset one bad month with two better periods. The intent is not to keep financial information away from the bank; rather, to avoid triggering short-term panic attacks that will soon be offset by the next month's results.

Bank Fees

Banks charge many types of fees, which may not appear large on a monthly basis, but which will add up over time. The treasurer should be aware of the rates being charged, and track these rates on an annual trend line to discern any rate changes. Examples of the rates that may be charged include the following:

Per-Transaction Fees

- Automated Clearing House (ACH) fee per payment processed
- Check processing fee per check processed
- Deposit fee per deposit processed
- Lockbox fee per check processed
- Not sufficient funds fee
- Overdraft fee
- Printed report fee
- Wire transfer fee per payment transaction

Periodic Fees

- Monthly account fee
- Monthly cash concentration sweep fee
- Monthly lockbox fee
- Monthly wire transfer capability fee

The treasurer may be tempted to squeeze banking fees down to the absolute minimum, thereby earning kudos from senior management. However, bankers need to earn a living too, and so will look askance at any customer that routinely engages in penny pinching. They may not feel compelled to provide the best service to such a customer, and may not even want to continue doing business with it over the long term. Consequently, it can make sense to discuss fees with bankers, just to let them know that the fees are being watched – but to let them earn reasonable profits from their business with the company.

Despite having just pointed out that banks should be allowed a reasonable profit, we do not advocate allowing them to impose fees with no protest. Instead, keep track of which fees are resulting in the largest costs for the company, and make note of these fees during periodic meetings with bankers. For example, a hardware store allows its customers to pay with checks, which is a service that many of its customers take advantage of. The result is 1,000 checks per month, for which the company's bank charges a $0.20 processing fee, or $200 per month. This amount constitutes 30% of the company's total banking fees, so the treasurer regularly points out to the bank that this one fee is of the most concern to him. The bank also has an inordinately high wire transfer fee, but the treasurer does not care, since the company almost never issues wire transfers.

Loan Covenants

Bankers like to impose loan covenants, which essentially allow them to call a loan if the customer breaches the covenants. Examples of covenants are maintaining a certain minimum current ratio or cash balance, or not being able to pay dividends. If these covenants are set anywhere near their current actual levels, there is an excellent chance of a covenant breach. If there is a breach, the bank may impose additional fees, increase the interest rate on its line of credit, and add other covenants. An increase in fees is especially likely if a loan was originally granted at a somewhat below-market rate, since a covenant breach now allows the bank to increase its interest rate to a level closer to the market rate.

Given these issues, it is best to either avoid covenants entirely or (more likely) negotiate the most liberal possible covenants, so there is less risk of a breach. The best opportunity for avoiding covenants is to maintain a long-term relationship with the bank, since the bank is more likely in this case to waive covenant violations, with a view toward maintaining a profitable long-term relationship with the company.

Collateral

When setting up a line of credit and other debt for a customer, banks like to include in their loan agreements a comprehensive collateral clause, entitling them to virtually all company assets in the event of a loan payment default. This type of clause is to be avoided or at least so narrowly defined that the bank is only permitted access to certain asset classes. By doing so, the company can still use certain assets as collateral on other loans, such as a factoring arrangement in which a factor uses the company's accounts receivable as collateral.

If the bank insists upon using all company assets as collateral, this presents a problem when the company approaches other lenders to obtain additional loans. Since these lenders cannot reduce their risk by gaining access to collateral, they must instead charge higher interest rates.

Account Signers

A potential administrative burden for the treasurer is the accuracy of the list of account signers. When a new person is authorized by the company to sign checks, a signature card must be forwarded to the applicable bank. In addition, the bank may require a copy of a Board resolution, authorizing the addition of the person to the account.

Changes in account signers may seem minor, but can be a notable problem when there are many bank accounts. If a person leaves the company but is not removed as an authorized signer, this leaves open the risk of the departing person taking check stock with him and illegally signing additional checks. Also, if a bank does not receive notice of a replacement signer, the bank may reject submitted checks that contain the replacement person's signature. To avoid these issues, have the human resources staff include a point in their employee termination checklist, reminding them to notify the relevant banks if a departing employee was a check signer.

> **Tip:** It can make sense to include in the treasurer's work schedule a note to verify the check signer records at quarterly intervals.

Credit Assessment

A bank usually conducts a credit assessment on its customers at annual intervals. This assessment is conducted more frequently if there are special events that may impact the perceived creditworthiness of a customer. Examples of these special events are:

- A major acquisition
- The reporting of an unusually large loss
- A large unplanned capital expenditure

Assessments follow a standard pattern of reviewing the financial statements and forecasted budget for a customer, possibly coupled with a bank audit that conducts a more detailed examination of the customer's financial records. In addition, the bank discusses the projected cash requirements of the customer for the upcoming year. There is a particular emphasis on the size and reliability of cash flows, since cash flows support debt repayments.

When the relationship involves a substantial line of credit, the bank may elect to conduct a more detailed analysis. This may include a walk-through of the customer's facilities, discussions with management regarding company prospects, and perhaps the use of independent analyst reports (for publicly-held entities). Items of particular concern that can impact cash flows may be examined in detail, such as:

- The accounts receivable aging, with an emphasis on older unpaid invoices
- Details of bad debts recognized in the past year
- The accounts payable aging, with an emphasis on older unpaid invoices
- The inventory detail, with an emphasis on low-turnover items
- The historical ability to achieve forecasted results
- Any outstanding lawsuits, with an emphasis on likely outcomes and the size of payouts

- The amount of risk exposure that has not been mitigated with insurance
- The adequacy of fixed asset replacement plans
- The quality of assets used as collateral
- The credit ratings given to the company's debt instruments by credit agencies

Based on the outcome of this credit assessment, the bank settles upon a maximum line of credit that it is willing to offer the customer, perhaps accompanied by several covenants. In addition, the bank may require a certain amount of collateral in order to mitigate its risk. Further, the bank may mandate that the customer purchase from it all associated banking products, such as all checking accounts, savings accounts, lockboxes, wire transfer services, and so forth.

Causes for Change

It is relatively rare event to switch away from the relationship bank. The activities and systems of the treasury department are so interwoven with those of the bank that a change can be a wrenching experience. For example, all bank accounts must be shifted to the replacement bank along with all data feeds, while debt arrangements must be renegotiated. Consequently, there are few reasons sufficiently large to make it worthwhile to institute a change. Some possible situations that may call for a change are:

- *Acquisitions.* One or more acquisitions are made that rapidly expand the banking requirements of the company well beyond what its relationship bank can offer. For example, an acquisition may be located in a region where the bank has no branches, or a spate of acquisitions suddenly makes it necessary to use a cash concentration product – which the bank does not have.
- *Lending shortfalls.* The company wants to grow quickly, and the existing bank is unwilling to provide the additional loans needed to help fund the expansion. Alternatively, the bank is unwilling to part with certain restrictive collateral or covenant requirements. This is one of the more common reasons for changing to a new bank.
- *Gradual expansion.* There may be no single event that triggers a change to a new bank. Instead, the treasurer finds that the business is gradually expanding in size, which increases its need for borrowing services. The company will likely engage in workarounds for a certain period of time, but eventually concludes that the effort of maintaining a relationship exceeds the benefits being gained from it.

Summary

The key to bank relations is to treat a relationship like a well-organized speech. Use a reasonable forecast to tell the bank how the company is going to perform, and then report back that the company produced the expected results. This is similar to a speech, where the speaker tells the audience what to expect, and then delivers on the promise.

If results are worse than expected, do not hold back this information. The bank should be informed as soon as possible, and then kept in the loop while the management team takes corrective action. This keeps the trust level very high, and makes it easier to engage in a long-term relationship, despite the occasional performance bump.

Chapter 3
Cash Concentration

Introduction

A key treasurer task is to collect and concentrate incoming cash as quickly as possible, so that it is made available for operational and investment purposes. There are several cash aggregation services available from banks that can assist in this process. One approach, called cash sweeping, moves cash into a central concentration account; this is useful for centralized payment and investment systems. An alternative, notional pooling, aggregates cash from multiple accounts for investment purposes, without actually shifting the cash into a concentration account. We will explore the mechanics of these two cash concentration systems in this chapter, as well as other topics related to these systems.

Related Podcast Episode: Episode 220 of the Accounting Best Practices Podcast discusses how many bank accounts to use. It is available at: **accounting-tools.com/podcasts** or **iTunes**

The Need for Cash Concentration

Many organizations have a large number of highly dispersed locations that collect or disburse cash. The classic example is a chain of retail stores, each of which collects cash and checks every day, and forwards them to a local bank account. If the treasurer were to leave the cash in these accounts untouched, they would not earn any interest income for the company. In these situations, it is necessary to find a way to concentrate the balances in the various accounts in order to maximize use of the cash.

There is a temptation *not* to concentrate cash balances, for concentration requires either an automated bank system (for which the fees are significant) or the ongoing daily monitoring and movement of cash balances by the treasurer. However, the cost of unused cash can be quite substantial. Follow these steps to determine the cost of cash that remains in non-interest-bearing bank accounts:

1. *Determine the average account balance.* This information is available as an end-of-day account balance on the most recent bank statement. Add up the end-of-day balances for all days in the month and divide by the number of reported days.
2. *Determine the interest rate.* If the company has debts that it could pay down with the excess cash, then use the interest rate that the company is paying on this debt. If there is no debt, use the interest rate that the company is current-

ly earning on its short-term investments (which is usually lower than the debt interest rate).

3. *Calculate lost earnings.* Multiply the average account balance by the interest rate to arrive at the cost of unused cash.

In most cases, the treasurer will want access to residual cash to cover periodic spikes in the demand for cash. This means that the interest rate on short-term investments is the most reasonable rate to use for determining the cost of residual cash, rather than the interest rate on debt; the treasurer would never actually use the cash to pay down debt, since doing so creates a risk of not having enough cash on hand.

Another way of looking at the cost of a widely-dispersed set of bank accounts is the cost of overdrafts charged by the bank when an account balance turns negative. In the current market conditions, a company is lucky to obtain 2% interest on its short-term investments, but will be charged at least 10% interest on any bank overdrafts. If there is no cash concentration system in place, the bank is entitled to charge interest on all overdraft situations. Conversely, a cash concentration system will set all account balances to no worse than zero, so that overdraft charges are no longer possible. Thus, if a company has a history of debit balances in some of its bank accounts, the elimination of expensive overdraft interest charges may justify the cost of a cash concentration system.

EXAMPLE

Suture Corporation has four subsidiaries, all of which are allowed to manage their funds locally. Subsidiary D has a history of having negative cash balances, which has led to a significant amount of bank overdraft charges. In the past year, the average account balance and interest income or expense associated with each subsidiary is noted in the following table, where interest income is earned at 2% and overdrafts are charged at 10%:

Subsidiary	Average Cash Balance	Applicable Interest Rate	Annual Interest Income / Expense
A	$82,000	2%	$1,640
B	30,000	2%	600
C	17,000	2%	340
D	-45,000	10%	-4,500
Totals	$84,000		-$1,920

In short, the 5x difference between the interest income paid by the bank and its bank overdraft charge virtually eliminates all interest income that the company might otherwise earn.

The treasurer investigates the possibility of a cash concentration system, and finds that a key benefit is the automatic cross-funding of accounts with negative balances from those accounts with credit balances, thereby eliminating the overdraft charge. For the past year, the result would have been a 2% rate of income on the entire $84,000 company-wide average cash balance, which is $1,680. Thus, there would have been a net increase of $3,600 in interest income by switching to a cash concentration system, where Suture goes from $1,920 of net interest expense to $1,680 of interest income. This increase in interest income is calculated prior to the imposition of any bank fees related to running the cash concentration system.

Yet a third benefit of cash concentration is the reduction in investment fees. When a single large investment is made from a concentration account, a company pays only a single transaction fee to initiate the transaction. If, however, cash is invested locally from many accounts, a transaction fee will be imposed for each investment made from every account. Thus, investment costs can be radically reduced when cash is pooled into a single location.

Cash Sweeping

A cash sweeping system (also known as physical pooling) is designed to move the cash in a company's outlying bank accounts into a central concentration account, from which it can be more easily invested. Cash sweeps are intended to occur at the end of every business day, which means that quite a large number of sweep transactions may arise over the course of a year.

Cash sweeping can be fully automated as long as a company keeps all of its bank accounts with a single bank, where the bank can monitor account balances. Since several banks now span entire countries, it is not especially difficult to locate banks that can provide comprehensive sweeping services across broad geographic regions.

The Zero Balance Account

One way to implement a cash sweeping system is the *zero balance account* (ZBA). A ZBA is usually a checking account that is automatically funded from a central account in an amount sufficient to cover presented checks. To do so, the bank calculates the amount of all checks presented against a ZBA, and pays them with a debit to the central account. Also, if deposits are made *into* a ZBA account, the amount of the deposit is automatically shifted to the central account. Further, if a subsidiary account has a debit (overdrawn) balance, cash is automatically shifted from the central account *back* to the subsidiary account in an amount sufficient to bring the account balance back to zero. In addition, subsidiary account balances can be set at a specific target amount, rather than zero, so that some residual cash is maintained in one or more accounts.

There are three possible ZBA transactions, all of which occur automatically:

- Excess cash is shifted into a central account
- Cash needed to meet payment obligations is shifted from the central account to linked checking accounts
- Cash needed to offset debit balances is shifted from the central account to linked accounts

The net result of a ZBA is that a company retains most of its cash in a central location, and only doles out cash from that central account to pay for immediate needs.

EXAMPLE

Suture Corporation has a ZBA arrangement where three accounts used by local facilities are linked to a cash concentration account. At the end of Monday, the three accounts have the following balances, along with associated transfer activity:

Account	Ending Balance	To/From Concentration Account	Transferred Amount	Ending Account Balance
A	$45,000	To	-$45,000	$0
B	-12,000	From	+12,000	0
C	39,000	To	-39,000	0
	$72,000		-$72,000	$0

The ZBA system has extracted funds from accounts A and C to bring their balances down to zero, and added funds to account B in order to bring its balance *up* to zero.

A company's bank will charge a monthly service fee to manage a ZBA, and may add additional charges for each individual automated transaction to move cash into or out of a ZBA.

A ZBA may transfer cash across national boundaries, which can cause tax issues that the tax department should monitor. If there is a national prohibition on cash transfers across borders, it may not be possible to create a cross-border ZBA.

Multiple Sweep Arrangements

An alternative to sweeping in cash from outside a bank's system is to have a separate sweeping system for each bank that the company uses. Thus, it may have one bank servicing its stores in the western half of a country, and design a system that sweeps cash from those accounts into a concentration account that is still within the same bank. The same approach could be used for each of a company's banks. This approach minimizes sweeping costs, but does require that more concentration accounts be monitored for investment purposes.

Multiple sweeping arrangements may be necessary when there are accounts within different countries. Depending on the situation, cross-border transfers can be time-consuming, and may even be restricted by government rules. If so, a reasonable alternative is to conduct sweeps within each country. This may mean that the funds concentrated through each sweeping system are also invested within the same country.

In situations where there is no prohibition on cross-border cash concentrations, but cash is administratively difficult to move across borders, the treasurer can still plan for occasional transfers that are manually initiated. These moves should be coordinated with the company's tax planning staff, to ensure that the company is complying with all local tax laws when shifting funds into or out of a country.

Manual Sweeping

There may be situations where the bank operating a cash sweep cannot automatically initiate a sweep for an account located outside of its system. If so, the treasurer can resort to a more manual approach where the person responsible for the account notifies the treasurer of the most recent deposit amount or account balance; this triggers an ACH debit transaction to move the funds out of the outlying account and into an account located within the sweep system. For those parts of the world where ACH debits are not available, a more expensive alternative is to move the funds with a wire transfer. Given the high cost of a wire transfer, it may be more cost-effective to let cash pile up and then initiate wire transfers at longer intervals.

Tip: A manual deposit reporting system is subject to error, which can trigger an overdraft charge if a company withdraws an excessive amount from an account. Consequently, review all overdraft notices in detail, to determine what problem caused them to occur.

Sweeping Rules

A number of rules can be set up in a cash sweeping system to fit the cash requirements of the business entity using each account, as well as to minimize the cost of the system. Rules usually address:

- *Frequency*. Cash can be swept from some accounts at longer intervals than for other accounts. Some accounts accumulate cash very slowly, and only require an occasional sweep.
- *Threshold sweeps*. Cash can be swept only when the cash balance in an account reaches a certain level. This minimizes the cost of initiating sweeps for very small amounts of cash.
- *Target balances*. A designated amount of cash can be left in an account to ensure that a certain balance is always available. This may require that cash be sent *into* an account, rather than the usual outbound sweep. Target balances are useful when day-to-day operating needs are being met locally through an account. For example, a local bank may automatically extract its

monthly service fee from an account, and will charge an overdraft fee if the account contains no cash with which to pay the service fee. Also, a balance may be needed in order to meet banking covenants or regulatory requirements.

Sweep Problems

Cash sweeping is not to be engaged in lightly when cash is being moved among the accounts of multiple business entities, and especially when cash is being moved across national boundaries. Cash sweeping can cause all of the following problems:

- *Thin capitalization.* The automated extraction of cash from a subsidiary may result in a covenant breach with a lender, since the subsidiary has replaced cash with a loan receivable.
- *Recognition of interest income.* Some local tax jurisdictions will take exception if a business recognizes all of its interest income at the corporate level, since the cash that generated the interest income is located at the subsidiary level. To offset this problem, all interest earned should be allocated back to the subsidiaries based on the amount of their cash that was used to generate the income.
- *Recognition of interest expense.* As was the case with interest income, some tax jurisdictions want to see an interest charge recorded against those subsidiaries that required a cash infusion to avoid an overdraft situation. The interest charge should be based on the interest rate paid by the company for its debt; in the absence of any debt, use the market interest rate.
- *Sweep timing.* Cash is swept from an account near the end of each business day. Depending on sweep timing, it is possible that a late deposit into an account will not be swept into the concentration account until the following day, so that one day of interest income is lost.

> **Tip:** Always document how interest income and expense is allocated back to and recorded by subsidiaries, since tax auditors may want to review this information.

Sweep Costs

Banks charge high service fees for cash sweeps, which should be factored into whether the service should be used. For example, a typical monthly sweep charge is $150 (which is $1,800 per year), while the interest income earned from sweeps is relatively low. The following table notes the cash balance breakeven point for different interest rates, assuming the $1,800 annual bank fee.

Cash Sweeping Breakeven Analysis

Annual Bank Fee	Interest Rate	Cash Required to Breakeven
$1,800	1.0%	$180,000
1,800	1.5%	120,000
1,800	2.0%	90,000
1,800	2.5%	72,000
1,800	3.0%	60,000
1,800	3.5%	51,000
1,800	4.0%	45,000
1,800	4.5%	40,000
1,800	5.0%	36,000

At the low interest rates that frequently apply in today's credit markets, the preceding table shows that a company probably needs to have an average cash balance of at least $100,000 on an ongoing basis before it should even consider using a bank's cash sweeping service.

EXAMPLE

A subsidiary of Suture Corporation is located in a country that does not allow the transfer of cash outside of its borders, so the subsidiary's treasurer investigates the use of a cash sweep for the 10 Suture bank accounts located within the country. In the past three months, these accounts averaged an aggregate cash balance of $127,000. The subsidiary can earn 2.2% on its short-term cash investments. The company will be charged $2,000 per year by its bank for cash sweeping services. Thus, if the company were to create an in-country cash sweep, the result would be:

($127,000 Cash balance × 2.2%) - $2,000 Annual fee = $794 Net profit

The profits from the prospective sweep arrangement are quite small but are still positive, so the treasurer elects to proceed with the arrangement.

The cost of individual sweeps is minimal if all of the accounts are administered by the same bank, since the bank can simply shift the funds with an entry in its own accounting records. However, if an account is being swept that is *not* within the bank's system, the cost of doing so over time can be substantial. An ACH debit transaction is the least expensive alternative, but this method is not available in many parts of the world, and also involves a one-day lag. A wire transfer will work, but is much more expensive than an ACH debit.

EXAMPLE

Suture Corporation's treasurer learns that a $50,000 wire transfer has just been made into an outlying account that is not automatically swept by the company's primary bank. If the treasurer initiates a $20 wire transfer, the funds will be shifted into the company's concentration account the same day, and so will be available for investment in a bond that yields 4% interest. Alternatively, he can initiate the transfer by ACH, which costs only $0.50, but which requires a one-day delay. If the cash remains in its existing account overnight, it will earn a 1% earnings credit that will offset bank fees charged against the account.

The difference between the interest rates that can be earned from the two investment options is 3%, which is worth the following amount of interest income for a single day of investment:

$$(\$50,000 \text{ Cash} \times 3\%) \div 365 \text{ Days} = \$4.11/\text{day}$$

Since the incremental difference in earnings from the two investment options is so small, the most cost-effective sweeping arrangement is to initiate an ACH to move the funds with a one-day delay.

Summary

Cash sweeping is a rather expensive way to move cash into a central concentration account for investment purposes. Given the minimal interest rates now available on short-term investments, the decision to use cash sweeping mandates a detailed cost-benefit analysis. If a company does not expect to maintain a reasonably large aggregate cash balance across all of its accounts, it is entirely possible that a sweeping arrangement will actually *lose* money for a company. Also, and due to the same low interest rates, it is rarely cost-effective to use wire transfers to sweep in cash from outlying accounts. Instead, consider using less expensive alternatives that may require one or more days to centralize the excess cash.

Notional Pooling

Cash sweeping can be considered an intrusive cash concentration system, since it moves cash among accounts. Local managers may complain that they do not have control over their cash, since it is being moved out from under their direct supervision. An alternative is to allow cash to remain where it is and under local control, but to record it at the bank as though the cash has been centralized. This is called *notional pooling*. If a bank offers notional pooling, it simply combines the ending balances in all of a company's accounts to arrive at an aggregate net balance. If the result is a positive cash balance, the bank typically invests the funds automatically and pays the company interest income on the amount invested. If the result is a negative cash balance, the bank charges interest on the net negative amount.

The notional pooling concept is particularly useful when individual accounts are owned by subsidiaries that want control over their cash, and do not want to see it commingled in a central concentration account.

Another advantage of notional pooling is that a few banks offer pooling across currencies, where there is a notional transfer into the currency of choice. This means that interest is earned on cash holdings denominated in multiple currencies, without ever having to engage in any foreign exchange conversions into a single investment currency. Instead, the bank conducts a notional buy-sell swap, where there is simply an economic calculation by the bank – no foreign exchange transaction actually takes place.

Some banks offer the automated allocation of interest income back to the accounts where cash is stored, based on the actual amount of interest earned and the relative proportions of cash in the various accounts included in the pooling arrangement.

Notional Pooling Problems

Though notional pooling initially may appear to be an ideal solution, there are some problems that limit its use. These issues are:

- *Availability*. Notional pooling systems are prohibited in some countries, and are impractical in others where banking systems are not sufficiently integrated to allow for the virtual aggregation of funds. The reason for the prohibition of notional pooling is that some governments believe that such pooling constitutes a co-mingling of funds from different entities. Notional pooling is allowed in most European countries, but is not allowed in the United States.
- *Legal restrictions*. Even when notional pooling is allowed, some countries restrict its use to wholly-owned subsidiaries. Other countries do not allow notional pooling to include accounts located in other countries.
- *Single bank network*. The approach only works within the account network of a single bank, since the bank must have the capability to "see" all account balances. If a company uses multiple banks, it can instead employ a separate notional pooling arrangement with each bank, or a mix of notional pooling and cash sweeps.
- *Recognition of interest income and expense*. A notional pooling system awards interest income to the corporate parent. As was the case with cash sweeping, this means that some tax jurisdictions will want that interest income to be allocated back to the subsidiary level. The same allocation is needed for interest expense, if an account carries a debit balance. These allocations should be fully documented, since they may be perused by tax auditors.

For the first three reasons just noted, notional pooling tends to be a partial solution that works well in some areas, and is not available or allowed in others. Consequently, and despite the attractiveness of the concept, it is more likely to be implemented in a patchwork manner, with different systems installed in different parts of the world.

Notional Pooling Costs

The cost of notional pooling is lower than for cash sweeps, since no transactions are used to move cash between accounts. Also, the time that might be required by the treasurer to manually move funds is eliminated. Finally, the bank overdraft expense that might otherwise be charged on accounts having negative balances is eliminated, since the debit and credit positions in all accounts are merged through notional pooling; ideally, credit positions will exceed the amount of any debit account balances.

Summary

When it is available, notional pooling is administratively simple and allows for the retention of cash in accounts at the local level. However, the system is not allowed in some countries, and cannot be used as a single system where accounts are being administered by multiple banks. The latter issue is addressed in the next section, Multi-Tiered Banking.

Multi-Tiered Banking

There may be situations where a company has long-standing relationships with certain local banks that it wants to maintain, perhaps due to connections with local business partners. It is quite possible that these local banks cannot be linked into a company's worldwide cash concentration system on an automated basis. If so, an alternative is to have the company's primary bank open an account on behalf of the company within every country where the company does business, and then periodically shift funds from the local bank accounts into the designated accounts of the primary bank.

The result is a two-tiered structure, where the lowest level of banks is responsible for the local receipt and payment of day-to-day operating transactions. Excess cash is siphoned off to the higher tier of banks, which are then used to concentrate the cash on either a sweep or notional pooling basis for investment purposes. Cash transfers between the two tiers of banks may have to be manually initiated, in which case it may be more cost-effective to concentrate cash at longer intervals.

The two-tiered structure is subject to local banking regulations, and so may not be universally applicable. Nonetheless, the concept can bring additional centralization to a dispersed system of accounts that might at first appear to resist centralization.

Hybrid Pooling Solutions

It may be possible to combine the best aspects of cash sweeping and notional pooling in situations where a business has multiple subsidiaries. In this case, there can be a two-step arrangement, which is as follows:

1. *Subsidiary cash sweep.* There may be a large number of bank accounts controlled by a subsidiary, perhaps being used by individual store locations. The excess funds in these accounts are periodically swept into a concentration account for the subsidiary – not for the entire corporation. This approach keeps cash within the subsidiary entity, so there are no issues with reducing the capitalization of each entity.
2. *Corporate pooling.* Once all cash has been swept at the subsidiary level, notional pooling is used to link the cash concentration accounts of the subsidiaries. Centralized investment activities are then conducted at the corporate level, with interest income being apportioned back to the subsidiaries from which the cash was notionally taken. This approach eliminates the need for intercompany loans, as would be needed if the cash were to be physically shifted to the corporate entity.

Cash Concentration Best Practices

Irrespective of the type of cash concentration system being used, the treasurer should periodically review a number of structural issues involving a company's use of bank accounts. These issues are:

- *Examine low-usage accounts.* Review accounts having extremely low transaction volumes to see if the transaction activity can be shifted into a more active account. This can eliminate account servicing fees, and makes it easier to concentrate cash for investment purposes.
- *Review the accounts of acquired businesses.* Include on the company's acquisition checklist a reminder to review the bank accounts of every acquired business. There are likely to be opportunities for account reduction within these inherited accounts.
- *Mandate deposit cutoff times.* Review the company's procedures for depositing cash, to ensure that cash is deposited by a certain cutoff time each day. If deposits are made late, they may not be picked up by a bank's automated cash sweep, and so will not earn interest income until the following business day.
- *Administration charges.* Charge back a reasonable amount of treasury expenses to the company subsidiaries if there are significant expenses traceable to cash concentration activities. By doing so, the company can realize tax savings when its subsidiaries are located in high-tax regions. The strategy is less useful when subsidiaries are located in low-tax regions where there is little benefit to be gained from an expense allocation.

EXAMPLE

The treasurer of Suture Corporation is conducting a routine review of open bank accounts and notices that an account from a recent acquisition is still open. The account contains a balance of $5,000, and has essentially no activity. The bank is charging $50 per month to keep the account open. Suture is currently earning 3% on its short-term investments. Based on this information, the annual cost of the account is:

($5,000 Account balance × 3% Earnings rate) + ($50/Month fee × 12 Months)

= $750

Thus, the cost of maintaining this stray account balance is 15% of its current account balance. The treasurer decides to close the account at once and move the funds into a more heavily-used account.

The ongoing concentration of accounts has an additional benefit, which is that the smaller number of remaining banks will see that more cash is being stored in their accounts, which may give a company slightly more bargaining power with its banks.

Cash Concentration Alternatives

A cash concentration system is not a requirement. It is extremely helpful in situations where there are many scattered accounts that are not under central control, but is not cost-effective where that specific scenario does not arise. In particular, consider alternatives to or modifications of cash concentration under the following circumstances:

- *Small local balances.* There may be a number of small accounts in which modest credit balances are maintained. This scenario is most common where there are small-scale retail operations at the local level. It is too expensive to use cash sweeps for such a large number of accounts. Notional pooling may not be possible if there are a number of accounts operated by different banks. In short, this scenario probably calls for locally controlled accounts.
- *Independent subsidiaries.* Senior management may have implemented a corporate structure that is essentially "hands off," allowing local managers considerable leeway to conduct operations as they see fit. If so, instituting any type of cash concentration system may be seen as the first step in the redistribution of power to the corporate staff, and so will not be allowed. A possible alternative is to use notional pooling, where cash concentration is essentially invisible at the local level.
- *Slow cash buildup.* What if the amount of cash in some accounts only builds up over a long period of time? It could be overkill to continually extract small-dollar balances from these accounts on a daily or even weekly basis. Instead, consider a manual review of these accounts at very long intervals,

such as quarterly or semi-annually, with a manually-initiated cash sweep at that time.

- *Country restrictions.* A company may operate within a country that imposes severe restrictions on cash flows into or out of the country. If so, cash concentration systems can still be attempted within the country, as long as cash is never shifted to pools outside of the country.

Summary

The need for a cash concentration system depends upon the structure of a business. If the organization is designed to be top-down, with tight oversight by a corporate group, then there will probably be a cash concentration system that is managed from above. Conversely, if senior management goes to great lengths to diffuse responsibility down into an organization and keep the corporate group lean, then the management philosophy of the company may keep it from ever installing a cash concentration system – irrespective of any cost-benefit analysis.

If the decision is made to engage in cash concentration, the treasurer needs to decide upon the level of automation that will be used. Any system that requires the ongoing, detailed attention of the treasurer on a frequent basis is likely to fail, simply because there are so many accounts to be monitored every day. Instead, the best solutions are either those handled automatically by the company's bank, or only at long intervals on a manual basis.

Finally, there are distinct differences between the cash sweeping and notional pooling methods of cash concentration. Use the following table to determine which one is the better alternative for your specific circumstances:

Comparison of Cash Sweeping and Notional Pooling

Operational Issue	Cash Sweeping	Notional Pooling
Administrative effort	Considerable effort is needed to track intercompany loans arising from sweep activities	Minimal, since there are no cash transfers or intercompany loans
Interest allocation to subsidiaries	The calculation can be automated	The calculation can be automated
Cross-border transactions	Foreign currency conversions are required	Foreign currency conversions not required
Prohibitions on cross-border cash transfers	Can keep cash sweeps from taking place	Is not a limitation, since cash is not moved
Accounts with multiple banks	Can still be accomplished, though manually-initiated transactions may be required	Generally not possible for accounts located outside of the bank providing notional pooling services
Local control of cash	Not possible, since cash is being physically centralized	Possible, since cash is not being moved
Legality	Generally allowed in most countries	Prohibited or restricted in some countries

The preceding table shows that notional pooling is the generally preferred approach for most decision points involving cash concentration systems. However, since it only works for accounts administered by a single bank and is not allowed in some countries, it is quite possible that a business will need to install a mix of the two systems. Finally, be sure to explore the tax aspects of cash concentration before implementing any of these solutions, to avoid any unpleasant surprises.

Chapter 4
Cash Forecasting

Introduction

The treasurer is responsible for having funds available and investing excess funds, but can do neither one effectively without a cash forecast. The treasurer needs to know the timing and amount of cash flows, and preferably also the currencies in which these cash flows will occur.

A cash forecast is designed to give the treasurer insights into the state of cash inflows and outflows over the next few weeks and months. A well-constructed forecast should give the treasury staff sufficient information to ensure that there is enough cash available to meet the ongoing needs of a business on a day-to-day basis. The forecast should be sufficiently reliable for the treasurer to invest funds in somewhat longer-term investments, without being concerned that there will be a sudden need for the cash prior to the maturity dates of the investments.

Clearly, it is imperative to have a cash forecast that is completely reliable. In this chapter, we cover the details of how to create such a forecast, the reliability of the source information used within it, and how to improve the document on an ongoing basis.

Related Podcast Episode: Episode 187 of the Accounting Best Practices Podcast discusses cash forecasting accuracy. It is available at: **accounting-tools.com/podcasts** or **iTunes**

The Cash Forecast

The treasurer needs to know the amount of cash that will probably be on hand in the near future, in order to make fund raising and investment decisions. This is accomplished with a cash forecast, which should be sufficiently detailed to inform the treasurer of projected cash shortfalls and excess funds on at least a weekly basis. This section covers the details of how to create and fine-tune a cash forecast.

The cash forecast can be divided into two parts: near-term cash flows that are highly predictable (typically covering a one-month period) and medium-term cash flows that are largely based on revenues that have not yet occurred and supplier invoices that have not yet arrived. The first part of the forecast can be quite accurate, while the second part yields increasingly tenuous results after not much more than a month has passed. It is also possible to create a long-term cash forecast that is essentially a modified version of the company budget, though its utility is relatively low. The following exhibit shows the severity of the decline in accuracy for short-term and medium-term forecasts. In particular, there is an immediate decline in accuracy as soon as the medium-term forecast replaces the short-term forecast, since less reliable information is used in the medium-term forecast.

Variability of Actual from Forecasted Cash Flow Information

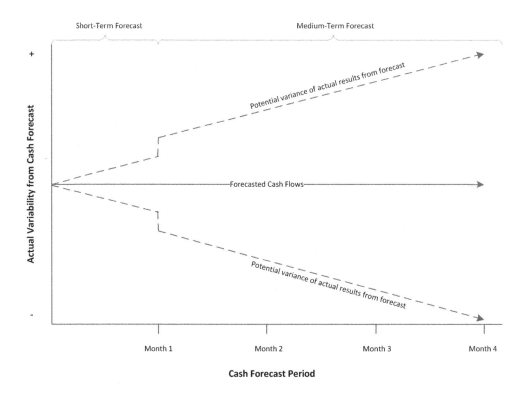

Through the remainder of this section, we will deal separately with how to construct the short-term and medium-term portions of the cash forecast, along with related topics.

The Short-Term Cash Forecast

The short-term cash forecast is based on a detailed accumulation of information from a variety of sources within the company. The bulk of this information comes from the accounts receivable, accounts payable, and payroll records, though other significant sources are the treasurer (for financing activities), the CFO (for acquisitions information) and even the corporate secretary (for scheduled dividend payments). Since this forecast is based on detailed itemizations of cash inflows and outflows, it is sometimes called the *receipts and disbursements method*.

The forecast needs to be sufficiently detailed to create an accurate cash forecast, but not so detailed that it requires an inordinate amount of labor to update.

Consequently, include a detailed analysis of only the *largest* receipts and expenditures, and aggregate all other items. The detailed analysis involves the manual prediction of selected cash receipts and expenditures, while the aggregated results are scheduled based on average dates of receipt and payment (see the comments at the end of this section about the use of averaging).

> **Tip:** Use detailed analysis of cash items in the cash forecast for the 20% of items that comprise 80% of the cash flows, and use aggregation for the remaining 80% of items that comprise 20% of the cash flows.

The following table notes the treatment of the key line items in a cash forecast, including the level of detailed forecasting required.

Cash Forecast Line Items

+/-	Line Item	Discussion
+	Beginning cash	This is the current cash balance as of the creation date of the cash forecast, or, for subsequent weeks, it is the ending cash balance from the preceding week. Do not include restricted cash in this number, since you may not be able to use it to pay for expenditures.
+	Accounts receivable	Do not attempt to duplicate the detail of the aged accounts receivable report in this section of the forecast. However, you should itemize the largest receivables, stating the period in which cash receipt is most likely to occur. All other receivables can be listed in aggregate.
+	Other receivables	Only include this line item if there are significant amounts of other receivables (such as customer advances) for which you expect to receive cash within the forecast period.
-	Employee compensation	This is possibly the largest expense item, so be especially careful in estimating the amount. It is easiest to base the compensation expense on the amount paid in the preceding period, adjusted for any expected changes.
-	Payroll taxes	List this expense separately, since it is common to forget to include it when aggregated into the employee compensation line item.
-	Contractor compensation	If there are large payments to subcontractors, list them in one or more line items.
-	Key supplier payments	If there are large payments due to specific suppliers, itemize them separately. You may need to change the dates of these payments in the forecast in response to estimated cash positions.
-	Large recurring payments	There are usually large ongoing payments, such as rent and medical insurance, which can be itemized on separate lines of the forecast.

+/-	Line Item	Discussion
-	Debt payments	If there are significant principal or interest payments coming due, itemize them in the report.
-	Dividend payments	If dividend payments are scheduled, itemize them in the forecast; this tends to be a large expenditure.
-	Expense reports	If there are a large number of expense reports in each month, they are probably clustered near month-end. You can usually estimate the amount likely to be submitted.
=	Net cash position	This is the total of all the preceding line items.
+/-	Financing activities	Add any new debt, which increases cash flow, or the reduction of debt, which decreases cash flow. Also add any investments that mature during the period.
	Ending cash	This is the sum of the net cash position line item and the financing activities line item.

The following example illustrates a cash forecast, using the line items described in the preceding table.

EXAMPLE

The treasurer of Suture Corporation constructs the following cash forecast for each week in the month of September.

+/-	Line Item	Sept. 1-7	Sept. 8-14	Sept. 15-22	Sept. 23-30
+	Beginning cash	$50,000	$30,000	$2,000	$0
+	Accounts receivable				
+	Alpha Pharmaceuticals	120,000		60,000	
+	St. Joseph's Burn Center		85,000		52,000
+	Third Degree Burn Center	29,000		109,000	
+	Other major receivables	160,000	25,000	48,000	60,000
+	Other receivables	10,000		5,000	
-	Employee compensation	140,000		145,000	
-	Payroll taxes	10,000		11,000	
-	Contractor compensation				
-	Bryce Contractors	8,000		8,000	
-	Johnson Contractors	14,000		12,000	
-	Key supplier payments				
-	Chico Biomedical	100,000		35,000	
-	Stanford Research	20,000	80,000	29,000	14,000
-	Other suppliers	35,000	40,000	30,000	48,000
-	Large recurring payments				
-	Medical insurance				43,000
-	Rent				49,000
-	Debt payments		18,000		
-	Dividend payments			20,000	
-	Expense reports	12,000	0	0	21,000
=	Net cash position	$30,000	$2,000	-$66,000	-$63,000
+/-	Financing activities			66,000	63,000
=	Ending cash	$30,000	$2,000	$0	$0

The forecast reveals a cash shortfall beginning in the third week, which will require a cumulative total of $129,000 of additional financing if the treasurer wants to meet all scheduled payment obligations.

The format is designed with the goal of giving sufficient visibility into cash flows to reveal the causes of unusual cash shortfalls or overages, without burying the reader in an excessive amount of detail. To meet this goal, note the use of the "Other receivables" and "Other suppliers" line items in the exhibit. They are used to aggregate smaller projected transactions that do not have a major impact on the forecast, but which would otherwise overwhelm the document with an excessive amount of detail if they were listed individually.

A possible addition to the cash forecast is the use of a *target balance*. This is essentially a "safety stock" of cash that is kept on hand to guard against unexpected cash requirements that were not planned for in the cash forecast. All excess cash above the target balance can be invested, while any shortfalls below the target balance should be funded. If a target balance had been incorporated into the preceding cash forecast example in the amount of $10,000, the amount would have been listed for the week of September 1-7 as a deduction from the ending cash position, leaving $20,000 of cash available for investment purposes.

The model we have outlined in this section requires a weekly update. It only covers a one-month period, so its contents become outdated very quickly. Ideally, the treasurer should block out time in the department work schedule to complete the forecast at the same time, every week. Unless there is an extremely tight cash flow environment, we do not recommend daily updates of cash forecasts – the time required to create these forecasts is excessive in comparison to the additional precision gained from the more frequent updates.

Tip: Do not schedule an update of the cash forecast on a Monday or Friday, since too many of these days involve holidays. Instead, schedule the forecast update on any other business day, thereby increasing the odds of completing a new forecast every week.

The very short-term portion of the cash forecast may be subject to some tweaking, usually to delay a few supplier payments to adjust for liquidity problems expected to arise over the next few days. To incorporate these changes into the forecast, the treasurer may use a preliminary draft of the forecast to coordinate changes in the timing of payments with the controller, and then record the delays in the forecast before issuing the final version.

The Medium-Term Cash Forecast

The medium-term cash forecast extends from the end of the short-term forecast through whatever time period the treasurer needs to develop investment and funding strategies. Typically, this means that the medium-term forecast begins one month into the future.

The components of the medium-term forecast are largely comprised of formulas, rather than the specific data inputs used for a short-term forecast. For example, if the sales manager were to contribute estimated revenue figures for each forecasting period, then the model could derive the following additional information:

- *Cash paid for cost of goods sold items*. Can be estimated as a percentage of sales, with a time lag based on the average supplier payment terms.
- *Cash paid for payroll*. Sales activity can be used to estimate changes in production headcount, which in turn can be used to derive payroll payments.

- *Cash receipts from customers*. A standard time lag between the billing date and payment date can be incorporated into the estimation of when cash will be received from customers.

A possibly more precise method for deriving cash paid for cost of goods sold items is based on the presence of a constraint somewhere in the company's production or administrative systems that chokes the flow of orders. If this bottleneck exists, estimate sales based on the capacity of the constraint; at a minimum, do *not* forecast for cash flows derived from sales that exceed the capability of the constraint, since it is impossible for the system to generate these additional amounts.

The concept of a formula-filled cash forecast that automatically generates cash balance information breaks down in some parts of the forecast. In the following areas, the treasury staff will need to make manual updates to the forecast:

- *Fixed costs*. Some costs are entirely fixed, such as rent, and so will not vary with sales volume. The treasury staff should be aware of any contractually-mandated changes in these costs, and incorporate them into the forecast.
- *Step costs*. If revenues change significantly, the fixed costs just described may have to be altered by substantial amounts. For example, a certain sales level may mandate opening a new production facility. A more common step cost is having to hire an overhead staff position when certain sales levels are reached. The treasury staff should be aware of the activity levels at which these step costs will occur.
- *Seasonal / infrequent costs*. There may be expenditures that only arise at long intervals, such as for the company Christmas party. These amounts are manually added to the forecast.
- *Contractual items*. Both cash inflows and outflows may be linked to contract payments, as may be the case with service contracts. If so, the exact amount and timing of each periodic payment can be transferred from the contract directly into the cash forecast.

The methods used to construct a medium-term cash forecast are inherently less accurate than the much more precise information used to derive a short-term forecast. The problem is that much of the information is derived from the estimated revenue figure, which rapidly declines in accuracy just a few months into the future. Because of this inherent level of inaccuracy, do not extend the forecast over too long a time period. Instead, settle upon a time range that provides useful information for planning purposes. Any additional forecasting beyond that time period will waste staff time to create, and may yield misleading information.

The Long-Term Cash Forecast

There can also be a long-term cash forecast that extends for an additional one or two years past the end of the medium-term forecast. It can be extremely difficult and time-consuming to develop and maintain a sales forecast for this period, so the most common approach is to instead adapt information from the corporate budget, and update it regularly to coincide with management's best estimates of long-term results.

The cash flows indicated by a long-term cash forecast should be considered only approximate values, so the treasurer is probably justified in not using it as the basis for any investment activities having specific maturity dates. However, the long-term forecast may be of more use in dealing with projected cash shortfalls. For lack of any better information, the treasurer can use it to obtain approximations of how much cash may be needed, and to plan on acquiring debt or selling stock to meet the shortfall.

The Use of Averages

There can be a temptation to use averages for estimated cash flows in the cash forecast. For example, it may seem reasonable to divide the average cash collections for receivables in a month by four, and then enter the resulting average cash receipts figure in each week of the forecast. This is not a good idea in the short-term portion of the forecast, since there are a number of timing differences that will make actual results differ markedly from average results. The following bullets contain several cash flow issues that can have sharp spikes and declines in comparison to the average:

- The receipt of payment for an unusually large invoice
- The designation of a large invoice as a bad debt
- Once-a-month payments, such as rent and medical insurance
- Sporadic payments, such as for dividends and property taxes

It is particularly dangerous to use averaging to estimate accounts receivable. In many companies, there is a disproportionate amount of invoicing at the end of each month, which means that there is a correspondingly large amount of cash receipts one month later (assuming 30-day payment terms). In short, it is quite common to have billing surges cause payment surges that vary wildly from average cash receipt numbers.

If a treasurer were to rely upon an averages-based cash forecast, there would be a high risk of routinely having cash shortfalls and overages. After all, the treasurer is responsible for ensuring liquidity *every day*, not just on average. Thus, we strongly recommend against the use of averages when forecasting the larger items in a short-term cash forecast.

The situation is different in a medium-term forecast, since the time period is sufficiently far into the future to make it impossible to predict cash flows with any degree of precision. In this case, the treasurer must estimate based on averages, though with three enhancements:

- Insert specific cash flows that the treasurer is sure of, such as contractually-mandated payments or receipts.
- Insert specific cash flows that have historically proven to be reliable. For example, if a customer has proven to be consistent in paying on a certain

day of the month, assume that these payments will continue with the same timing.

- It may be possible to substitute actual cash flow information for averages in the least-distant time periods. This is particularly likely for cash outflows, such as payroll, where there is not a significant amount of change in the amount paid from period to period.

Automated Cash Forecasting

Some accounting software packages include a feature that estimates cash balances in the near future, based on outstanding accounts receivable and accounts payable and when they are supposed to be paid. The feature should be used with caution in cash forecasting, given the following pluses and minuses associated with how they operate:

- *Cash outflow estimates.* The systems can be quite accurate in estimating accounts payable, since they draw upon the mandated payment terms listed in the vendor master file in the accounting system. However, the accounting department must be very good at entering all accounts payable into the system immediately upon receipt, to ensure that these items are properly reflected in the cash forecast.
- *Cash collection estimates.* Cash receipt estimates will necessarily be less accurate, since customers do not always pay in accordance with the payment terms listed in the customer master file. Also, customer accounts payable departments may be irregular in making payments around major holidays, which an automated system does not account for.
- *Available for use information.* Automated cash forecasting systems project cash balances based on the issuance or receipt of payments, which differ from the availability dates of the underlying checks.
- *Undocumented cash outflows.* Many companies have short-term cash outflow requirements related to fixed asset purchases, legal settlements, acquisitions, and so on that are not entered into the accounts payable system until the day when payment is to be made. These payments can unexpectedly alter the results of an automated system by a substantial amount.

An automated system that relies upon accounts payable to determine cash outflows is probably only accurate through a time period of about two to three weeks. To extend the accuracy of the forecast, consider routing requests for all larger purchases through the purchasing department; doing so allows for the creation of purchase orders that incorporate pricing and delivery dates, which can then be integrated back into the cash forecast. The result should be a cash forecast whose cash outflow information is accurate for a few more weeks into the future.

Given these issues, the treasury staff will likely need to modify the results provided by an automated cash forecasting system, especially in regard to projected cash receipts from customers. For medium-term forecasts, the detailed cash receipt and disbursement information used by these systems is not available, rendering them much less effective.

The Reliability of Cash Flow Information

After building cash forecasts for a few months, it will become apparent that certain information is highly reliable, while other types of information vary considerably from expectations. It is useful to identify which types of information are *least* reliable, so that the most time can be spent monitoring them. Highly reliable information can be copied forward into successive versions of the cash forecast with minimal cross-checking. The following table notes the reliability of different types of cash flow information.

Reliability of Cash Flow Information

Cash Flow Item	Reliability	Comments
Cash Inflows		
Credit sales	Average	If there are many small invoices, it should be possible to calculate the time periods within which certain proportions of all billed invoices will be paid. The situation is more dire if there are a few large invoices, since reliability is subject to the whims of a few customers. Timing is particularly problematic for payments coming from international customers, since there are more ways in which payments can be held up in transit.
Investments	Very high	If an investment has a specific maturity date, the related cash receipt can be scheduled with high confidence.
Cash Outflows		
Payroll	High	If a company uses a third party payroll supplier, the full amount of the payroll will be extracted from the company's account on a specific date. If payroll is handled in-house and especially with check payments, then the reliability of payments will be high within a period of a few days.
Suppliers	High	The payment dates for supplier payments are based on negotiated payment terms, which make the reliability of this information quite high. The reliability can be eroded if there are payment disputes with suppliers that delay payments.
Income tax payments	Varies	Quarterly income tax payments can be based on prior year payments, and so are very predictable. However, the final annual payment is based on annual net profits, which may be considerably less predictable.
Other tax payments	High	Sales tax remittances are usually compiled several weeks in advance, and can also be predicted as a percentage of sales.
Dividends	Very high	The amount and timing of dividends are determined several months in advance by the board of directors.
Debt payments	Very high	Debt repayment schedules are usually quite rigidly enforced. The lender may even use an ACH debit to extract debt payments from the company's bank account on specific dates.

The preceding table points out that the credit sales component of cash inflows can have the most problematic reliability. Thus, this is likely to be the area in which the treasury staff should focus its attention when developing a cash forecast.

Information used in the forecast is more likely to be unreliable when it is manually forwarded from another department. These other departments have no stake in the accuracy of the cash forecast, and so are less concerned with forwarding information that is accurate in terms of both cash amounts and payment or receipt timing. The following are all possible techniques for improving the reliability of such information:

- Develop a data entry system that forwards the information. When there is a formal system for entering the required information, as well as a supporting procedure, it is more likely to yield more reliable information.
- Design a bonus system that rewards targeted individuals for the accuracy of the information they forward to the treasury department, and penalizes them for unreliable information.
- The treasury department can be given formal responsibility over the area that produces the information. This is a drastic step, since it smacks of empire building.
- Make presentations to the various departments to impart to them the importance of providing reliable information. This approach tends to have a good short-term impact, but then fades over time.
- Change the underlying processes to circumvent the departments providing information. For example, if cash receipts forecasts from the sale of assets were coming from the individual departments selling the assets, consider centralizing this task with the purchasing department.

The Impact of Special Events

There are a number of special events that can have a profound (and usually negative) impact on the cash forecast. From the perspective of cash management, it is critical to identify these events and incorporate them into the cash forecast as early as possible. Doing so improves the likelihood that sudden cash shortages can be avoided. Here are several examples of special events that can impact cash flows:

- *Commodity price spikes.* The price of a key commodity suddenly increases, and the company is unable to pass the increase through to its customers. This will cause a significant jump in cash outflows in 30 days, when supplier invoices are due for payment. This will impact the transitional period in the cash forecast between the end of the short-term forecast and the start of the medium-term forecast.
- *Competing product introduction.* A competitor unexpectedly introduces an excellent competing product at a low price point, which immediately drives down the company's market share. This will impact the medium-term cash forecast, as sales drop and cash inflows decline.

- *Supply chain disruption.* A flood destroys a key supplier facility. It will take three months to mitigate the supply chain damage. In the meantime, existing buffer stocks of finished goods will be drawn down and sales will then terminate for all goods containing the parts provided by the supplier. This will not impact the short-range cash forecast, but may trigger a massive decline in cash inflows from customers over the medium term.
- *War.* An insurgency impacts deliveries into a key market in the Middle East, cutting off the company from its distributors. All sales are expected to cease until the insurgency can be put down. This will certainly impact the medium-term forecast, and may even roll into the short-term forecast, if the impacted distributors cannot make payments on outstanding invoices.

These examples of special events all impact the cash forecast to a major extent. It is entirely possible that a business may be subjected to at least one of these events every year or so. Given the reasonable probability of these occurrences, it is of some importance to maintain strong lines of communication with everyone in the company who is most likely to be best informed about these events. This means having ongoing discussions with the purchasing manager to understand changes in the supply chain, as well as with the sales manager to learn firsthand what is happening with the company's products and distribution systems. This enhanced level of communication allows for the more rapid inclusion of special events in the cash forecast.

Cash Forecasting Documentation

There are several source documents from which cash forecasting information is extracted, such as the aged accounts receivable report and the aged accounts payable report. The treasury staff should use a standard checklist of these source documents to find the information it needs to update the cash forecast. As long as the same checklist is used to compile every forecast, there should be no need to store the supporting documentation, for several reasons. First, forecasts may be updated frequently, so creating a documentation package for each one is excessively burdensome. Second, the treasury staff may shift the timing of anticipated cash flows "on the fly," based on their best estimates; it is too time-consuming to document the reasons for each of these timing changes. A treasurer who has been promoted into the position from the accounting side of a business may be uncomfortable with this minimal level of documentation, since the accounting staff is accustomed to more rigorous documentation standards.

The Foreign Currency Cash Forecast

The cash forecast is particularly useful when a company deals with large amounts of foreign currency. In these cases, consider maintaining a separate cash forecast for each foreign currency. By doing so, it is much easier to identify possibly excessive exposures to large foreign currency holdings or payment requirements, which may trigger a variety of hedging activities.

> **Tip:** It may be possible to develop a consolidated cash forecasting system that is comprised of separate foreign currency forecasts that roll up into a corporate-level forecast.

Cash Forecast Reconciliation

No matter how excellent a job the treasury staff may do in constructing a cash forecast, the result will never exactly match actual results. Either the amount or timing of actual cash inflows and outflows will differ from the prediction. Because of these differences, the people responsible for generating each cash forecast should routinely conduct a forecast reconciliation. The reconciliation should encompass the following activities:

- Investigate items that were expected to occur, but which did not
- Investigate items that were entirely unanticipated, or which were accelerated
- Investigate items that occurred in unanticipated amounts

The result can be a formal reconciliation document, but the main point is for the cash forecast preparers to gain experience with any permutations in the company's cash flows. The gradual accumulation of knowledge about such matters as the speed with which certain business partners pay the company or cash its checks is key to the improvement of cash forecasts.

> **Tip:** The best time to conduct a cash forecast reconciliation is immediately prior to generating the next forecast, so that any identified issues can be immediately incorporated into the next forecast.

There may be rare cases where the reconciliation process uncovers a check payment that was fraudulently issued. Though these occasional discoveries may qualify the cash forecast reconciliation as a weak detective control, it is not designed to be a control. Consequently, do not incorporate into the reconciliation a detailed investigation of the nature of every check paid by the business. Instead, the focus should be on improving the accuracy of the forecast.

Summary

It can take several months to achieve a forecasting process that generates reliable cash forecasts. It is not sufficient to reach this level of success and then move on to other projects. Instead, build review systems that constantly monitor forecasts to see if accuracy levels start to decline, and use this information to correct the forecasting model at once. This high level of watchfulness is needed in every company, since the alteration of company systems that is triggered by new lines of business, new software, acquisitions, and so forth will eventually alter the inputs to the cash forecast, making its results less reliable.

Chapter 5
Clearing and Settlement Systems

Introduction

From a treasury management perspective, it is not critical to understand the exact details of how payments move through the various national and international payment settlement systems. Accordingly, we have provided in this chapter a more general overview of how the clearing and settlement process works, and noted a number of the more prominent systems. All countries operate their own domestic clearing and settlement systems, which follow the general operational patterns described below for the representative systems.

The Clearing and Settlement Process

Clearing is the recordation of transactions between the various members of a *clearing channel*. An example of a clearing channel is the Clearing House Interbank Payments System (as discussed later in this chapter). *Settlement* is achieved between the member's accounts located at the Federal Reserve Bank (Fed), or at the central or similar bank of any country operating a settlement system. Thus, clearing is the recordation phase of transferring funds, and settlement is the actual movement of funds between parties. There are many clearing and settlement systems, which are usually constructed at the national level.

For a clearing and settlement system to work, participating banks must have an account with the clearing and settlement entity. Settlement then occurs between these accounts. The banks move funds in and out of these accounts as necessary to fulfill their obligations through the settlement system. If a bank does not have an account with a settlement system, it must work through a correspondent bank (see the next section) that has such an account.

Conceptually, settlement is the process of shifting funds from the account of the payer to the account of the payee. Settlement can occur on a net basis or a gross basis. When settlement is on a *net basis*, all transactions between participating banks are tallied, and only the net difference between their total positions is transferred. When settlement is on a *gross basis*, the full amounts of funds required by a payment transaction are shifted between banks for each individual transaction. Net settlement is clearly more efficient in terms of the total amount of cash paid out, but takes more time to complete. As examples of these settlement systems, the Fedwire system is on a gross basis, and the Automated Clearing House (ACH) system operates on a net basis.

Banks have most of their liquidity tied up in loans and other investments, and so prefer to transfer away the minimum amount of cash as part of the settlement process. Thus, from a liquidity perspective, a net settlement system is the preferred approach for a bank. A gross settlement system could require the outbound transfer of a significant amount of cash, which may not immediately be offset by inbound cash transfers related to inbound payments, and which may therefore require a bank to liquidate some invested funds in order to pay for the outbound transfer.

The risk of bank failure has differing impacts on gross and net settlement systems. In a gross system, settlement is immediate and simultaneous, so there is no risk of a bank failure interfering with a payment. However, settlement under a net system can require several business days, which introduces the risk of a bank failure interfering with payments. This is called *settlement risk*, or *Herstatt risk*, after a small German bank, Bankhaus Herstatt, which failed in June 1974. Herstatt accepted a payment of Deutsche Marks in Frankfurt in exchange for a delivery of U.S. dollars in New York. Because of the time zone difference between the two cities, the counterparty banks incurred estimated losses of $620 million when regulators shut down the bank before the offsetting dollar payment was made in New York.

Because of this settlement risk, there is a tendency for high-value payments to be made through gross settlement systems, leaving lower-value payments to be made through net settlement systems. Some net settlement systems have been gradually reducing the time required to calculate net settlements, thereby reducing settlement risk for participating banks.

Correspondent Banks

What if a bank is asked to handle a transaction that is located outside of its normal service area? The usual solution is to enter into a relationship with a bank authorized to do business in the required area, which is called a *correspondent bank*. A correspondent bank acts as an agent, handling transactions, accumulating documents for forwarding, accepting deposits, and so forth. The correspondent bank concept is especially important for transactions taking place in foreign countries. Some of the larger banks have thousands of these correspondent banking relationships, which allows them to handle any banking transaction, anywhere in the world through a correspondent bank, without having to incur the expense of opening up their own branch offices in distant locations.

Check Clearing

When a company issues a check payment, the payee deposits the check with its own bank. The payee's bank collects information from each check by scanning the bottom line of information on the check. This information is encoded using magnetic ink character recognition (MICR), which makes it easier to extract information from the check with a check scanner. The MICR line contains the routing information needed to route the check back to the payer's bank for reimbursement. The following information is encoded on the MICR line:

- *ABA number*. Contains the identification number of the bank on which the check was drawn. Also known as a transit routing number, or TRN. "ABA" is an acronym for American Bankers Association.

- *Account number*. Contains the number of the account assigned to the payer by the bank.
- *Check number*. States the number of the check, which is also shown in the upper right corner of the check.
- *Payment amount (optional)*. States the payment amount listed on the check. This code can be created by the payer when the check is printed, or by the payee when preparing the check for deposit. Most commonly, it is added by the bank at which the check is deposited.

A sample of the MICR information encoded on a check is shown in the following exhibit.

MICR Information on a Check

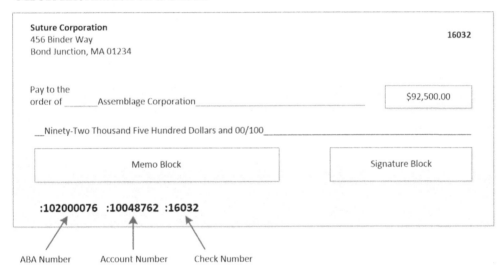

The payment amount stated on a check does not immediately appear in the payee's bank account, since the payee's bank has not yet received the funds from the payer's bank. Instead, the payee's bank makes a notation of the amount in the payee's account, and sets a date by which the funds will be available for use by the payee (known as the *value date*). A bank sets value dates based on its own availability schedule, which states the number of business days required before the cash stated on various types of checks will be made available to payees. Availability dates should approximately follow these timelines:

- *Zero-day delay*. *On-us* checks, which are checks deposited in the same bank on which they were drawn. U.S. Treasury checks should also be assigned a zero-day delay.
- *One-day delay*. Checks drawn on local banks or on banks located in major cities.
- *Two-day delay*. Checks drawn on more distant locations.

The payee's bank then has a choice of four possible methods for clearing the check, which are:

- *Clearinghouse.* Send the check to a check clearinghouse that aggregates and nets check payments forwarded from multiple banks.
- *Direct send.* Forward the check directly to the payer's bank.
- *Federal Reserve.* Send the check to the Fed's clearing service.
- *On-us processing.* Process the payment internally, if the check was drawn on an account with the same bank.

If the check is moving between banks, then ultimately the Fed will remove cash from the account of the payer bank with a debit, and deposit the cash in the account of the payee bank with a credit.

The following exhibit shows the process flow for clearing a check, assuming that the payment is drawn on a different bank from the payee's bank.

Check Clearing Process Flow

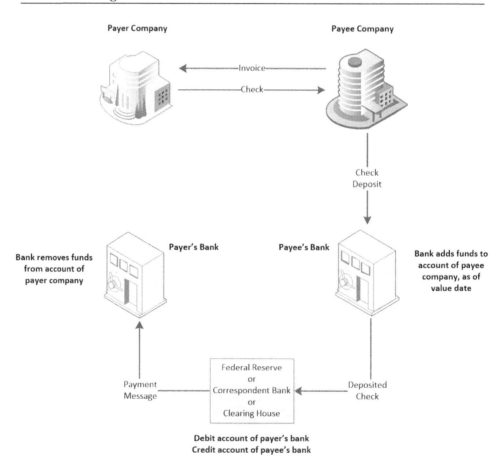

Foreign Check Clearing

There are inevitable delays in the settlement of currencies, for every currency must be settled in its country of origin. Thus, if a check is paid out of the account of a bank that is not part of the U.S. payment system, the check is sent back to the payer's bank for collection. The payer's bank pays an in-country correspondent bank, which in turn remits the funds by electronic transfer to the payee's bank. This settlement process is very time-consuming and expensive, and may mean that the check recipient will not have access to the cash amount stated on the check for weeks.

There are countries in which there is heavy usage of a particular foreign currency – usually the U.S. dollar. In these cases, there are systems in place to clear locally drawn checks within those countries, using a local commercial settlement bank. For example, U.S. dollar clearing is available in Tokyo, Hong Kong, and the Philippines. These local settlement systems create a credit risk for the participants in a check clearing transaction, because the local settlement bank could fail while checks are being cleared, leaving liabilities outstanding between the payer and payee.

> **Tip:** A few banks offer immediate availability of the cash noted on a check that originates in another country, though at a discount to the face value of the check. Cash availability will be based on the size of the payment, the currency in which it is denominated, and how important the payee is to its bank. If the payee's bank cannot collect from the payer's bank, the payee will be liable to its bank for repayment.

The Automated Clearing House System (ACH)

The Automated Clearing House System is much better known as ACH. The system is designed for high-volume, low-value payments, and charges fees low enough to encourage the transfer of low-value payments. The system is designed to accept payment batches, so that large numbers of scheduled payments can be made at once. Given its convenience and reliability, the ACH system has replaced check payments to a considerable extent.

The ACH system is designed for the domestic transfer of payments. It does not operate in other countries, though variations on the system have been installed in many countries. Some major banks operate portals that link a number of these ACH-like systems, so that a "global" system with ACH characteristics is currently operational.

ACH is a net settlement system, so settlement is delayed for up to two days, and there is some settlement risk. The system allows for the transfer of a limited amount of additional information along with payment instructions, though this information may be stripped away if a transaction is being transferred into a different national ACH system that does not allow for additional payment information.

ACH is primarily used to process payments from businesses to individuals. For example, ACH is used for payroll direct deposit payments, as well as for pension and annuity payments. In the reverse direction, businesses use ACH debits to extract a variety of payments from the bank accounts of individuals. There is also increasing usage of ACH for accounts payable payments from one business to another.

The basic process flow for the ACH system is as follows:

1. The payer submits a file to its bank, containing a batch of payment information.
2. The bank immediately pays any amounts directed to payee accounts within the bank, using an internal book transfer.
3. The bank assembles all remaining payments into a batch and sends it to the regional ACH operator to which it has been assigned.
4. The ACH operator nets the payment information submitted by the banks in its region and notifies them of the settlement amounts for which they are responsible.
5. The ACH operator summarizes the remaining transactions involving payments to banks located outside of its processing region, and sends the summaries to the other regional ACH operators for further settlement, which are completed on a gross basis.
6. When payments arrive in the accounts of payee banks, those banks forward the payments to payees, while the payers' banks debit the payers' accounts for the related and offsetting payment amounts.

The following exhibit shows the process flow when several payroll payments to employees are made using the ACH system (and employing a *very* simplified view of ACH processing).

ACH Process Flow

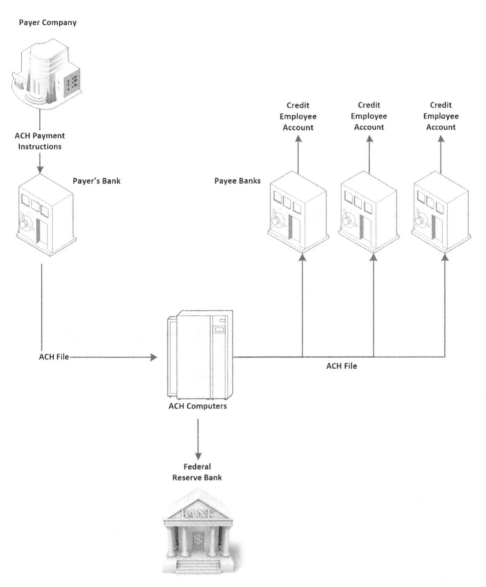

CHIPS

The Clearing House Interbank Payment System (CHIPS) is primarily used to settle foreign exchange transactions, move funds between banks, and make Eurodollar and letter of credit payments. The system handles nearly all interbank transfers involving international dollar payments. CHIPS is an end-of-day net settlement system, where system participants send and receive Fedwire transfers through a settlement account at the Fed. End-of-day settlement represents a reduced level of settlement risk. Once funds have been shifted to the payee in CHIPS, they cannot be recalled by the payer.

The basic process flow for the CHIPS system is as follows:

1. The payer sends payment instructions to its bank.
2. The bank forwards payment instructions to CHIPS, which aggregates these instructions from all submitting banks at the end of the day.
3. CHIPS nets all payment instructions and sends the results to the Fed.
4. The Fed debits the accounts of payer banks and credits the accounts of payee banks, as per the CHIPS instructions.
5. CHIPS sends payment instructions to the payee's bank, so that the bank can credit the account of the payee.

The CHIPS system is particularly frugal in using a bank's liquidity, since only net settlement amounts are transferred between banks.

An advantage of CHIPS is that it allows participants to attach a large block of remittance information along with their payments. The main downside to using CHIPS is that its transaction fee is higher than that of the ACH system.

CHIPS is operated by the New York Automated Clearing House, which in turn is owned by a group of banks. Membership in CHIPS is quite small, so access to the system is typically through a correspondent relationship with one of the member banks.

Fedwire

The Fedwire system is operated by the Federal Reserve System in the United States. Fedwire is a same-day gross settlement system. The system settles payments with a simultaneous same-day credit to the account of the payee's bank and a debit to the account of the payer's bank. The Fed guarantees all payments made through the Fedwire system. The Fedwire system is primarily used for high-value payments, partially because the per-transaction fee is quite high, and so is cost-prohibitive for smaller payments. Also, once funds have been shifted to the payee and confirmed by the Fed, they cannot be recalled without the permission of the payee.

The following exhibit shows the process flow when a payment is made using the Fedwire system.

Fedwire Process Flow

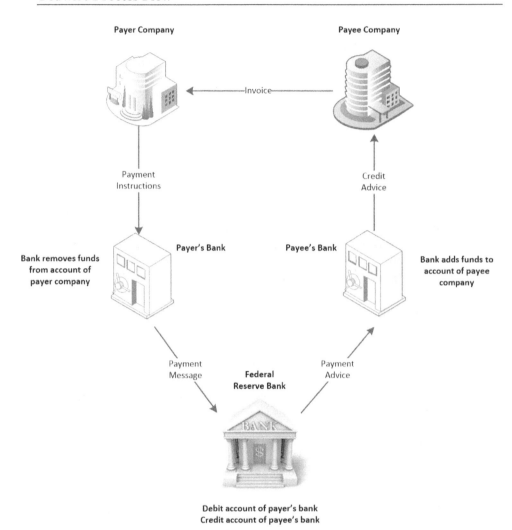

Debit account of payer's bank
Credit account of payee's bank

The basic process flow with the Fedwire system is for a company to send payment instructions to its bank, which removes the funds from the company's account and sends the payment instructions to the Fed. The Fed transfers the cash from the Fed account of the payer's bank to the Fed account of the payee's bank. The payee's bank then credits the bank account of the payee.

CHAPS

The clearing and settlement system for pound-denominated payments is the Clearing House Automated Payments System (CHAPS), which is operated by the CHAPS Clearing Company. This is a gross settlement system, which therefore offers same-day settlement. The system is owned and operated by a small number of member banks, with hundreds of other banks participating in the system.

CHAPS charges a high transaction fee, so its use is generally limited to high-value payments. The system is used for money transfers between banks, as well as businesses making high-value payments to their suppliers. Also, the system is used by attorneys on behalf of persons buying houses.

TARGET2

The Trans European Automated Real Time Gross Express Transfer System (TARGET2) is a real-time gross settlement system, which replaced the original TARGET system in 2007. TARGET2 connects the various real-time gross settlement systems in the Euro area. The system is designed to increase the efficiency of cross-border payments denominated in euros. Since it is used for all payments involving the Eurosystem (the monetary authority of the euro zone), it is one of the largest payment systems in the world, with more than 10,000 participating financial institutions.

All payments made through TARGET2 are final, and so cannot be reversed.

Continuous Linked Settlement

Continuous Linked Settlement (CLS) is a real-time net settlement system used by many international banks to settle foreign exchange transactions amongst themselves, and on behalf of their clients. The system is operated by CLS Bank, and currently handles transactions denominated in the currencies of 17 countries, which are noted in the following table.

Currencies Handled by CLS Bank

Australian dollar	Israeli shekel	Singapore dollar
British pound	Japanese yen	South African rand
Canadian dollar	Korean won	Swedish krona
Danish krone	Mexican peso	Swiss franc
Euro	New Zealand dollar	United States dollar
Hong Kong dollar	Norwegian krone	

The CLS system is designed to ensure that foreign currency payments and receipts are completed simultaneously, thereby avoiding settlement risk. CLS stands between the participating banks as the common counterparty. The system process flow is as follows:

1. Participating banks send their foreign exchange information to CLS until the daily cutoff time.
2. CLS aggregates the submitted information into a schedule of payments due to CLS from each bank, which it sends to the banks.

3. The participating banks submit the required amount of funds to CLS, which are credited to their CLS accounts. These accounts are set up with sub-accounts for each currency.
4. CLS settles payments with debits and credits to the CLS sub-accounts of the participants.
5. If a participating bank has not submitted sufficient funds to support all settlements, CLS postpones processing the related payment transactions until it receives the required funds. This means that CLS processes settlements using a direct link between both sides of a specific foreign exchange transaction (known as a *payment-versus-payment* procedure). Thus, if a participating bank needs to submit more funds, the related credit to the other side of the payment is not completed until such time as the required funds are sent to CLS.

All CLS processing is concluded within a five-hour time period that encompasses the business hours of the national settlement systems with which it is linked.

The CLS system is highly efficient for participants, since banks pay into it only the net obligation in each currency required for the hundreds or thousands of currency transactions that they handle each day, rather than the total amount of each trade being processed. This netting efficiency is typically in the vicinity of 95%, so that the participating banks only have to pay in roughly 5% of the aggregate transaction total. The system is made more efficient by allowing a debit balance in a sub-account for a certain currency for a bank participant, as long as the aggregate balance in all of the participant's sub-accounts still sums to a credit balance.

The system is managed by CLS Group Holdings, and has a number of member banks, each of which holds multi-currency accounts with CLS Bank. Based on transaction volume, CLS appears to be the market leader for the settlement of foreign exchange transactions.

SWIFT

SWIFT is an acronym for the Society for Worldwide Interbank Financial Telecommunications. It is a global system for transmitting financial information, using an array of specifically-formatted electronic messages. The system was originally restricted to messaging between financial institutions, but has since been modified to allow businesses to originate messages that are then routed through bank intermediaries.

There are electronic links between SWIFT and the clearing and settlement systems in many countries, which allows a bank to use SWIFT to initiate financial transactions in most parts of the world. Given the costs to set up SWIFT, it has traditionally only been used by banks, which process a sufficient volume of transactions to justify the cost. This means that corporations have routed their SWIFT transactions through banks. However, larger corporations with massive transaction volumes have found it cost-effective to become participants in the SWIFT system, and so have direct links into the system.

The primary categories of SWIFT messages that can be used are noted in the following table, with a large number of more specific messages available within each message series:

SWIFT Message Types

Message Series	Description
MT000	System messages
MT100	Customer payments and checks
MT200	Financial institution transfers
MT300	Treasury markets
MT400	Collection and cash letters
MT500	Securities markets
MT600	Treasury markets – Metals and syndications
MT700	Documentary credits and guarantees
MT800	Traveler's checks
MT900	Cash management and customer status

Examples of SWIFT messages related to cash management are the bank transfer to its own account (MT200), interbank payment (MT202), advice to receive (MT210), foreign exchange confirmation (MT300), and loan confirmation (MT320).

These messages are highly regimented, containing a closely-defined set of fields unique to each transaction type. The following table shows the fields comprising an MT300 foreign exchange confirmation. The intent is to note the extreme level of detail required to ensure that each SWIFT message is properly executed as intended by the parties to a transaction.

MT300 Foreign Exchange Confirmation Fields

Field	Field Name and Comment
20	*Sender's reference*. A unique identifier assigned by the sender to unambiguously identify the message.
21	*Related reference*. Contains the identification of the message to which the current message is related.
22C	*Common reference*. A unique value containing portions of the sender and receiver codes, plus the last digits of the exchange rate.
22A	*Type of operation*. Specifies the function of the message, such as a new transaction, a cancellation, or an amendment.
94A	*Scope of operation*. Specifies the roles of the sender and receiver.
17T	*Block trade indicator*. Specifies whether the deal is a block trade.

Field	Field Name and Comment
17U	*Split settlement indicator.* Specifies whether the amount is to be settled as a whole or in several parts, and indicates relevant account names, account numbers, routing codes, and bank names.
82A	*Party A.* Identifies the client.
83A	*Account number.* Specifies the funds or beneficiary customer.
87A	*Party B.* Identifies Party B.
33B	*Currency, amount.* Specifies the currency type and the amount sold by Party A.
32B	*Currency, amount.* Specifies the currency type and amount bought by Party A.
53A	*Delivery agent.* Identifies the financial institution from which the payer will transfer the purchased amount.
57A	*Receiving agent.* Identifies the financial institution and account where the payee will receive the purchased amount.
58A	*Beneficiary institution.* Specifies the institution to which the payment is to be made.
36	*Exchange rate.* Specifies the exchange rate of the transaction.
30T	*Trade date.* Notes the date on which the parties agreed to the transaction.
30V	*Value date.* Specifies the value date of the transaction.
56A	*Intermediary.* Notes the intermediary institution for the transfer of funds.
72	*Sender to receiver information.* States the time and venue at which the transaction was concluded.

Be sure to completely fill out a SWIFT message form. Otherwise, the automated processing system of the bank handling the transaction will shunt the message into a manual processing queue. Manual processing can delay a transaction, and one or both of the parties to the transaction may also be charged by the bank for the additional processing labor.

Summary

From a treasury perspective, the key issue involving clearing and settlement systems is the amount of time required for a payment to transit the relevant system. This time period can be brief, if a gross settlement system is used, or can take an inordinate amount of time, if a check payment is made across international borders. This information can be useful for cash forecasting purposes.

Another issue with clearing and settlement systems is the fee charged by one's bank for the type of settlement system used. For example, the fee required for an ACH payment is minimal, while a wire transfer can be inordinately expensive. Consequently, it is useful to understand how the fees associated with a clearing and settlement system will be passed through to the payer, and sometimes also to the payee.

Chapter 6
Investment Management

Introduction

Any company will have occasional surges in cash flow, while wealthier ones may have substantial cash reserves. The treasurer should have a system in place for investing this cash, with a number of restrictions that are primarily designed to protect the cash and make it readily accessible. In this chapter, we discuss the guidelines used for investing, cash availability scenarios, various investment strategies, and the investment instruments most commonly used.

Investment Guidelines

Though this chapter is entirely concerned with investments, we must emphasize that an organization keep cash reserves available for operational use; this is much more important than maximizing the return on investment. The following guidelines are designed to meet this cash availability goal:

- *Protect the cash.* Above all, do not lose the cash. No investment should be so risky that the company is unable to recover the cash that it initially placed in the investment. This is a particularly important consideration in situations where a company has a short-term operational need for cash, and is only parking it in an investment for a short time in order to gain some assured income.
- *Ready conversion to cash.* It should be easy to convert an investment into cash on little notice. It is critical to satisfy any short-term operational need for cash, even if it was not planned for in the cash forecast. This means that there should be an active secondary market for all investments, where someone else can readily be found to acquire an investment instrument held by the company.
- *Earn a return.* After the preceding two factors have been dealt with, it is then permissible to optimize the return on investment. This means that, if there are two possible investments that have identical risk profiles and liquidity, pick the one having the greater return on investment.

An additional investment consideration is the taxability of investment income. The interest earned on different types of federal, state, and municipal obligations may not be taxable. Taxability may be a consideration when making investments, but usually the preceding guidelines for protecting cash and cash convertibility override a possible boost in net interest income.

The interplay between these guidelines changes in relation to the duration of an investment. For example, a portfolio of investments that all have long-term maturities usually have returns associated with them that are locked in (assuming they are held to maturity), so there is a reduced risk related to the return that will be earned. Conversely, and depending upon the existence of a secondary market, it may be more difficult to liquidate these longer-term investments. For comparison purposes, a short-term investment is at risk of a change in the rate of return, for the company is constantly buying new investments, each reflecting the most recent market rate of return; however, the shorter associated maturity makes it easier to liquidate these investments to meet short-term cash needs.

We must make it clear that it is critical to be exceedingly risk averse when investing company cash. All but the largest and wealthiest corporations will be harmed by an investment loss, so do not attempt to gain outsized returns on an investment when the accompanying risk level is too high.

Tip: There should be a formal investment policy that confines the company to a narrow range of possible investments that are considered to be at low risk of default. A sample policy is listed later in this section.

There are a few steps that can be taken to reduce the risk of losing invested funds, and which should be considered when engaging in investment activities. They are:

- *Diversification.* Only invest a limited amount of cash in the securities of a single entity, in case that entity defaults on its obligations. Similarly, only invest a limited amount in securities originating within one industry, in case economic circumstances lead to multiple defaults within the industry.
- *FDIC insurance.* The Federal Deposit Insurance Corporation (FDIC) protects depositors of insured banks against the loss of their deposits and accrued interest if an insured bank fails. This coverage includes deposits in checking accounts, savings accounts, money market deposit accounts, and certificates of deposit. The coverage does not include cash invested in stocks, bonds, mutual funds, life insurance proceeds, annuities, or municipal securities. The amount of this coverage is limited to $250,000 per depositor, per insured bank. Consequently, it may be worthwhile to monitor account balance levels and shift funds above the insurance cap to accounts in other banks. By doing so, a company can achieve an FDIC coverage level that is substantially higher than $250,000.

These risk reduction steps guard against admittedly unusual circumstances that a business may never experience. Nonetheless, if a counterparty were to fail, the potential loss could be quite large. Consequently, give strong consideration to these options when engaging in investment activities.

To ensure that investment guidelines are followed, they should be codified in a formal investment policy that is approved by the board of directors. The internal audit department can monitor compliance with this policy. A sample policy follows.

EXAMPLE

Suture Corporation's board of directors adopts the following investment policy.

General

In general, investments in securities with low liquidity levels shall be restricted to 15% of the company's total investment portfolio. There must be an active secondary market for all other investments.

Debt Investments

Debt investments are subject to the following restrictions:

- May only be made in high-quality intermediate or long-term corporate and Treasury bonds
- No more than 20% of the total debt investment can be made in a single industry
- Investments cannot comprise more than 5% of the debt issuances of the investee
- The average term to maturity cannot exceed __ years
- An investment must be terminated within one month if its Standard & Poor's credit rating drops below BBB
- Any bank acting as a counterparty shall have a capital account of at least $5 billion
- Short-term investments shall be pre-qualified by the investment advisory committee for the placement of funds

Equity Investments

Equity investments are subject to the following restrictions:

- May only be made in the common stock of companies trading on the New York Stock Exchange
- No more than 20% of the total equity investment can be made in a single industry
- Investments cannot comprise more than 5% of the capitalization of the investee

Control of Securities

All securities over which the company has physical control shall be consigned to an accredited third party.

Prohibitions

The company is prohibited from investing in any of the following types of investments without the prior approval of the board of directors:

- Commodities
- Foreign equity investments and commercial paper
- Leveraged transactions
- Real estate
- Securities with junk ratings
- Short sales or purchases on margin
- Venture capital

It is useful to periodically compare the company's investment policy to the actual structure and performance of its investment portfolio over the past few months, for the following reasons:

- *Compliance.* To ensure that employees have followed the guidelines set forth in the policy.
- *Performance.* To see if the company might have achieved better returns if the policy had been somewhat less restrictive.
- *Risk management.* To determine whether the company avoided or mitigated risks by adhering to the policy.
- *Liquidity.* To see if adherence to the policy allowed the company to routinely meet its liquidity requirements.

This analysis should be conducted by someone not directly associated with the treasury department, in order to avoid any bias in the results.

Cash Availability Scenarios

Before considering the type of investment strategy to follow, first determine the historical availability of cash that can be invested. A mix of the following situations will likely apply:

- *Daily operational needs.* For many organizations that operate at low profitability levels, nearly all cash on hand may be called upon to service the daily operational needs of the business. If so, the main emphasis is on highly liquid investments that will likely be called upon within the next few days.
- *Untouched cash.* If a business routinely has a baseline level of cash that is never used, these funds can be invested in longer-term and/or less liquid investments that have a higher rate of return. However, the duration of these investments should not exceed the end date of the corporate cash forecast, so that the organization is not caught in an investment when there is a need for funds.
- *Seasonal cash balances.* It is relatively common for a business to build up its cash balance following a seasonal spike in sales, and then use the accumulated funds during those parts of the year that experience lower activity levels. These changes in the seasonal accumulation and use of cash can be quite predictable. Investments should be tailored to make cash available as of the periods when cash outflows are anticipated.
- *Planned expenditures.* If there are upcoming capital purchases of significant size, a business may accumulate cash in advance in order to pay for these purchases. This means there is a target date on which a specific amount of invested funds must be converted to cash. In this situation, the type of investment made must conform to the requirements of the planned expenditure.
- *Contingent expenditures.* A business may be anticipating a large cash outflow for which there is not a specific payout date, and needs to accumu-

late funds for that payment. An example of this situation is an anticipated payout from a lawsuit that the organization expects to lose. This situation calls for an investment of funds that is extremely liquid, so that it can be converted to cash on very short notice.

- *Corporate growth rate.* The rate at which an entity grows or shrinks will dictate the amount of cash available for investment, and the timing for when cash is needed. A rapidly-growing business will likely have an enormous need for cash that is fueled by rapid increases in working capital and fixed assets. In this situation, investment durations should be extremely short, so that cash can be put to use at once. Conversely, when a business is shrinking, there will be a gradual decline in working capital, which is converted back into cash. This can result in a large pool of cash for which there is no particular need; unless distributed to investors, this cash can be parked in longer-term investments.
- *Trapped cash.* Cash may be located in a country or other jurisdiction where cash flows are restricted, or where there are severe tax penalties associated with moving the cash elsewhere. If so, the cash will likely need to be invested locally. In this case, all of the preceding cash availability scenarios come into play. The proper investment will depend upon the level of planned or contingent expenditures, the corporate growth rate, and the variability of cash flows – but using local investments.

Investment Strategy

Within the preceding guidelines and cash availability scenarios, what strategy should the treasurer follow when investing cash? Several possibilities are noted in the following bullet points. When considering the options, please note that the more active ones require accurate cash forecasts, which may not be available.

- *Earnings credit.* The simplest investment option of all is to do nothing. Cash balances are left in the various bank accounts, where they accrue an earnings credit that is offset against the fees charged by the bank for use of the accounts. If cash balances are low, this can be an entirely acceptable strategy, since more active management of a small amount of cash will probably not glean a significantly larger return. However, the earnings credit can only be applied to fees charged in the current period; if the fees are less than the credit, the company loses the difference. This consideration puts a cap on the amount of funds that should be left in a bank account.

EXAMPLE

Suture Corporation has an African division that is in startup mode, and so has little excess cash. Currently, the division maintains an average of only $20,000 in its sole bank account. Its bank offers a 1.5% earnings credit on retained cash balances, which is $25 per month that can be offset against account fees. The best alternative is a money market fund that earns 2%, but which requires the manual transfer of funds several times per month.

Given the minor amount of the balance and the low return on other investment alternatives, the treasurer elects to accept an earnings credit, rather than taking any more aggressive investment actions.

- *Automated sweeps*. Sweep all excess cash into a central account, and shift the funds in that account to an overnight investment account. This strategy requires no staff time, but yields a low return on investment, since banks charge significant fees to manage this process. This approach works very well when the short-term need for cash is uncertain.
- *Laddering*. The laddering strategy involves making investments of staggered duration, so that the company can take advantage of the higher interest rates typically associated with somewhat longer-term investments. For example, a treasurer can reasonably forecast three months into the future, so she invests in a rolling set of investments that mature in three months. To begin this strategy, she invests a block of funds in an investment having a one-month maturity, another block in an investment with a two-month maturity, and yet another block in an investment with a three-month maturity. As each of the shorter investments matures, they are rolled into new investments having three-month maturities. The result is an ongoing series of investments where a portion of the cash is made available for operational use at one-month intervals, while taking advantage of the higher yields on three-month investments.
- *Match maturities*. An option requiring manual tracking is to match the maturities of investments to when the cash will be needed for operational purposes. This method calls for a highly accurate cash forecast, both in terms of the amounts and timing of cash flows. To be safe, maturities can be planned for several days prior to a forecasted cash need, though this reduces the return on investment.
- *Tiered investments*. If a business has more cash than it needs for ongoing operational requirements, conduct an analysis to determine how much cash is never or rarely required for operations, and use this cash in a more aggressive investment strategy. For example:
  - o *Continual cash usage*. Cash usage levels routinely flow within a certain range, so there must be sufficient cash available to always meet these cash requirements. The investment strategy for the

amount included in this investment tier should be concentrated in highly liquid investments that can be readily accessed, with less attention to achieving a high rate of return.

- o *Occasional cash usage.* In addition to cash usage for daily operating events, there are usually a small number of higher cash usage events that can be readily predicted, such as a periodic income tax or dividend payment. The strategy for this investment tier should focus on maturity dates just prior to the scheduled usage of cash, along with a somewhat greater emphasis on the return on investment. There should be a secondary market for these types of investments.
- o *No planned cash usage.* If cash usage levels have never exceeded a certain amount, all cash above this maximum usage level can be invested in longer-term instruments that have higher returns on investment, and perhaps with more limited secondary markets.

EXAMPLE

The treasurer of Suture Corporation wants to adopt a tiered investment strategy. He finds that the company routinely requires a maximum of $200,000 of cash for various expenditures on a weekly basis. In addition, there are scheduled quarterly dividend payments of $50,000 per quarter, and quarterly income tax payments of $100,000, which fall on the same date. There have not been any instances in the past three years where cash requirements exceeded these amounts. Currently, Suture maintains cash reserves of $850,000 on a weekly basis. Based on the preceding information, the treasurer could invest the cash in the following ways:

Investment Tier	Amount	Investment Type
Continual cash usage	$200,000	Money market
Occasional cash usage	150,000	Certificates of deposit, commercial paper
No planned cash usage	500,000	Bonds
Total	$850,000	

The tiered investment strategy requires close attention to the cash forecast, particularly in regard to the timing and amount of the occasional cash usage items. Otherwise, there is a risk of being caught with too much cash in an illiquid investment when there is an immediate need for the cash.

- *Ride the yield curve.* A treasurer could buy investments that have higher interest rates and longer maturity dates, and then sell these investments when the cash is needed for operational purposes. Thus, the treasurer is deliberately buying investments that cannot be held until their maturity dates. If the yield curve is inverted (that is, interest rates are lower on longer-maturity investments), one would instead continually re-invest in very short-term instruments, no matter how far in the future the cash is actually needed again by the company.

EXAMPLE

The treasurer of Suture Corporation has $300,000 available to invest for the next 90 days. He notes that the interest rate on 3-month T-Bills is 2.0%, while the rate on 6-month T-Bills is 2.25%. He elects to take advantage of this 0.25% difference in interest rates by investing the $300,000 in 6-month T-Bills, and then selling them on a secondary market in 90 days, when he needs the cash for operational purposes.

A variation on all of the preceding strategies is to outsource the investment task to an experienced third party money manager. This option works well if a company is too small or has too few cash reserves to actively manage its own cash. If outsourcing is chosen, be sure to set up guidelines with the money manager for exactly how cash is to be invested, primarily through the use of lower-risk investments that mitigate the possibility of losing cash. A variation on the outsourcing concept is to invest primarily in money market funds, which are professionally managed.

Types of Investments

Once an investment strategy has been decided upon, the next step is to shift funds into a preferred set of investments. In this section, we describe the most common types of investments, along with the characteristics of each one.

Repurchase Agreements

A repurchase agreement is a package of securities that an investor buys from a financial institution, under an agreement that the institution will buy it back at a specific price on a certain date, typically the next business day. The repurchase price incorporates the interest rate paid to the investor during the investor's holding period. It is most commonly used for the overnight investment of excess cash from a company's cash concentration account, which can be automatically handled by a company's primary bank.

The interest rate earned on this investment is equal to or less than the money market rate, since the financial institution takes a transaction fee that reduces the rate earned. Despite the low return, the automated nature of repurchase agreements makes them a popular investment choice for a business that does not want to spend the time manually entering into a short-term investment for residual funds.

Time Deposits

A time deposit is a bank deposit that pays a fixed interest rate, and requires an investment for a specific period of time, usually anywhere from one week to one year. This is essentially a loan from the company to a bank, with interest set at a level close to the interbank rate. Time deposits have the advantage of being set at fixed interest rates, so there is no risk of an interest rate decline. However, the interest rate is typically quite low.

Certificates of Deposit

A certificate of deposit (CD) is an interest-bearing certificate that is issued by a bank as a receipt for deposits invested with it. A CD can have a maturity of as little as a few weeks to several years. There is a secondary market for some CDs, so this type of investment can be liquidated relatively quickly. CDs are available in multiple currencies. In particular, two variations on the concept are:

- *Eurodollar CDs.* Denominated in U.S. dollars, and issued by entities outside the United States.
- *Yankee CDs.* Denominated in U.S. dollars, and issued by foreign entities with operations in the United States.

A CD is issued at its face value, with additional interest due to the investor in addition to the face amount. A shorter-term CD is usually issued at a fixed interest rate, with interest being paid at the end of each year or the maturity of the instrument.

A longer-term CD may instead use a floating interest rate that is based on a major benchmark interest rate, such as LIBOR. If so, the interest rate is usually re-set every three or six months.

Bankers' Acceptances

A banker's acceptance arises when a bank guarantees (or accepts) corporate debt, usually when it issues a loan to a corporate customer, and then sells the debt to investors. These acceptances are sold at a discount, and redeemed upon maturity at their face value. Because of the bank guarantee, a banker's acceptance is viewed as an obligation of the bank. If the bank has a good reputation, the acceptance can be re-sold in an open market, at a discount to its face value. A banker's acceptance is considered to be a very safe asset, and is used extensively in international trade. A banker's acceptance usually has a term of less than 180 days.

Commercial Paper

Commercial paper is a promissory note issued by a corporation, usually with a maturity of less than 180 days; thus, it is a short-term bond. The short maturity is designed to avoid the extra cost of registration with the Securities and Exchange Commission that would be required if the term were to exceed 270 days. Typical issuers of commercial paper include:

- Financial entities
- Industrial companies

- Insurance companies
- Public utilities

Entities issuing commercial paper have usually obtained a credit rating from one of the major credit rating agencies, such as Standard & Poor's, Moody's Investors Service, or Fitch Ratings. If the credit rating of an issuer were to decline, then the value of its commercial paper would decline as well (and vice versa), which can impact the value of investments if they are to be sold on a secondary market.

Commercial paper is usually sold at a discount from its face value, which means that the investor buys it at a discounted price, and is repaid on the maturity date at its face value. Most commercial paper is unsecured, which means that this type of investment carries a higher interest rate to reflect the increased level of risk associated with it – though the rate is still quite low. Commercial paper can be acquired directly from the issuing companies, but is also commonly available through banks that act as dealers.

Money Market Funds

A money market fund is a pool of short-term financial instruments operated by a fund manager, for which investors can purchase shares. A money market fund usually invests solely in federal government debt issuances, such as T-Bills and T-Notes. It is quite easy to invest in and move cash out of a money market fund, and so is ideal for extremely short-term investments. To attract investors, many of these funds offer late cutoff times for new investments, which allows a company to wait until later in the day to concentrate cash positions before making an investment in a fund.

There are some discernible differences in the risk associated with different money market funds, which is caused by some fund managers taking risks in order to outperform the market. Conversely, other fund managers do an excellent job of investment diversification in order to reduce risk. Some funds may also be able to defer redemptions under certain conditions. For these reasons, be sure to examine the stated objectives and rules of a fund before investing in it.

U.S. Government Debt Instruments

Despite the continuing increases in the debt of the United States government, its debt instruments are still considered among the lowest-risk in the world. The ones most commonly used by corporations for investment are Treasury Bills (T-Bills) and Treasury Notes (T-Notes). T-Bills have 3, 6, and 12-month maturities. T-Bills having maturities of 3 and 6 months are auctioned on a weekly basis, while T-Bills with 12-month maturities are auctioned once a month. T-Bills are sold at a discount, and redeemed upon maturity at their face value. There is a very active secondary market in T-Bills, so it is easy to sell them prior to their maturity dates.

The maturities of T-Notes range from 1 to 10 years. Two-year T-Notes are issued on a monthly basis, while T-Notes with other maturities are issued on a quarterly basis. T-Notes are available as both inflation-indexed and fixed-rate investments. Interest on T-Notes is paid semi-annually. T-Notes are traded on secondary markets at premiums or discounts to their face values, to reflect the current market interest rate.

Treasury Bonds are also available. Bonds have similar characteristics to T-Notes, but have longer maturities. Maturities are generally in the range of 10 to 30 years.

Paradoxically, the trouble with U.S. government debt instruments is their safety – the United States government can obtain the lowest possible interest rates, so there is little return on funds invested in these instruments.

State and Local Government Debt

An interesting investment option is the debt obligations issued by state and local governments. These debt instruments are usually issued in conjunction with the revenue streams associated with large capital projects, such as airport fees and tolls from toll roads. Other instruments are based on general tax revenues. The maturities of these obligations are typically multi-year, so a company in need of cash must rely upon a vigorous aftermarket to liquidate them prior to their maturity dates. The returns on state and local debt obligations are higher than the yields on federal government issuances, and income from these investments is usually exempt from federal taxation.

Though it is rare for a state or local government to default on its debt, such cases are not unknown, so be mindful of the reliability of the cash flows supporting debt repayment.

Bonds

A bond is an obligation to pay a fixed amount to the bond holder, usually in the amount of $1,000 per bond, as of one or more dates specified in a bond agreement. The maturities of bonds can be extremely long, sometimes extending to 30 or even 40 years in the future.

There are many variations on the bond concept, but the two key types are based on differing methods for paying the bond holder. They are:

- *Coupon bond.* Each bond comes with a set of coupons, which are submitted to the issuer for payment of interest at regular intervals. The company does not track bond holder contact information for coupon bonds.
- *Registered bond.* The issuer maintains an updated list of the holders of its bonds, and sends interest payments to them at regular intervals.

The coupon bond is designed to be more easily transferrable between bond holders. This is of some importance, since there is an active secondary market in many bonds. The presence of a secondary market is critical for investors, especially when the maturity date is many years in the future, and the holder is uncertain of how long it wants to retain possession of the bond.

Several variations on bonds are noted below:

- *Secured/unsecured.* Some bond instruments provide specific collateral against which bondholders have a claim if the bonds are not paid. If there is a guideline to protect cash, then a business should only invest in secured bonds.
- *Convertible.* This is a bond that can be converted to stock using a pre-determined conversion ratio. This option is usually only available at set intervals, and conversion is at the discretion of the bondholder. The presence of conversion rights typically reduces the interest rate on a bond, since investors assign some value to the conversion privilege. If the main investment goal is obtaining a high return on investment, an organization should avoid convertible bonds, since they tend to have somewhat lower returns.
- *Callable.* This is a bond that the issuer can buy back prior to its maturity, usually because there has been a decline in interest rates since the issuance of the bond, and the issuer wants to refinance at a lower rate. The existence of a call provision tends to reduce the value of a bond, so investing organizations usually avoid this type of bond.

The Primary and Secondary Markets

A primary market refers to the original sale of a security to an investor. Whenever a security is sold thereafter among investors and market makers, it is referred to as the secondary market. The existence of a secondary market is critical to the investment operations of a business, since it allows for the liquidation of an investment prior to its maturity date. If there were no secondary market, investment activities would have to be limited to the most short-term investments, in order to ensure the availability of cash.

The secondary market is comprised of financial institutions and dealers. These entities can act as brokers, taking a commission on the transfer of an investment from a seller to a buyer. Alternatively, they can hold an inventory of investments on their own behalf, and sell them directly to buyers for a profit.

Secondary markets are particularly important when a company is aggressively investing in longer-term investments that generate higher interest rates. This activity, known as "riding the yield curve," is only possible if a business can promptly liquidate an investment well before its maturity date.

The Discounted Investment Formula

Some investments, such as T-Bills and T-Notes, are sold at a discount and redeemed at their face value. The calculation used to determine the correct discount to pay for one of these instruments is:

$$\text{Face value} \times \text{Discount rate} \times \frac{\text{Day count}}{\text{Annual basis}} = \text{Amount of discount}$$

For example, a company wants to buy a 90-day $10,000,000 T-Bill at a discount of 2.5%. The calculation is:

$10,000,000 Face value	×	0.025 Discount rate	×	90 Days / 360 Days	=	$62,500 Discount

When the discount is subtracted from the face value of the T-Bill, the amount to be paid is:

$10,000,000 Face value - $62,500 Discount = $9,937,500 Purchase price

Summary

While there are many investment alternatives available, it is entirely likely that an efficient treasury department will elect to concentrate its attention on just a few alternatives, and probably on those that are transactionally most efficient to engage in on a regular basis. For example, a business with modest cash balances may enter into an automated overnight repurchase arrangement with its primary bank, and essentially forget about any additional investment activities. An alternative where there is more investable cash on hand is to make all investments through an investment portal that conveniently links participants with a specific cluster of available investment instruments. Thus, convenience may prove to be the key reason for continually investing excess cash in the same types of investments.

If there is an interest in looking beyond the most convenient investments and exploring other options, the next most critical element of the investment decision will likely be the presence of an active secondary market. If there is such a market, it is much easier to liquidate an investment before its maturity date. The result can be a broader range of choices when cash is available for investment even over a relatively short period of time.

Chapter 7
Equity Financing

Introduction

The treasurer might find it expedient to sell shares to investors. This is most necessary when a business already has a high proportion of debt to equity, or if the business does not have sufficiently consistent cash flows to warrant the risk of taking on debt. In this chapter, we describe several possible equity financing methods, including Regulation D and Regulation A+ stock sales. Another alternative for a business that has successfully followed the classic capital raising path is the seasoned equity offering, which is described near the end of the chapter. Several related topics are also covered, including accredited investors, the rights offering, and dilution.

Regulation D Stock Sales

The requirements for registering shares are so onerous that a company may want to explore other alternatives that can bring in needed funds with less effort. One option is the sale of restricted stock under Regulation D to accredited investors. This approach is commonly used by businesses not willing to go public just yet, but can also be employed by organizations that have already gone public.

> **Related Podcast Episode:** Episode 89 of the Accounting Best Practices Podcast discusses Regulation D stock sales. The episode is available at: **accounting-tools.com/podcasts** or **iTunes**

Regulation D provides an exemption from the normal stock registration requirement. This is an exceedingly useful exemption, since unregistered shares can be sold to investors with a minimal amount of reporting to the SEC. Thus, the administrative aspects of registering shares are almost entirely eliminated.

Regulation D Rules

The detailed aspects of Regulation D are described in the SEC's Rules 504, 505, and 506. In general, to sell shares under Regulation D, a company must follow these rules:

- Only sell shares to accredited investors (as described in a later section).
- Investors cannot be contacted through a general solicitation, such as advertising or free seminars open to the public.
- If shares are sold over a long time period, prove that all sales are covered by Regulation D (rather than being separate offerings). This can be done by

documenting a financing plan, selling the same type of stock to all investors, showing that all shares are sold for the same type of consideration, *and* by proving that the sales are being made for the same general purpose.

Regulation D Process Flow

Because of the inability to advertise a stock sale, companies usually turn to investment bankers, who contact their clients to see who is interested in buying shares. The bankers impose a fee for this service, which is a percentage of the amount of funds generated.

If a prospective investor is interested in buying shares, the company sends them a boilerplate questionnaire to fill out, in which they state that they are accredited investors. This form provides the company with legal protection, in case the SEC questions whether the stock issuance is protected by Regulation D. The questions posed by this questionnaire typically include the following:

- *Knowledge and experience.* The investor has sufficient knowledge of and experience in financial matters to be able to properly evaluate the merits and risks of the stock offering.
- *Restricted nature of shares.* The investor understands that the securities are restricted, and so cannot be sold until they have been registered.
- *Ability to invest.* The investor affirms that his/her total commitment to unregistered investments is not out of proportion to his/her net worth. Further, the investor has sufficient liquidity to provide for personal needs, and does not expect a change in liquidity that will require the sale of these securities at a later date.
- *Personal ownership.* The investor will hold the securities for his/her personal account, not with the intent of selling them to a third party.
- *Questions asked.* The investor affirms that he/she can question the company concerning the securities prior to purchasing them, and that these questions have been asked prior to the purchase.
- *Completeness of information.* The investor affirms that the information he/she provides in this questionnaire is complete and accurate.
- *Accredited investor qualifications.* The questionnaire also includes yes/no affirmations of each line item in the definition of an accredited investor, as described in a following section. This information is used to determine whether a prospective investor falls within the definition of an accredited investor, and so can purchase shares from the company under Regulation D.

Investors then send their money to an escrow account that is maintained by a third party, until such time as the total amount of funding meets the minimum requirement set by the company. The investment banker extracts its fee from the escrowed funds, the company collects its cash, and the company's stock transfer agent sends stock certificates to the investors.

Shares issued under Regulation D are not initially registered, which means that a restriction statement appears on the back of each certificate. This statement essentially prohibits the shareholder from selling to a third party. A sample statement is:

> The shares represented by this certificate have been acquired for investment and have not been registered under the Securities Act of 1933. Such shares may not be sold or transferred or pledged in the absence of such registration unless the company receives an opinion of counsel reasonably acceptable to the company stating that such sale or transfer is exempt from the registration and prospectus delivery requirements of said Act.

This restriction on the resale of stock is usually a major concern for all but the most long-term investors. Accordingly, investors like to see one or more of the following guarantees being offered by a company:

- *Piggyback rights*. The company promises to include their shares in any stock registration statement that it may eventually file with the SEC. This is a near-universal inclusion in a Regulation D offering, since it does not impose an immediate obligation on the company.
- *Registration promise*. The company promises to file a registration statement with the SEC by a certain date. If the company is currently privately held, this promise essentially requires it to become publicly-held, along with the various ongoing SEC filing requirements that are part of being a public company. A more onerous agreement will even require the company to issue additional stock if it does not obtain SEC approval of the registration statement by a certain date.

The downside of using a Registration D stock sale is that investors typically want something extra in exchange for buying unregistered stock. This may take the form of a reduced price per share. In addition, investors may demand warrants, which are a formal right to buy additional company stock at a certain exercise price.

EXAMPLE

Hegemony Toy Company sells 10,000 shares of its common stock for $10.00, along with 10,000 warrants to buy additional shares of the company for the next three years at $10.00 per share. The price of the company's stock later rises to $17.00, at which point the investor uses his warrant privileges to buy an additional 10,000 shares at $10.00 each. If he can then have the shares registered and sells them at the $17.00 market price, he will pocket a profit of $70,000 on his exercise of the warrants.

A company is paying a steep price if it issues warrants and then experiences a sharp increase in its stock price, since the recipient of the warrants will eventually buy shares from the company at what will then be an inordinately low price. If the company had not issued warrants, it would instead be able to later sell shares at the full market price.

If an investor wants one warrant for every share purchased, this is called 100% warrant coverage. If an investor agrees to one warrant for every two shares purchased, this is called 50% warrant coverage. These are the two most common warrant issuance terms, though any proportion of warrants to shares purchased may be agreed to.

An even more serious downside of using Regulation D is when prospective investors insist upon buying preferred stock, rather than common stock. Preferred stock may include a number of oppressive terms, such as favorable conversion rights into common stock, the payment of dividends, and perhaps even override voting privileges concerning the sale of the company or other matters.

Given the number of rights that investors may demand in a Regulation D stock sale, it is best to only use this approach when the company is operating from a position of strength, where it does not have an immediate need for cash.

The Form D Filing

An organization that sells shares under the provisions of Regulation D must file a report with the SEC concerning the sale. This is the Form D, which must be filed by the securities issuer no later than 15 calendar days after the date on which securities were first sold. This date is considered to be when the first investor is irrevocably contractually committed to invest. Examples of first sale dates are:

- When the entity receives a stock subscription agreement from an investor
- When the entity receives a check from an investor to pay for shares

An amendment to this form must be filed annually, if the entity is continuing to sell shares under the offering contained within the original notification. An amendment is also needed if there is a material mistake of fact or error in the preceding filing, or if there is a change in the information provided (with certain exceptions). The main types of information to be described on the Form D are:

- *Identity*. The name and type of entity of the issuer.
- *Contact information*. The location and contact information for the issuer.
- *Related persons*. The executive officer, directors, and promoter of the issuer, as well as their contact information.
- *Industry type*. The industry group in which the issuer is situated.
- *Issuer size*. The revenue range or aggregate net asset value range of the issuer.
- *Exemptions*. The federal exemptions or exclusions claimed, under which the shares are being sold.
- *Investment*. The minimum investment amount to be accepted from investors.
- *Sales compensation*. The identification of anyone receiving compensation as part of the stock sales, and the states in which solicitations are being made.
- *Offering and sales amounts*. The total offering amount, the amount sold, and the amount remaining to be sold.

- *Expenses*. The amounts of any sales commissions and finder's fees to be paid as part of the offering.
- *Use of proceeds*. The uses to which the resulting funds are to be put.

The amount of information required by the Form D is relatively small, compared to the much more comprehensive requirements of a formal securities registration document.

Rule 506(c)

One of the exemptions from the SEC's registration requirements is located in Rule 506(c) of the SEC's Regulation D. Under this Rule, the amount of funding that can be raised is unlimited and sales are restricted to accredited investors. The downside of limiting investors in this manner is that the pool of potential investors will be relatively small. Further, the fundraising entity must verify that investors actually qualify as accredited investors. Prior to this Rule, the burden of proof was on the investor, who would usually fill out a form in which they certified that they were accredited. Now, the issuer must take reasonable steps to verify that all investors are properly classified as being accredited. The SEC offers two ways in which this verification can be accomplished. They are:

- *Principles-based approach*. The issuer uses its judgment to decide whether an investor is accredited. This means looking at the nature of the investor, the type of accredited investor the individual purports to be, the kind of information on hand about the investor, how the investor was reached, and the terms of the offering. The problem here is that the SEC may decide that the issuer's judgment was flawed, which could result in the loss of its 506(c) exemption.
- *Formal verification*. The issuer determines an investor's accredited status based on "hard" documentation, which is the safer approach for verifying accredited status. This can include the following:
  - o Review the investor's tax returns to verify income over the past two years.
  - o Obtain a written statement from the investor regarding income expectations for the current year.
  - o Review the investor's consumer credit report, bank statements, brokerage statements, and/or real estate appraisals to estimate net worth.
  - o Obtain a written confirmation from a registered or licensed professional, such as a certified public accountant or a securities attorney, that the investor is verified as being accredited.

Despite these issues, Rule 506(c) actually represents a favorable regulatory environment for fund raising. Those websites that usually assist in raising funds already have procedures in place to satisfy the accreditation requirement. For example, a fundraising portal may require prospective investors to provide substantiation of their income or net worth. This pre-existing base of accredited investors is quite useful, for a business is allowed under the Rule to advertise their fundraising activities. By combining advertising with a base of accredited investors that is already available through a fundraising portal, a business may be able to reach a wider audience of investors. Further, there is no ceiling on the amount of funds that can be raised under this Rule.

In short, Rule 506(c) provides one of the most cost-effective ways to raise money through a restricted form of crowdfunding. This is especially the case when a business does not already have relationships with entities that might be interested in investing.

The Accredited Investor

An accredited investor qualifies under SEC rules as being financially sophisticated. The SEC definition of an accredited investor is:

1. A bank, insurance company, registered investment company, business development company, or small business investment company;
2. An employee benefit plan, within the meaning of the Employee Retirement Income Security Act, if a bank, insurance company, or registered investment adviser makes the investment decisions, or if the plan has total assets in excess of $5 million;
3. A charitable organization, corporation, or partnership with assets exceeding $5 million;
4. A director, executive officer, or general partner of the company selling the securities;
5. A business in which all the equity owners are accredited investors;
6. A natural person who has individual net worth, or joint net worth with the person's spouse, that exceeds $1 million at the time of the purchase, excluding the value of the primary residence of such person;
7. A natural person with income exceeding $200,000 in each of the two most recent years or joint income with a spouse exceeding $300,000 for those years and a reasonable expectation of the same income level in the current year; or
8. A trust with assets in excess of $5 million, not formed to acquire the securities offered, whose purchases a sophisticated person makes.

This definition comes from Rule 501 of the SEC's Regulation D.

A questionnaire is used to ascertain whether a prospective investor is accredited; elements of this questionnaire were noted earlier in the Regulation D Stock Sales section. The company should go to some lengths to ensure that all investors who intend to buy shares under Regulation D have completed and signed the questionnaire, since this represents the company's only evidence that it has sold shares to accredited investors.

Regulation A+ Overview

The preceding discussion of Regulation D was oriented toward stock sales to accredited investors. What if a company does not have access to this group of wealthy investors, or cannot find any who are willing to invest? An alternative is available under the Regulation A+ exemption.

Under Regulation A+, a company can issue securities under two tiers. The more essential requirements associated with each tier are noted in the following table.

Regulation A+ Tiers

	Tier 1	Tier 2
Amount raised per year	$20 million maximum	$50 million maximum
Investment limitations	None	For non-accredited investors, 10% of the greater of income or net worth, per offering
Non-accredited investors allowed	Yes	Yes
Audited financials required	No	Yes
Registration required with SEC	Yes	Yes
Shares freely tradable	Yes	Yes
Ongoing reporting requirements	No	Yes (semi-annual)

The Regulation A+ exemption is not available to a number of types of companies. They are investment companies, foreign companies, oil and gas companies, public companies, and companies selling asset-backed securities.

If a company qualifies for this exemption, the basic process flow is to issue an SEC-reviewed offering circular to attract investors, then file a Form 1-A with the SEC, then sell shares, and then file a Form 1-Z to document the termination or completion of the offering. If the company is in Tier 2, it must then file a Form 1-K annual report that includes audited financial statements, a discussion of its financial results, and information about its business and management, related-party transactions, and share ownership. The Form 1-K is estimated to require 600 hours to complete. A Tier 2 company must also file a Form 1-SA semi-annual report that includes interim unaudited financial statements, as well as a discussion of the company's financial results. The Form 1-SA is estimated to require 187 hours to complete. Finally, a Tier 2 company must file a Form 1-U within four business days of certain events, such as a bankruptcy, change in accountant, or change in control.

A key feature of Regulation A+ stock sales is that shares are freely tradable. This might initially appear to be an exceedingly valuable feature for investors. However, because the shares are not being traded on a public exchange, it still may be difficult for investors to sell their shares.

In short, Regulation A+ can be considered a miniature version of an initial public offering. It allows a business to raise a fairly significant amount of money, but incurs significant reporting burdens in exchange.

Private Investments in Public Equity

When a publicly-held company's equity is sold to accredited private investors, this is referred to as a private investment in public equity (PIPE). Private investors are usually willing to engage in such a transaction when they are offered a discount from the market price of a company's stock, typically in the range of a 10% to 25% discount. The sale of securities under a PIPE can be structured in a number of ways, including the following:

- Common stock sold at a specific price point
- Common stock sold with warrants having fixed exercise prices
- Common stock sold with warrants having resettable exercise prices
- Common stock sold at a variable price point
- Convertible preferred stock
- Convertible debt

A major advantage of a PIPE is that it is considered a private investment by the SEC under Regulation D, so the shares do not have to be immediately registered with the SEC. Since no registration is required, the offering can be completed quickly and with minimal administrative hassles. A further advantage for the issuing company is that shares are typically sold in large blocks under a PIPE transaction to longer-term and more knowledgeable investors.

However, there are some disadvantages to entering into a PIPE transaction, from the perspective of the company. Consider the following issues:

- *Additional shares.* The company may have to guarantee the issuance of additional shares to PIPE investors if the market price of the shares subsequently falls below a threshold amount.
- *Rapid sell-off.* Unless the company is careful about which investors are allowed to buy shares in a PIPE deal, it may find that the investors sell off their shares as soon as possible after the shares have been registered, thereby driving down the market price of the stock.
- *Registration obligation.* The company is typically obligated to file a registration statement with the SEC shortly after the sale is completed, so that the investors can eventually have the restrictions removed from their stock certificates and can then sell their shares.
- *Short seller manipulation.* If the company is obligated to issue more shares to investors if the stock price declines, short sellers could take advantage of the situation by continually driving down the stock price, which triggers the issuance of more and more shares. This *death spiral PIPE* can even result in majority ownership of the company by the PIPE investors. The scenario can

be avoided by specifying a minimum stock price below which no additional compensatory shares will be issued.

- *Warrants.* Investors may demand that they also be granted warrants, so that they can participate in any upside growth in the price of the company's stock.

Crowdfunding

The JOBS Act was passed in 2012, with the intent of making it easier for companies to raise small amounts of capital, both by opening up stock sales to the general public and by reducing the reporting requirements of businesses.

> **Related Podcast Episode:** Episode 242 of the Accounting Best Practices Podcast discusses crowdfunding. The episode is available at: **accountingtools.com/podcasts** or **iTunes**

When Congress passed the JOBS Act, it required the SEC to create a regulation that embodied the requirements of the Act. Accordingly, the SEC issued Regulation Crowdfunding in 2016. The key provisions of this regulation are noted in the following sub-sections.

Requirements

An organization can only use the crowdfunding exemption if it meets all of the following requirements, where monetary amounts have been adjusted for inflation as of 2017:

- *Aggregate limitation.* The firm is limited to raising a maximum amount of $1,070,000 in a 12-month period. This limit includes the amount it has already sold during the preceding 12-month period and the amount it intends to raise in this offering. This total does not include other exempt (non-crowdfunding) offerings during the period. We discuss these exemptions in the next chapter.
- *Investor limitations.* The aggregate amount that can be sold to any single investor cannot exceed:
  - The greater of $2,200 or five percent of the annual income or net worth of the investor, if the annual income or net worth of the investor is less than $107,000; and
  - Ten percent of the annual income or net worth of the investor, not to exceed a maximum aggregate amount sold of $107,000, if either the annual income or net worth of the investor is equal to or greater than $107,000.

EXAMPLE

An investor has annual income of $150,000 and a net worth of $80,000. The individual can invest the greater of $2,200 or 5% of $80,000. Therefore, the maximum possible investment is $4,000.

An investor has annual income of $200,000 and a net worth of $900,000. The individual can invest 10% of the $200,000 income, which is a $20,000 investment.

- *Intermediary*. An entity acting as an intermediary in a crowdfunding sale of securities must register with the SEC and FINRA[1] as a broker-dealer or a funding portal, that will provide investors with investor-education information, affirm that investors understand that they are risking the loss of their entire investments, and take steps to reduce the risk of fraud with respect to these transactions. Fraud reduction includes obtaining a background and securities history check on each officer, director, and person holding more than 20 percent of the outstanding equity of the issuing entity. No later than 21 days prior to the first day on which securities will be sold by an issuer, the intermediary must make available to the SEC and to potential investors any information provided by the issuer. Also, the entity can only forward funds to the issuer when the aggregate capital raised from all investors equals or exceeds the target offering amount.
- *Ineligible entities*. The following types of organizations are not eligible to use the Regulation Crowdfunding exemption:
  - Non-U.S. companies
  - Companies already subject to the reporting requirements of the Exchange Act
  - Certain types of investment companies
  - Companies that are disqualified under the Regulation's disqualification rules (see the following Bad Actor Disqualification sub-section)
  - Companies that have not met the Regulation's annual reporting requirements during the preceding two years
  - Companies that have no specific business plan
  - Companies that plan to engage in unidentified mergers or acquisitions

Disclosures

When an organization plans to conduct an offering under the Regulation, it must electronically file its offering statement on Form C, via the SEC's EDGAR[2] system, as well as with the entity that is acting as the intermediary in the offering. The Form C is essentially an abbreviated version of the much longer filing required when a

---

[1] The Financial Industry Regulatory Authority
[2] EDGAR is short for the Electronic Data Gathering, Analysis and Retrieval System

firm wants to register shares with the SEC for a public offering. The Form C is estimated to require about 50 hours to complete. Its main information requirements are:

- Information about the firm's officers, directors, and owners of 20% or more of its shares
- A description of the business
- A description of how the proceeds from the offering will be used
- The price at which the shares will be offered, or the method used to determine the price
- The target offering amount
- The deadline by which the offering amount must be reached
- Whether the firm will accept investments in excess of the target amount
- A description of certain related-party transactions
- A discussion of the firm's financial condition and financial statements

If the firm plans to raise $107,000 or less, it must provide its income tax return for the most recently completed year, and its financial statements (to be certified by the principal executive officer). However, if the firm has either audited or reviewed financial statements, it must provide these statements instead.

If the firm plans to raise more than $107,000 but not more than $535,000, it must provide financial statements that have been reviewed by an independent public accountant. However, if the firm has audited financial statements, it must provide these statements instead.

If the firm plans to raise more than $535,000 and it is a first-time user of the Regulation Crowdfunding exemption, it must provide financial statements that have been reviewed by an independent public accountant. However, if the firm has audited financial statements, it must provide these statements instead.

If the firm plans to raise more than $535,000 and it has previously used the Regulation Crowdfunding exemption, it must provide financial statements that have been audited by an independent public accountant.

There may be cases in which an organization has material updates to the information it has provided to the SEC. If these changes occur while an offering is not yet complete, the firm should include the changes in a Form C/A. Also, the firm must reconfirm any outstanding investment commitments within five business days, or else the commitment will be considered cancelled.

The firm must provide periodic updates to the SEC on the Form C-U. This report must be filed within five business days of reaching 50% of the targeted funding amount, as well as when the 100% threshold has been reached. If the firm accepts proceeds in excess of the target amount, it must file yet another Form C-U that states the total amount of securities sold in the offering.

When a firm sells securities under the Regulation Crowdfunding exemption, it must provide an annual report to the SEC, using the Form C-AR. This report must be filed no later than 120 days after the end of the firm's fiscal year. The firm must also post the completed Form on its website. The content of this Form is similar to what was required for the Form C, though there is no requirement to have the firm's financial statements audited or reviewed. These annual report filings must continue into the future until one of the following happens:

- The firm is required to file reports under Exchange Act sections 13(a) or 15(d)
- The firm has filed at least one annual report and has fewer than 300 holders of record
- The issuer has filed at least three annual reports and has total assets of not greater than $10 million
- The firm or another party purchases or repurchases all of the securities, including any payment in full of debt securities or any complete redemption of redeemable securities
- The firm liquidates itself

When a firm is terminating its annual reporting obligation, it must file a Form C-TR with the SEC, stating that it will no longer be providing annual reports.

Limits on Advertising and Promoters

An issuer is not allowed to advertise the terms of a Regulation Crowdfunding offering, except to issue a statement that sends investors to the intermediary's platform. This statement can only include the following information:

a) A statement that the issuer is conducting an offering pursuant to Section 4(a)(6) of the Securities Act, the name of the intermediary through which the offering is being conducted, and a link directing the potential investor to the intermediary's platform;
b) The terms of the offering, which means the amount of securities offered, the nature of the securities, their price, and the closing date of the offering period; and
c) Factual information about the legal identity and business location of the issuer, which is limited to the name of the issuer, its address, phone number, and website, the e-mail address of a representative of the issuer, and a brief description of its business.

It is allowable for the issuer to communicate with investors about the terms of the offering through communication channels provided on the intermediary's platform.

An issuer is allowed to compensate third parties to promote its crowdfunding offerings through communication channels provided by the intermediary, but only if the issuer ensures that the promoter discloses the compensation in each communication made.

Restrictions on Resale

When securities are sold in a crowdfunding transaction, they cannot be resold for one year. The only exceptions are when the securities are transferred to the issuer, or an accredited investor, or as part of an offering registered with the SEC, or to a member of the family of the purchaser or to a trust controlled by the purchaser.

Exemption from Section 12(g)

Section 12(g) of the Exchange Act states that an issuer having total assets of more than $10 million and a class of securities held by either 2,000 persons or 500 persons who are not accredited investors must register those securities with the SEC. However, securities issued under Regulation Crowdfunding are exempt from this requirement, as long as the following conditions are met:

- The issuer is current in its ongoing reporting requirements to the SEC; and
- The issuer has assets as of the end of its last fiscal year of $25 million or less; and
- The issuer has engaged the services of a transfer agent that is registered with the SEC.

If these requirements are not met, the issuer has a two-year transition period in which to register its securities with the SEC, as long as it continues to file all required reports with the SEC in a timely manner.

Bad Actor Disqualification

The SEC will disqualify an offering if the issuer or other covered persons have experienced a disqualifying event. Issuers must conduct an inquiry to determine whether any covered person has had a disqualifying event. Covered persons include the following:

- The issuer
- The issuer's directors, officers, general partners, or managing members
- Beneficial owners of 20% or more of the issuer's outstanding voting equity securities
- Promoters associated with the issuer
- Persons compensated for soliciting investors

These disqualifying events must have occurred after May 16, 2016, and include the following:

- Certain criminal convictions
- Certain court injunctions and restraining orders
- Certain final orders of state and federal regulators
- Certain SEC disciplinary orders
- Certain SEC cease and desist orders
- Suspension or expulsion from membership in a self-regulatory organization, such as FINRA
- SEC stop orders and orders suspending the Regulation A+ exemption
- U.S. Postal Service false representation orders

The regulation contains an exemption from disqualification when the issuer can demonstrate that it did not know, and could not have known that a covered person with a disqualifying event had participated in an offering.

Seasoned Equity Offerings

A follow up to the initial public offering discussed in the preceding chapter is the seasoned equity offering (SEO). This refers to any issuance of securities where the securities have been previously issued. Publicly-held companies tend to be cautious about issuing new SEOs, since the investment community tends to take the stance that more shares will water down their existing holdings, and so will bid down the price of the company's stock. A company may gain back this initial loss over time, if it can use the proceeds from the SEO to create a disproportionate increase in earnings (see the Dilution section later in this chapter).

Despite the possible short-term negative effect of an SEO, this is a more cost-effective approach to raising capital than the initial public offering. The company is already in compliance with the various mandates of the SEC, and so will incur no additional internal labor costs as a result of the SEO. Also, the company is presumably already listed on a stock exchange, so the incremental listing cost associated with the additional shares will be relatively small. Further, investment bankers usually charge a somewhat smaller fee than the hefty underwriting discount that they charge for an initial public offering. Consequently, if a public company continues to require additional funds that it does not want to obtain through more debt, an ongoing series of SEOs can be a reasonable way to obtain the funds.

A common method followed for an SEO is to use a *shelf registration*. This is a new issuance of securities registered with the SEC, where the issuance is to be made sometime during the next three years. This approach means that a business has pre-registered securities in hand, which it can issue on short notice. The CFO can maximize the funds raised from an equity shelf registration by waiting until the company's stock price is at a high point, and selling shares to investors at that point. This approach is easiest for a well-known seasoned issuer (WKSI), for which the shares associated with a shelf registration are declared effective as soon as the registration document is filed with the SEC. An organization qualifies as a WKSI if the market value of its stock owned by non-affiliates is at least $700 million, or it has issued at least $1 billion of non-convertible debt securities during the last three years.

The Rights Offering

The articles of incorporation of an organization may mandate that any new issuance of shares first be offered to existing shareholders. This requirement is designed to concentrate ownership among the existing shareholders, rather than watering down their investments as new investors acquire shares in the business.

An issuance of shares to existing shareholders is called a *rights offering*. In essence, a rights offering is an option to purchase shares. Under the terms of this option, a shareholder can purchase a certain number of shares at a designated price. The option expires on a specific date, after which the company can sell shares to outside investors. An option is exercised when a shareholder sends the required payment to the subscription agent handling the offering on behalf of the company.

EXAMPLE

Eskimo Construction, maker of energy-efficient homes, has 5,000,000 shares of common stock outstanding. These shares are currently selling on a stock exchange at $11 per share, which implies a market value for the company of $55 million. Management plans to use a rights offering to raise an additional $10 million.

Eskimo sets the price of the offering at $10. Doing so attracts the attention of the current investors, since they can buy at a price that is $1 below the market rate. Since management wants to raise $10 million at a price of $10 per share, it will be necessary to sell an additional 1,000,000 shares. To raise this sum, Eskimo will need to issue 1,000,000 rights.

A rights offering has value, since it typically allows the holder to buy shares at a below-market price. In the preceding example, a $1 discount per share was available to each rights holder. However, this advantage is only available until the termination date of the rights offering. This means that someone purchasing a company's shares should pay more for those shares up until the rights termination date, in order to account for the increased value associated with the attached rights offering. The price of the stock should decline immediately thereafter, to reflect the termination of the rights offering.

A company that engages in a rights offering usually sets the price sufficiently low that any declines in the market price of the stock during the offering period will not fall below the subscription price. Doing so essentially ensures that the rights will be used by shareholders, so that the company receives the full amount of proceeds from the offering. A business can guarantee its receipt of the expected funds by entering into a standby underwriting arrangement with an underwriter, which will commit to purchase all unsubscribed shares for a fee. The fee charged for this service is essentially a form of insurance against the loss of funds.

Dilution

When raising capital, the existing shareholders may be concerned that their ownership interest in the business will be diluted, since shares will now be sold to a new set of shareholders. This inherent level of dilution can be avoided with a rights offering, where the current investors are first given the opportunity to purchase additional shares.

EXAMPLE

Mr. Smith is one of the founding shareholders of Blitz Communications, maker of office phones. He originally purchased 10,000 shares, which represented a 10% share of the total number of shares outstanding.

The management of Blitz needs to raise capital, and proposes selling an additional 100,000 shares to the public. If Mr. Smith does not purchase any of these new shares, his ownership interest in the company will decline to 5%, which is calculated as follows:

10,000 Shares held ÷ 200,000 Total shares outstanding = 5% Ownership interest

The company elects to initiate a rights offering arrangement, where the existing shareholders are given the opportunity to purchase shares at a rate of one new share for each share currently held. Mr. Smith elects to purchase his full allotment of 10,000 additional shares. His ownership interest in the company is now 10%, which is calculated as follows:

20,000 Shares held ÷ 200,000 Total shares outstanding = 10% Ownership interest

---

A valid concern may be raised that shareholders will suffer a reduction in the value of their shares if new shares are sold. There are numerous factors that influence the market price of a share, but certainly among the more crucial factors are earnings per share and cash flow per share. If a company sells shares to raise capital and then invests the new funds in activities that generate a lower incremental level of earnings or cash flow, then investors will likely be less inclined to invest in the shares, and their market price will decline.

EXAMPLE

Creekside Industrial currently has 5,000,000 shares of common stock outstanding, which sell on a national stock exchange for $20 per share. The company currently produces income of $25,000,000, which is $5.00/share. This means that investors are buying the stock at a 4x multiple of the earnings per share.

The management team believes that there is a golden opportunity to manufacture batteries for hybrid cars, and needs $10,000,000 of capital to construct a battery production facility for this purpose. Accordingly, the board of directors authorizes the sale of 500,000 shares of common stock to raise the required amount of capital. The money is raised, and is invested in the facility. However, the company finds that foreign competition is driving down the price of hybrid car batteries, so the new facility can only break even.

The result is no change in company income, which remains at $25,000,000. However, there are now 5,500,000 shares of common stock outstanding, so the earnings per share figure has declined to $4.55. Assuming that investors are still assigning a 4x multiple to the earnings per share figure, this means that the market value of the company's stock has now declined to $18.20.

Stock price dilution is a particular concern among investors when shares are being sold to pay for an acquisition. The majority of acquisitions do not achieve initial expectations, so the additional shares issued are not likely to trigger an increase in earnings per share or cash flow per share. Consequently, it is not uncommon to see a market price decline for the shares of the acquirer, even before an acquisition has been completed – investors are simply making their expectations known by fleeing the stock.

Summary

The capital raising alternatives described in this chapter all have flaws or restrictions that limit their use. For example:

- *Regulation A.* The fatal flaw in Regulation A from the perspective of the issuer is that the organization is still required to produce a considerable amount of information for the Form 1-A, and yet can only obtain a maximum of $50 million for all of this effort. From the perspective of investors, they will obtain unrestricted stock, but the issuer is likely so small that there is not much of a market for the shares, making them difficult to sell.
- *Regulation D.* The Regulation D option does not result in registered stock, so investors cannot easily sell their shares. A common outcome is that the issuer must offer one or more enticements to prospective investors in order to convince them to buy shares. These enticements could be quite expensive, or force the issuer to take itself public at a later date.
- *Crowdfunding.* The annual crowdfunding limitation for a business is so small that it is likely to be a viable alternative only for the smallest startup companies. Further, a prospective issuer will likely compare the amount of money to be gained to the level of required information reporting, and conclude that the trade-off is not a reasonable one.
- *Seasoned equity offerings.* This is a fine, lower-cost approach to raising capital, but is only available to businesses that have already gone public. Consequently, an SEO is only a viable option for a small number of businesses.

Chapter 8
Debt Financing

Introduction

A business may not be able to obtain additional funding through the issuance of equity, or its owners may be reluctant to do so. If this is the case, a common alternative is to instead obtain debt financing. In this chapter, we review the different types of debt. The bulk of the debt alternatives available are based upon the assets of a business, which imposes a limitation on the total amount of debt that can be obtained. A smaller number of unsecured financing choices are available to businesses that have more robust financial results. These options are described in the following sections.

Related Podcast Episodes: Episodes 124 and 125 of the Accounting Best Practices Podcast discuss lender relations and refinancing debt, respectively. They are available at: **accountingtools.com/podcasts** or **iTunes**

Overview of Debt Financing

If a business cannot meet its funding requirements by internally generating cash or selling shares, then the best remaining option is to obtain debt funding. There are several types of debt financing, which fall into these categories:

- *Asset-based financing*. Company assets are used as collateral for this type of debt. Examples are the line of credit, invoice discounting, factoring, receivables securitization, inventory financing, loan stock, purchase order financing, hard money loans, and mezzanine financing.
- *Unsecured financing*. No company assets are used as collateral. Instead, lenders rely upon the cash flows of the business to obtain repayment. Examples are long-term loans and bonds.

Examples of these types of debt financing are noted through the remainder of this chapter.

If a company obtains financing, it must pay interest on the amount borrowed. The interest percentage may be variable, with the rate adjusting in accordance with a benchmark rate at regular intervals. If the rate is variable and may rise suddenly, a company is at some risk of incurring much higher interest expenses. These costs are mitigated by the tax deductibility of interest expense. For example, if a company incurs $100,000 of interest expense and is in the 35% incremental income tax bracket, it can use the $100,000 interest deduction to reduce its income tax liability (if any) by $35,000.

There may also be a fee for an annual audit of the company's books by a bank-designated auditor, as well as an annual facility fee for keeping open a line of credit.

When reviewing the following types of debt, take note of any administrative charges that may also be billed to the company. This is a particularly large issue for financings involving accounts receivable or inventory as collateral, and can noticeably increase the total borrowing cost.

The Line of Credit

A line of credit is a commitment from a lender to pay a company whenever it needs cash, up to a pre-set maximum limit. A line of credit is generally secured by company assets, which the lender can take if the company is unable to pay back the line of credit. The lender will not allow a drawdown against a line of credit if the total amount lent will then exceed the amount of assets pledged as collateral against the line (known as the *borrowing base*). Any debt made available under a line of credit can be accessed multiple times over the course of the debt agreement. The lender may also block out a portion of a line of credit for letter of credit transactions where the borrower is committing to pay a supplier a predetermined amount on a future date. A line of credit is a highly useful form of financing for a business that does not have sufficient cash reserves to fund its day-to-day needs.

A larger and more credit-worthy business may be able to avoid any collateral; if so, the lender is relying on the general credit quality of the company. The usual agreement under which a line of credit is granted requires the company to pay an annual fee in exchange for the lender's commitment to keep a certain amount of debt available for the company's use; this is called a *committed* line of credit. It is also possible to have a less formal arrangement at a lower cost, where the lender is not obligated to make funds available to the company. This latter arrangement is called an *uncommitted* line of credit, and is useful for rare lending needs when a company has several sources of funds from which to choose.

When a bank offers a line of credit, it is typically under the agreement that the bank will also handle the company's other banking business, such as its checking accounts and lockboxes. This arrangement can be useful, since the staff can monitor cash balances and routinely transfer borrowed funds back to the bank through an inexpensive intrabank transfer transaction. Doing so on a frequent basis minimizes the interest cost of the line of credit.

When entering into a line of credit arrangement, be sure to also obtain separate debt funding to handle all of the company's long-term debt needs. The reason is that a line of credit is intended to be a source of short-term funding *only*, which means that the line of credit balance is expected to drop to zero at some point each year. Otherwise, it will appear that the company is using the line as part of its long-term borrowing arrangements.

The Borrowing Base

A borrowing base is the total amount of collateral against which a lender will lend funds to a business. This typically involves multiplying a discount factor by each type of asset used as collateral. For example:

- *Accounts receivable*. 60% to 80% of accounts receivable less than 90 days old may be accepted as a borrowing base. Receivables from related parties and foreign entities are excluded.
- *Inventory*. A smaller percentage of finished goods inventory may be accepted as a borrowing base. Raw materials and work-in-process, as well as custom-made goods and slow-moving finished goods are usually not allowed, since they are more difficult to liquidate.

It is also common for a lender to only use the accounts receivable of a borrower as collateral - it may not accept *any* inventory as part of the borrowing base.

If the business is a small one, the lender issuing a line of credit will probably also want a personal guarantee from the owner of the business, in addition to the underlying collateral.

A business that borrows money under a borrowing base arrangement usually fills out a *borrowing base certificate* at regular intervals, in which it calculates the applicable borrowing base. A company officer signs the certificate and submits it to the lender, which retains it as proof of the available amount of collateral. If the borrowing base stated on the certificate is less than the amount that the company is currently borrowing from the lender, then the company must pay the difference to the lender at once.

EXAMPLE

Hammer Industries enters into a line of credit arrangement that has a maximum lending limit of $6 million. The amount of the accounts receivable to be used in the borrowing base is limited to 80% of all trade receivables less than 90 days old. The amount of the inventory to be used is limited to finished goods. The amount of finished goods to be used in the borrowing base is limited to 65%.

At the end of March, there are $4.8 million of accounts receivable outstanding, of which $200,000 are more than 90 days old. Hammer also has $6.5 million of inventory on hand, of which $3.5 million is finished goods. The amount of debt that has been drawn down on the line of credit is $5 million. Based on this information, the treasurer of Hammer constructs the following borrowing base certificate:

Hammer Industries	
Borrowing Base Certificate	as of 3/31/20x3
Total accounts receivable	$4,800,000
Less: Receivables > 90 days old	-200,000
Eligible accounts receivable	$4,600,000
× Advance rate	80%
= Collateral value of accounts receivable	$3,680,000
Total finished goods inventory	$3,500,000
× Advance rate	65%
= Collateral value of finished goods inventory	$2,275,000
Total collateral	$5,955,000
Total debt outstanding	5,000,000
Excess collateral	$955,000

Careful monitoring of the borrowing base is of particular importance in seasonal businesses, since the inventory portion of the base gradually builds prior to the selling season, followed by a sharp increase in the receivable asset during the selling season, and then a rapid decline in all assets immediately after the season has been completed. It is necessary to balance loan drawdowns and repayments against these rapid changes in the borrowing base to ensure that a company does not violate its loan agreement.

Invoice Discounting

Invoice discounting is the practice of using a company's unpaid accounts receivable as collateral for a loan, which is issued by a finance company. Invoice discounting essentially accelerates cash flow from customers, so that instead of waiting for customers to pay within their normal credit terms, cash is received almost as soon as an invoice is issued.

This is an extremely short-term form of borrowing, since the finance company can alter the amount of debt outstanding as soon as the amount of accounts receivable collateral changes. The amount of debt issued by the finance company is less than the total amount of outstanding receivables (typically 80% of all invoices less than 90 days old).

The finance company earns money both from the interest rate it charges on the loan (which is well above the prime rate), and a monthly fee to maintain the arrangement. The amount of interest that it charges the borrower is based on the amount of funds loaned, not the amount of funds available to be loaned.

Invoice discounting is impossible if another lender already has blanket title to all company assets as collateral on a different loan. In such cases, the other lender needs to waive its right to the accounts receivable collateral, and instead take a junior position behind the finance company.

From an operational perspective, the borrower sends an accounts receivable report to the finance company at least once a month, aggregating receivables into the categories required by the finance company. The finance company uses this information to adjust the amount of debt that it is willing to loan the borrower. The borrower retains control over the accounts receivable, which means that it is responsible for extending credit to customers, invoicing them, and collecting from them. There is no need to notify customers of the discounting arrangement.

Invoice discounting works best for companies with relatively high profit margins, since they can readily absorb the higher interest charges associated with this form of financing. It is especially common in high-profit businesses that are growing at a rapid rate, and need the cash flow to fund additional growth. Conversely, this is not a good form of financing for low-margin businesses, since the interest on the debt may eliminate any prospect of earning a profit.

Invoice discounting tends to be a financing source of last resort, because of the substantial fees associated with it. It would normally be used only after most other forms of financing have been attempted.

Factoring

Another type of asset-based lending is factoring. A company that engages in factoring sells its accounts receivable to a third party, known as the *factor*. As was the case with invoice discounting, factoring is only an option if a company has not allowed other parties to attach its receivables as collateral on other loans. The pricing arrangement for a factoring deal includes the following components:

- *Advance*. This is a proportion of the face amount of the invoices that the factor pays to the company at the point of sale.
- *Reserve*. This is the remaining proportion of the face amount of the invoices, which the factor retains until collections have been completed.
- *Fee*. This is the cost of the factoring arrangement, which is deducted from the reserve payment.

Once the factor owns a company's receivables, customers are notified to send their payments to a lockbox controlled by the factor. Payments made into the lockbox are retained by the factor. If the factoring arrangement is *with recourse*, the factor can pursue the company for any unpaid customer invoices. If the arrangement is *without recourse*, the factor absorbs any bad debt losses. A without recourse arrangement is more expensive, to compensate the factor for bad debt losses.

The total amount of fees associated with a factoring arrangement can be substantial, so this is generally considered a fund-raising arrangement of last resort.

Receivables Securitization

A larger organization can convert its accounts receivable into cash at once by securitizing the receivables. This means that individual receivables are aggregated into a new security, which is then sold as an investment instrument. A securitization can result in an extremely low interest rate for the issuing entity, since the securities are backed by a liquid form of collateral (i.e., receivables). In essence, a receivables securitization is accomplished with these steps:

1. Create a special purpose entity (SPE). An SPE is designed to acquire and finance specific assets, while separating the risk associated with those assets from any risks associated with the parent entity.
2. Transfer selected accounts receivable into the SPE.
3. Have the SPE sell the receivables to a bank conduit.
4. Have the bank conduit pool the company's receivables with those from other companies, and issue commercial paper backed by the receivables to investors.
5. Pay investors back based on cash receipts from the accounts receivable.

These process steps indicate that the securitization of accounts receivable is complex, and so is reserved for larger companies that can attend to the many steps. Also, the receivables included in a pool should be widely differentiated (so there are many customers), with a low historical record of customer defaults. Despite the complexity, securitization is tempting for the following reasons:

- *Interest cost.* The cost to the issuer is low, because the use of the SPE isolates the receivables from any other risks associated with the company, typically resulting in a high credit rating for the SPE. This credit rating must be assigned by a rating agency, which will take into account such factors as the historical performance of the receivables in the pool, unusually large debtor concentrations in the pool, and the conservatism of the issuing company's credit and collection policies.
- *Non-recordation.* The debt incurred by the company is not recorded on its balance sheet, since the debt is passing through an SPE.
- *Liquidity.* The flow of cash into the business can be accelerated, rather than waiting for customers to pay their bills.

The low interest cost of a receivables securitization can only be achieved and maintained if there is considerable separation between the SPE and the company. This is accomplished by designating the transfer of receivables to the SPE as a nonrecourse sale, where creditors of the company cannot access the transferred receivables. In short, the company cannot be allowed to regain control over any transferred receivables.

Inventory Financing

The preceding Invoice Discounting and Factoring sections discussed how to use accounts receivable as collateral for different types of loan arrangements. The same approach can be applied to inventory. To make this arrangement work to the satisfaction of the lender, the inventory being used as collateral is placed in a controlled area and under the supervision of a third party that only releases inventory with the approval of the lender. The lender is paid from the proceeds of inventory sales. Under a less controlled environment, the lender may agree to periodic inventory reports by the borrower, with occasional inspections of the inventory to ensure that the counted amounts match the borrower's reports.

There must be a sufficient amount of insurance in place to ensure that the lender will be paid back if the inventory is destroyed or damaged. Also, depending on state laws, it may be necessary to post notices around the collateralized inventory, stating that a lien has been imposed on the inventory. Further, the inventory cannot be used as collateral on any other loans, unless they are subordinate to the arrangement with the inventory financing company.

If the amount of inventory being used as collateral drops below the amount of the loan associated with it, the borrower must immediately pay the lender the difference.

Because of the cost of third party monitoring, inventory financing is one of the more expensive forms of financing available and can also be quite intrusive, so it is used only after less-expensive alternatives have been explored. The sole advantage of this form of financing is that the lender relies exclusively on the inventory asset to ensure that it is repaid; it does not impose covenants on the borrower.

Floor planning is a method of financing inventory purchases, where a lender pays for assets that have been ordered by a distributor or retailer, and is paid back from the proceeds from the sale of these items. The arrangement is most commonly used when large assets, such as automobiles or household appliances, are involved.

The entity at risk in this arrangement is the lender, who is relying upon the sale of the underlying assets in order to be repaid. Accordingly, the lender may demand the following:

- That all assets acquired under the floor planning arrangement be sold at a price that is no lower than its original purchase price.
- That the inventory of assets in stock is regularly counted and matched against the records of the lender.
- That the lender be repaid at once if there is any shortfall in the inventory count.
- That the loan be paid back no later than a certain date, thereby avoiding the risk of product obsolescence.

Floor planning may be a valid option when the seller of the goods does not have adequate financing to use other options.

Loan Stock

Loan stock is shares in a business that have been pledged as collateral for a loan. The lender may require that it retain physical control of the shares for the duration of the loan, and will return the shares to their owner once the loan has been paid off. If the borrower defaults on the loan, the lender can then retain the shares. This type of collateral is most valuable for a lender when the shares are publicly traded on a stock exchange and are unrestricted, so that the shares can be easily sold for cash. This arrangement is of less use when a business is privately held, since the lender cannot easily sell the shares.

Loan stock can be a problem from a corporate control perspective, since a loan default means that the lender acquires the shares, and therefore the related ownership percentage in the business, along with all associated voting rights.

A loan stock arrangement can be risky for the lender, since the market value of the shares being used as collateral may decline. If a portion of the loan principal is being paid back on an ongoing basis, this is less of a problem, since the loan balance will be declining over time. If the loan is being paid off incrementally, there may be a clause in the lending agreement under which some portion of the shares are returned to the borrower before the end of the lending arrangement.

Purchase Order Financing

Purchase order financing is applicable when a company receives an order from a customer that it cannot process with its existing working capital. A lender accepts the purchase order as collateral, which allows the borrower to obtain sufficient funds to buy the materials and labor required to complete the order. This arrangement is risky for the lender, since the borrower must perform under the contract in order to receive payment from the customer. Given the extra risk, the borrowing cost is much higher for purchase order financing.

Hard Money Loans

A hard money loan is a short-term, high-interest rate loan. This type of loan is typically extended to businesses whose financial situations are poor, and so cannot qualify for lower-cost forms of debt. A hard money loan typically has the following characteristics:

- *High interest rate.* The rate may be several multiples of the prime rate, and is intended to cover the much higher risk that the lender takes on in this type of arrangement.
- *Short term.* The intent of the loan is to keep the borrower solvent for a short period of time. In essence, this is a bridge loan.
- *Collateral.* The lender typically bases repayment on the assets of the borrower, rather than the borrower's cash flow. This means the lender is willing to shut down the borrower's organization and liquidate its assets in order to obtain repayment of the loan and any outstanding interest.

Banks do not engage in hard money lending, since these loan characteristics go well beyond the normal borrowing rules of a bank. Instead, this type of loan is more likely to be offered by wealthy individuals or smaller firms that are willing to accept a high degree of risk. Given their high fee structures, these lenders are more likely to compete based on the rapid turnaround of loan applications than to offer lower interest rates.

A borrower must have substantial assets in order to take on a hard money loan. Otherwise, a prospective lender will see no obvious way to be repaid. Consequently, this type of financing arrangement is rare in the services industries, which are traditionally light on assets. These loans are more commonly found in the real estate industry, which is asset intensive.

Mezzanine Financing

Mezzanine financing is positioned partway between the equity and debt financings used by a business. It is designed to provide cash to an existing business that requires the funds to grow, or for a leveraged buyout, or a corporate restructuring. The borrower in a mezzanine financing situation is usually not publicly-held, and so does not have access to the public markets as a more ready source of cash. This type of financing is usually obtained from smaller lenders who specialize in mezzanine financing, rather than from more traditional banking institutions. Mezzanine financing is typically structured as:

- Convertible debt that can be swapped by the lender for company stock if the price of the stock rises.
- Debt with a significant number of attached warrants that allow the lender to acquire company stock if the price of the stock rises.
- Preferred stock that earns a dividend, and which may have special voting rights, the ability to convert to common stock, or other special features.

Mezzanine financing, if structured as debt, is usually junior to the debt of a company's more traditional lenders, such as the bank that issues its line of credit or any long-term loans. This means that, in the event of company cash flow troubles, the holders of senior debt are paid first from available cash, while those in a junior position are paid only from any residual cash available once the claims of all senior lenders and creditors have been satisfied.

Given the increased riskiness of being in a junior position, the lender of mezzanine financing wants to earn an unusually high return that is usually in the range of 20% to 30% per year. The lender may also charge a large up-front arrangement fee. A borrower may not be in a position to make ongoing interest payments in the 20% to 30% range on an ongoing basis, which is why the use of warrants and conversion features are heavily used to give the lender an alternative method for achieving its return on investment goal. This also means that principal is not scheduled to be repaid until the end of the loan period, and may be paid back with company stock, if the lender can realize an adequate return from taking this form of payment.

Mezzanine financing can also be used in a leveraged buyout situation, where it is used as a stopgap measure to provide short-term financing until a lower-cost and longer-term arrangement can be made.

Though mezzanine financing can provide a large amount of cash, it has a number of downsides. First, the lender may impose a number of restrictive covenants to protect its investment. Second, the lender may end up being a large shareholder in the business, and so is in a position to influence decisions made by the company. Third, it is one of the most expensive forms of financing available. And finally, mezzanine financing is only available after a prolonged investigation by a prospective lender.

The Long-Term Loan

When a company finds that it is unable to draw its line of credit down to zero at any point during the year, this means that its funding needs have become more long-term. If so, it should apply to a lender for a long-term loan that will be paid off over a number of years.

The following points may clarify whether it is even possible to obtain such a loan, and whether one would want to do so:

- *Banking services*. The provider of a long-term loan may insist on providing a complete package of banking services, to maximize its profits. If so, expect to shift all bank accounts, lines of credit, lockboxes, and other services to the lender.
- *Cash flow*. The lender is particularly sensitive to the historical and projected performance of the business, since the loan must be repaid from continuing cash flows. If positive cash flows have been a rare event, it will be very difficult to obtain a long-term loan. The lender may also want to see a budget for at least the next year.
- *Covenants*. The lender will probably impose covenants on the company that are designed to keep it from disbursing cash outside of the normal course of business. In particular, dividends may be restricted.
- *Creditor positioning*. A lender willing to commit to a long-term loan will certainly want to be designated as having the senior position among all creditors of the company, so that it will be more likely to be paid back in the event of a loan default. This positioning is necessary, because the lender is committing a large amount of funds over a long period of time, during which the company's financial results may change dramatically.
- *Personal guarantee*. In a smaller business where there are few owners, and especially where historical cash flow has been uncertain, the lender may insist on personal guarantees that allow the lender to pursue the owners for repayment.

A long-term loan can be configured as a series of fixed payments, or as interest-only payments with a large balloon payment due at the end of the loan. While the balloon payment option may appear tempting from a short-term cash flow perspective, it introduces the risk that credit conditions may have changed by the time it is due for payment, making it difficult to refinance.

The conditions associated with a long-term loan might leave management less inclined to pursue this option. However, a long-term loan allows a business to lock in debt for an extended period of time, without having to worry about the vagaries of the short-term credit markets. Thus, it can make sense to assign a portion of a company's debt to longer-term loans.

Bonds

When a business sells a fixed obligation to investors, this is generally described as a *bond*. The typical bond has a face value of $1,000, which means that the issuer is obligated to pay the investor $1,000 on the maturity date of the bond. If investors feel that the stated interest rate on a bond is too low, they will only agree to buy the bond at a price lower than its stated amount, thereby increasing the effective interest rate that they will earn on the investment. Conversely, a high stated interest rate can lead investors to pay a premium for a bond.

When a bond is registered, the issuer is maintaining a list of which investors own its bonds. The issuer then sends periodic interest payments directly to these investors. When the issuer does not maintain a list of investors who own its bonds, the bonds are considered to be *coupon bonds*. A coupon bond contains attached coupons that investors send to the issuer; these coupons obligate the company to issue interest payments to the holders of the bonds. A coupon bond is easier to transfer between investors, but it is also more difficult to establish ownership of the bonds.

There are many types of bonds. The following list represents a sampling of the more common types:

- *Collateral trust bond.* This bond includes the investment holdings of the issuer as collateral.
- *Convertible bond.* This bond can be converted into the common stock of the issuer at a predetermined conversion ratio. See the Debt for Equity Swaps section.
- *Debenture.* This bond has no collateral associated with it. A variation is the subordinated debenture, which has junior rights to collateral.
- *Deferred interest bond.* This bond offers little or no interest at the start of the bond term, and more interest near the end. The format is useful for businesses currently having little cash with which to pay interest.
- *Income bond.* The issuer is only obligated to make interest payments to bond holders if the issuer or a specific project earns a profit. If the bond terms allow for cumulative interest, then the unpaid interest will accumulate until such time as there is sufficient income to pay the amounts owed.

- *Mortgage bond.* This bond is backed by real estate or equipment owned by the issuer.
- *Serial bond.* This bond is gradually paid off in each successive year, so the total amount of debt outstanding is gradually reduced.
- *Variable rate bond.* The interest rate paid on this bond varies with a baseline indicator, such as the London Interbank Offered Rate (LIBOR).
- *Zero coupon bond.* No interest is paid on this type of bond. Instead, investors buy the bonds at large discounts to their face values in order to earn an effective interest rate.
- *Zero coupon convertible bond.* This variation on the zero coupon bond allows investors to convert their bond holdings into the common stock of the issuer. This allows investors to take advantage of a run-up in the price of a company's stock. The conversion option can increase the price that investors are willing to pay for this type of bond.

Additional features can be added to a bond to make it easier to sell to investors at a higher price. These features can include:

- *Sinking fund.* The issuer creates a sinking fund to which cash is periodically added, and which is used to ensure that bonds are eventually paid off.
- *Conversion feature.* Bond holders have the option to convert their bonds into the stock of the issuer at a predetermined conversion rate.
- *Guarantees.* The repayment of a bond may be guaranteed by a third party.

The following additional bond features favor the issuer, and so may reduce the price at which investors are willing to purchase bonds:

- *Call feature.* The issuer has the right to buy back bonds earlier than the stated maturity date.
- *Subordination.* Bond holders are positioned after more senior debt holders to be paid back from issuer assets in the event of a default.

Debt for Equity Swaps

In some cases, it may be possible to swap company shares for outstanding company debt securities. This is most common when a company issues convertible bonds that allow bond holders to convert their bonds into company stock at certain predefined exchange ratios. This option is only available to publicly-held companies.

In a privately-held company, a debt for equity swap usually occurs only when a company is in such dire financial straits that it is unable to repay its debt. If so, taking an equity interest in the company may be the only option remaining to the lender, other than writing off the debt as being uncollectible. This conversion to equity is more likely when the lender is an individual, rather than a bank, since banks may be constrained by their own lending rules from engaging in debt for equity swaps. A company that succeeds in converting debt to equity under these difficult financial circumstances may find that it can issue stock at such a low valuation that it is required by the accounting standards to book a profit on the conversion of debt to equity.

When a large public company issues convertible debt, any resulting conversions to equity are unlikely to be large enough to alter the debt-equity ratio of the business to a significant extent. The reverse is the case when a private company succeeds in converting debt to equity; it may be eliminating much of its debt, and had such little equity to begin with that it switches from having a dangerously unbalanced debt-equity ratio to one that gives the appearance of being solidly well-funded. Of course, the operational profitability of such a company is still questionable, but the debt for equity swap can repair its balance sheet.

Summary

Most of the forms of debt financing noted in this chapter can only be accessed in limited amounts that are defined by the amount of collateral, after which lenders will be extremely unwilling to advance additional funds. For really high debt levels, it will be necessary to obtain personal guarantees from the company owners, or the sale of stock to increase the amount of equity on hand.

If a business has extremely variable earnings, it may not make sense to have *any* debt, since it may be difficult to pay back the lender. In such a situation, it makes more sense to stockpile cash during periods when the company is flush with cash, or to rely primarily on the sale of stock to raise cash.

Chapter 9
Supply Chain Financing

Introduction

The suppliers that feed materials and services to a company should be well-funded. A financially healthy supplier is more capable of meeting its commitments to the company, and also has more cash to invest in facilities, as well as research and development activities. Such a business is also less likely to suddenly go bankrupt, leaving a hole in the company's supply chain. The treasurer can contribute to this level of funding by engaging in supply chain financing.

> **Related Podcast Episode:** Episode 143 of the Accounting Best Practices Podcast discusses supply chain financing. It is available at: **accountingtools.com/podcasts** or **iTunes**

Supply Chain Financing

Supply chain financing occurs when a finance company, such as a bank, interposes itself between a company and its suppliers and commits to pay the company's invoices to the suppliers at an accelerated rate in exchange for a discount (which is essentially a factoring arrangement). The following process flow shows the relationship between the parties.

Supply Chain Finance Process Flow

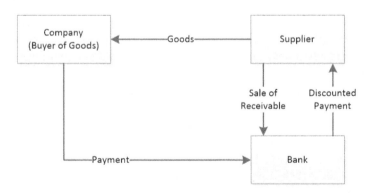

This approach has the following benefits for the entity that is paying its suppliers:

- The company can foster very close links with its core group of suppliers, since this can be a major benefit to them in terms of accelerated cash flow.

Because of the ready availability of cash, this may even mean that the company becomes the preferred customer for its supplier base.

- 100% of the invoice value is available for factoring, rather than the discounted amount that is available through a normal factoring arrangement.
- The company no longer has to deal with requests from suppliers for early payment, since they are already being paid as soon as possible.

Supply chain financing has the following benefits for suppliers:

- A cash-strapped supplier can be paid much sooner than normal, in exchange for the finance company's fee.
- The interest rate charged by the finance company should be low, since it is based on the credit standing of the paying company, not the rating of the suppliers (which assumes that the payer has a good rating).

The finance company acting as the intermediary earns interest income on the factoring arrangements that it enters into with the suppliers of the target company. This can represent an excellent source of income over a long period of time, so bankers try to create sole-source supply chain financing arrangements to lock in this income. In addition, the bankers can now develop relations with the entire group of suppliers that it is paying, which may result in an entirely new group of clients for a broad range of banking services.

Supply chain financing is usually begun by large companies that want to improve the cash flow situation for their suppliers. To convince a finance company to be involved in the arrangement requires the expectation of a considerable amount of factoring, which is why this approach is not available to smaller companies.

When first developing a supply chain financing arrangement, it can be difficult to make a reasonable estimate of the amount of financing that a group of suppliers will want. There are a number of factors that could drive the supplier need for cash, including the following:

- *General business environment.* If the economy is robust, suppliers will find that their customers are more likely to pay on time, and so will have less need for accelerated payments. Conversely, if the state of the economy is declining, they may be quite eager to take advantage of supply chain financing in order to assure themselves of a ready source of cash.
- *Existing terms.* If the company has negotiated lengthy payment terms with its suppliers (such as 60 or 90 days to pay), they will be more likely to take advantage of supply chain financing, since this represents a massive acceleration of their cash flow.
- *Interest rate.* If the interest rate being charged by the bank is too high, only the most desperate suppliers will take advantage of the financing.
- *Existing factoring arrangements.* Suppliers may already have long-standing factoring arrangements in place with other lenders, and so may be reluctant to shift their business over to the company's bank. This decision will probably be driven by a comparison of the factoring deals being offered.

There are on-line systems available on which a company can post its approved invoices, and which suppliers can access to select which invoices they want to have paid to them earlier than dictated by the standard payment terms.

Early Payment Discounts

A simpler version of supply chain financing is to eliminate the bank from the three-way payment flow, and just have the company directly interact with its suppliers. In this situation, cash payments to suppliers are accelerated when the company negotiates early payment discounts with each one. The trouble with this approach from the company's perspective is having to negotiate a separate discount with each supplier, and then keep track of the discount terms.

If the treasurer decides to follow this path, it will be necessary to calculate the interest rate being earned on early payment discounts, to see if the effective interest rate earned is acceptable. This rate should exceed the company's cost of capital. The effective interest rate calculation is:

$$(\text{Discount \%} \div (1 - \text{Discount \%})) \times (360 \div (\text{Allowed payment days} - \text{Discount days}))$$

Converted into the format of a procedure, this calculation is:

1. Calculate the difference between the payment date for those taking the early payment discount and the date when payment is normally due, and divide it into 360 days. For example, under "2/10 net 30" terms, one would divide 20 days into 360 to arrive at 18. Use this number to annualize the interest rate calculated in the next step.
2. Subtract the discount percentage from 100% and divide the result into the discount percentage. For example, under "2/10 net 30" terms, one would divide 2% by 98% to arrive at 0.0204. This is the interest rate being offered through the credit terms.
3. Multiply the result of both calculations together to obtain the annualized interest rate. To conclude the example, multiply 18 by 0.0204 to arrive at an effective annualized interest rate of 36.72%.

EXAMPLE

The treasurer of Suture Corporation has received an early payment offer from a supplier, where Suture can take a 1% discount on any invoices paid, as long they are paid within 10 days of the invoice date. Otherwise, the company must pay the full amount after 30 days have passed from the invoice date. Using this information, the calculation of the effective interest rate of the offer is:

$$(1\% \text{ Discount} \div (1 - 1\% \text{ Discount}))$$
$$\times (360 \div (30 \text{ Allowed payment days} - 10 \text{ Discount days}))$$

$$= 18.2\%$$

As long as the cost of capital of Suture is lower than 18.2%, this is an acceptable offer that the treasurer should authorize, if there is sufficient cash available to fund the early payment.

The table below shows some of the more common early payment discount terms, explains what they mean, and also notes the effective interest rate that suppliers are offering with each one.

Sample Credit Terms

Credit Terms	Explanation	Effective Interest Rate
1/10 net 30	Take a 1% discount if pay in 10 days, otherwise pay in 30 days	18.2%
2/10 net 30	Take a 2% discount if pay in 10 days, otherwise pay in 30 days	36.7%
1/10 net 60	Take a 1% discount if pay in 10 days, otherwise pay in 60 days	7.3%
2/10 net 60	Take a 2% discount if pay in 10 days, otherwise pay in 60 days	14.7%

The treasurer may choose to accept relatively poor early payment terms if a supplier is clearly in need of cash.

Summary

Supply chain financing is an easy way for a larger business to improve the cash flow of its suppliers. However, this option is only available to larger companies, so the suppliers of a smaller company will have to use their own factoring arrangements to achieve the same result. The trouble with independent factoring arrangements is that the cost to suppliers may be higher, and less than the full amount of each invoice may be made available for factoring. If a company wants to help its suppliers out of this situation, it could negotiate with them to reduce the number of days that it will wait before paying them, or accept relatively poor early payment discount terms. This does not have to be a unilateral reduction in payment terms; in exchange, the company could negotiate for preferred customer status, which would move it to the front of the queue for order placement, as well as for faster delivery times.

Chapter 10
Treasury Risk Management

Introduction

Risk equates to uncertainty regarding a future outcome. A business is filled with uncertainty, for there are few situations in which the outcome can be predicted with complete reliability. For example, a business has several thousand outstanding accounts receivable – exactly how many of them will become bad debts? Similarly, a business requires a key commodity as a raw material in the construction of a product – can it predict exactly what the price of this commodity will be in one year? Or, it will cost $250 million to develop a new drug and have it approved – but how certain is the approval? In these cases, it is impossible to predict the exact outcome.

Uncertainty is pervasive, and yet managers routinely ignore the concept of variable outcomes. Instead, they budget for a single view of the future, and are then perturbed when they cannot force their organizations to deliver results that precisely match the outcome predicted in the budget. This is because there may be thousands of uncertain events that all impact the financial results of a business. Despite management's best efforts, it is nearly impossible to deliver actual results that match the original budgeted prediction.

When people think about risk management, they probably consider treasury issues first. This part of a business contains a multitude of major risks related to funding, credit, investments, liquidity, foreign exchange, and interest rates. Some financially-oriented organizations consider treasury to be the *only* significant source of serious risk in their business models.

Treasury risks are considered so important because they can cause large losses and eliminate cash reserves within a short period of time, possibly resulting in bankruptcy. In the following sections, we cover risk management pertaining to funding, credit policy, credit exposure, credit concentration, foreign exchange, and interest rates. In addition, see the following chapters for additional discussions of risk:

- Investment Management chapter - risk related to investments
- Credit Management chapter – internal and external credit rating systems
- Insurance chapter – credit insurance

Benefits of Risk Management

There are a number of reasons why an organization should manage its risks. The central issues are the ability to smooth out earnings or to enhance earnings.

Risk management can be used to mitigate the occurrence of unusual expenses, so that the actual expenses incurred are much closer to budgeted expectations. This is particularly important for a publicly held company, which can then give the investment community reliable guidance about its future results. When a business consistently reports earnings that do not vary much from predictions, investors will probably keep the stock price within a relatively narrow range, and there will be no reason for investors to engage in short selling. Another benefit is that reliable earnings attract lenders, so that a business is more likely to be offered reasonable interest rates and longer-term lending arrangements. Lower interest rates reduce the cost of a firm's capital, so that it can invest in more projects that have lower projected returns. Having longer-term debt arrangements means that a business can more easily weather market crises, since it does not have to constantly roll over its debt into new loans.

One can enhance earnings by actively identifying opportunities that are risky, but which also generate high returns. For example, an organization might choose to start doing business in a country where profits could be substantial, but where there is also a risk of a currency devaluation. Taking this approach can result in higher profits, but those profits are also likely to be more variable – very high in some periods, but with notable losses in others. This use of risk management works well when the management team is willing to aggressively pursue profits.

The most likely scenario in a well-managed business is that management takes advantage of both types of risk management. They are well aware of the risks to which the business is subjected, and take steps to mitigate risks in certain areas while accepting the risk associated with selected business opportunities.

The amount of risk taken on by a business depends on the comfort level of the management team. Some may prefer a highly stable environment from which the probability of risk has largely been reduced, while others are more comfortable taking large chances in order to pursue the possibility of maximizing profits.

Funding Risk

A major concern with any corporate expansion is when the strategy calls for funding, and the treasurer cannot raise the money. This is particularly common in a tight credit market, where there is nothing fundamentally wrong with the company's creditworthiness. Instead, funds are simply not available. Here are several risk mitigation options:

- *Adopt a longer-term debt mix.* When funds are available in a looser credit market, obtain more long-term debt than the company actually needs. This could involve a mix of bank loans of medium-term duration and bonds that have a lengthy maturity. Doing so builds a cash reserve that can be accessed whenever needed for years to come.
- *Sweeten debt with equity instruments.* Offer convertible debt to investors. For example, a bond might have attached warrants, where the warrant exercise price is set low enough to be tempting to investors. In this case, inves-

tors will be more likely to buy the bonds, irrespective of the state of the credit market.

- *Adopt a DRIP plan.* If the company routinely pays dividends to its investors, offer a dividend reinvestment plan (DRIP) to investors, where the company can use their dividend payments to automatically purchase additional shares of company stock. Doing so diverts dividend payments straight back into the company's coffers. This is not an overly large source of funding.
- *Adopt an employee stock purchase plan.* Offer employees the opportunity to buy the company's stock at a modest discount from the market price. Payments are typically taken from employee paychecks as a standard deduction, so that stock purchases tend to run for a long period of time. This generally results in a relatively small amount of additional funding for the company.
- *Work with several lenders.* Have long-term lending arrangements with multiple lenders. By doing so, the company still has an established relationship with at least one lender if its main lender decides to cut off any further funding. This is not necessarily an easy tactic to follow, since the primary lender will try to maximize its profits by forcing the company to borrow solely from it.

An additional consideration when dealing with funding risk is how much cash a business should keep on hand to guard against unexpected losses. In a relatively staid business where cash flows are highly predictable and risks are intentionally kept low, there may be little need for a reserve of cash. However, an organization that has highly variable cash flows and a large appetite for risk may need to maintain substantial funding reserves. The concept of "funding reserves" does not necessarily mean maintaining a cash balance. A company could have little cash on hand but a large untapped line of credit that gives it significant funding reserves.

To expand upon the concept of a funding reserve, the management team may target having quite a high credit rating, which may be critical if it plans to engage in substantial borrowings and needs to acquire debt at the lowest possible interest rate. In this situation, the credit rating agency will only award a high credit rating if a business has a massive cash reserve (not just a large amount of available debt). A large cash balance allows an organization to absorb a number of large losses, and makes its debt instruments a safe investment. Conversely, if management is comfortable with a lower credit rating, it can maintain much lower cash reserves.

Credit Policy Risk

The corporate strategy may call for a loosening of credit terms in order to attract additional customers, and/or more orders from existing customers. For example, credit terms may be extended from net 15 days to net 60 days. If so, this represents a substantial increase in the amount of funding that will be required to support accounts receivable. If the company does not have the requisite amount of cash, the treasurer will be forced to look outside the company for more funding, which may not be available.

Another type of credit policy risk arises when the policy is not altered rapidly enough to account for changes in the financial condition of customers. For example, if there is a decline in general economic conditions, there may be a higher incidence of bankruptcy among customers, or at least longer days outstanding for receivables. This increased risk of bad debt losses and/or larger investment in working capital could have been reduced or eliminated if the credit policy were more frequently updated to match conditions.

Credit Exposure Risk

Even if a business routinely updates its credit policy and correctly enforces it, there is a risk that certain customers will unexpectedly be unable to pay their bills at all, resulting in bad debts. A certain number of bad debts are an expected part of doing business, and a reserve is created against the expectation of these occurrences. However, there is the risk that a large customer will suddenly and unexpectedly go out of business and be unable to pay its debts. This is a particular problem when a company gains most of its sales from a small number of large customers. There are several possible solutions, as outlined in the following sub-sections.

Terms Alterations

There may be situations where customers are less able to pay the company's bills in a timely manner, resulting in the credit manager reducing their available credit or even requiring them to pay in advance or on delivery. Here are several ways in which the treasurer can remain satisfied with the credit exposure risk that the company is undertaking, while still allowing the sales department to generate sales:

- *Find alternate payer*. Someone besides the customer agrees to also be liable for payments. This may involve a personal guarantee by the owner or a corporate guarantee that is extended by the corporate parent of the customer. It is sometimes possible to obtain a guarantee from a third party. This may be a related party that has an interest in the operations of the buyer, such as a member of its board of directors, a key supplier, a manager, or a family member. This type of guarantee can be quite valuable, since the assets of the third party may not be so closely tied to the fortunes of the buyer, and can survive the demise of the business.
- *Retain ownership*. It is possible to retain title to goods that are shipped to customers, and only transfer the title to buyers once payment has been made. This can be an effective risk reduction tool, but only if capital goods are being sold – the option is not practical for small-value items.
- *Pay early*. Require the acceleration of payment by customers, so that only smaller payments are at risk of default, and for shorter periods. For example, a customer requests $30,000 of credit on 30-day payment terms. The treasurer could instead offer $15,000 of credit on 15-day payment terms, which effectively reduces the risk of the company while still giving the customer the same amount of credit over a 30-day period.

Receivables Financing

When management concludes that the credit exposure being undertaken by the organization is too great, it could use a factoring arrangement to transfer the risk to a lender.

Under a factoring arrangement, a finance company agrees to take over a company's accounts receivable collections and keep the money from these collections in exchange for an immediate cash payment to the company. This process typically involves having customers mail their payments to a lockbox that appears to be operated by the company, but which is actually controlled by the finance company. Under a true factoring arrangement, the finance company takes over the risk of loss on any bad debts, though it will have the right to pick which types of receivables it will accept in order to reduce its risk of loss. A finance company is more interested in this type of deal when the size of each receivable is fairly large, since this reduces its per-transaction cost of collection.

If each receivable is quite small, the finance company may still be interested in a factoring arrangement, but it will charge the company extra for its increased processing work. The lender charges an interest rate, as well as a transaction fee for the processing of each invoice it receives. A company working under this arrangement can be paid by the factor at once, or can wait until the invoice due date before payment is sent.

Factoring can be considered a form of financing, since it accelerates the receipt of cash, but it is also a form of risk reduction, since the risk of nonpayment is accepted by the factor. However, the cost of factoring is quite high, making this a less cost-effective option, and probably not a practical one for a business whose margins are already small.

Outside Financing

When the goods being sold are high-cost fixed assets, it may be possible to arrange with a third-party lender to provide financing to the buyer to either buy or lease the items being sold. This type of arrangement shifts the credit risk to the lender. Of course, the lender will apply its own credit granting standards to buyers, and may not provide financing to those customers it considers being at an elevated risk of default.

Portfolio Approach to Risk

Thus far, we have discussed a variety of separate methods that can be used to reduce credit exposure risk. Another option is to summarize the total credit risk to which the business is exposed, and make a determination regarding how much risk to retain. For example, receivables can be categorized into some variation on low, medium, and high risk of nonpayment, and the estimated bad debt percentage calculated for each of these categories. If the total amount of expected bad debt is equal to or less than the amount that management considers to be acceptable, then the current portfolio of risk reduction techniques may be considered acceptable. This means that the treasurer may allow a certain number of higher-risk sales to proceed without risk reduction, as long as there are a large number of extremely low-risk transactions that sufficiently reduce the total credit risk for the company.

EXAMPLE

The treasurer of Laid Back Corporation (which sells business chairs) constructs the following table of estimated bad debts for the company's current portfolio of receivables. The management team has decided that bad debts can reach as much as 1½% of sales. Since the table indicates an expected bad debt percentage of 1.4%, the treasurer has a small amount of room to offer somewhat more credit to higher-risk customers and still remain within the guideline set by management.

Risk Category	Current Receivable Balance	Historical Bad Debt Percentage	Estimated Bad Debt by Risk Category
Low risk	$10,425,000	0.4%	$41,700
Medium low	6,100,000	1.3%	79,300
Medium high	2,350,000	3.8%	89,300
High risk	630,000	10.5%	66,150
Totals	$19,505,000	1.4%	$276,450

The portfolio approach to risk tends to increase earnings, as long as it is used judiciously, since the credit risk associated with customer orders is no longer assessed on an individual basis, but rather as a group of orders where some orders have a higher risk than others.

Cross-Selling Credit Exposure Risk

When a company has multiple lines of business, there is a natural temptation to try to cross-sell the customers of one set of products on the other lines of business. After all, the company has already expended a substantial amount to acquire the customers, and cross-selling is considered to be a relatively inexpensive way to generate additional sales. The trouble with this approach is that a portion of the customers subjected to cross-selling were not good customers to begin with, and their negative impact on the company is now multiplied by their additional purchases. This can have a profound impact on credit exposure risk and company profitability.

Credit exposure risk increases for this subset of customers if they are permitted additional credit. This is a common occurrence that is driven by the sales staff, under the obvious logic that cross-selling will not work unless sales are allowed to increase by providing more credit. The trouble is that the financial position of these customers does not permit them to make additional purchases, resulting in an inevitable increase in payment defaults.

In addition to this credit problem, the expansion of sales to these more difficult customers will also result in more returned goods and more administrative staff time to service their needs. These factors add up to an increase in expenses that, in total, completely offsets any increase in revenues.

The clear answer to the cross-selling conundrum is to carefully analyze all customers prior to initiating a cross-selling campaign, and to exclude the more problematic ones from the campaign. The analysis may even result in the termination of *all* business with these marginal customers.

Credit Concentration Risk

One of the most pervasive credit-related risks relates to the concentration of customers within a single industry. If there is a downturn within an entire industry, then a seller of goods and services into that industry could face a major increase in the number of customers that cannot pay their bills. In essence, the fortunes of the seller are inextricably tied to the welfare of a specific industry.

Many organizations are built around the idea of servicing one industry, so managers cannot see a way out of this type of risk – and there may not be one, if the strategy of the business is to continue servicing one industry. However, there may be opportunities to branch out into adjacent industries that do not suffer from the same economic factors. If so, sales to these other markets may buoy the sales of the business during those periods when the core market is stagnating.

Another way to deal with credit concentration risk is to deliberately acquire unrelated businesses, on the theory that a wide range of markets will eliminate this risk. While concentration risk may indeed be reduced, this approach will generate other issues, such as the inability to manage a diverse portfolio of businesses.

Foreign Exchange Risk Overview

There are several types of foreign exchange risks that can impact a company, and which are described below.

A company may incur *transaction exposure*, which is derived from changes in foreign exchange rates between the dates when a transaction is booked and when it is settled. For example, a company in the United States may sell goods to a company in the United Kingdom, to be paid in pounds having a value at the booking date of $100,000. Later, when the customer pays the company, the exchange rate has changed, resulting in a payment in pounds that translates to a $95,000 sale. Thus, the foreign exchange rate change related to a transaction has created a $5,000 loss for the seller. The following table shows the impact of transaction exposure on different scenarios.

Risk When Transactions Denominated in Foreign Currency

	Import Goods	Export Goods
Home currency weakens	Loss	Gain
Home currency strengthens	Gain	Loss

When a company has foreign subsidiaries, it denominates the recorded amount of their assets and liabilities in the currency of the country in which the subsidiaries generate and expend cash. This *functional currency* is typically the local currency of the country in which a subsidiary operates. When the company reports its consolidated results, it converts these valuations to the home currency of the parent company, which may suffer a loss if exchange rates have declined from the last time when the financial statements were consolidated. This type of risk is known as *translation exposure*.

EXAMPLE

Hammer Industries has a subsidiary located in England, which has its net assets denominated in pounds. The home currency of Hammer is U.S. dollars. At year-end, when the parent company consolidates the financial statements of its subsidiaries, the U.S. dollar has depreciated in comparison to the pound, resulting in a decline in the value of the subsidiary's net assets.

The following table shows the impact of translation exposure on different scenarios.

Risk When Net Assets Denominated in Foreign Currency

	Assets	Liabilities
Home currency weakens	Gain	Loss
Home currency strengthens	Loss	Gain

There are also several types of economic risk related to the specific country within which a company chooses to do business. These risks include:

- *Convertibility risk* is the inability to convert a local currency into a foreign currency, because of a shortage of hard currencies. This tends to be a short-term problem.
- *Transfer risk* is the inability to transfer funds across a national border, due to local-country regulatory restrictions on the movement of hard currencies out of the country. Thus, a company may find that a local subsidiary is extremely profitable, but the parent company cannot extract the profits from the country.

Country-specific risks call for strategic-level decisions in the executive suite, not in the treasury department. The senior management team must decide if it is willing to accept the risks of expropriation or of not being able to extract cash from a country. If not, the risk is eliminated by refusing to do business within the country.

Please note that the *type* of risk has an impact on the time period over which a company is at risk. For example, transactional risk spans a relatively short period, from the signing date of the contract that initiates a sale, until the final payment date. The total interval may be only one or two months. However, translation risk and the various types of economic risks can extend over many years. There tends to be an inordinate focus in many companies on the short-term transactional risk, when more emphasis should be placed on hedging against these other risks that can result in substantial losses over the long term.

Foreign Exchange Risk Management

As just noted, a company is at risk of incurring a loss due to fluctuations in any exchange rates that it must buy or sell as part of its business transactions. What can be done? Valid steps can range from no action at all to the active use of several types of hedges. In this section, we address the multitude of options available to mitigate foreign exchange-related risks. While perusing these options, keep in mind that the most sophisticated response is not necessarily the best response. In many cases, the circumstances may make it quite acceptable to take on some degree of risk, rather than engaging in a hedging strategy that is not only expensive, but also difficult to understand.

Take No Action

There are many situations where a company rarely engages in transactions that involve foreign exchange, and so does not want to spend time investigating how to reduce risk. There are other situations where the amounts of foreign exchange involved are so small that the risk level is immaterial. In either case, a company will be tempted to take no action, which may be a reasonable course of action, depending on the treasurer's tolerance for risk.

Avoid Risk

A company can avoid some types of risk by altering its strategy to completely sidestep the risk. Complete avoidance of a specific product, geographic region, or business line is an entirely reasonable alternative under the following circumstances:

- The potential loss from a risk condition is very high
- The probability of loss from a risk condition is very high
- It is difficult to develop a hedge against a risk
- The offsetting potential for profit does not offset the risk that will be incurred

For example, a company located in the United States buys the bulk of its supplies in China, and is required under its purchasing contracts to pay suppliers in yuan. If the company does not want to undertake the risk of exchange rate fluctuations in the yuan, it can consider altering its supply chain, so that it purchases within its home country, rather than in China. This alignment of sales and purchases within the same country to avoid foreign currency transactions is known as an *operational hedge*.

As another example, a company wants to sell products into a market where the government has just imposed severe restrictions on the cross-border transfer of funds out of the country. The government also has a history of nationalizing industries that had been privately-owned. Under these circumstances, it makes little sense for the company to sell into the new market if it cannot extract its profits, and if its assets in the country are subject to expropriation.

Shift Risk

When a company is either required to pay or receive payment in a foreign currency, it is taking on the risk associated with changes in the foreign currency exchange rate. This risk can be completely eliminated by requiring customers to pay in the company's home currency, or suppliers to accept payment in the company's home currency. This is a valid option when the company is a large one that can force this system of payment onto its suppliers, or when it sells a unique product that forces customers to accept the company's terms.

> **Tip:** Never give customers a choice of currency in which to pay the company, since they will likely pay with their home currency, leaving the company to bear the risk of exchange rate changes.

Another possibility is to charge business partners for any changes in the exchange rate between the date of order placement and the shipment date. This is an extremely difficult business practice to enforce, for the following reasons:

- *Continual rebillings*. There will always be some degree of variation in exchange rates between the order date and shipment date, so it is probable that a company would have to issue an invoice related to exchange rate adjustments for every order, or at least include a line item for the change in every invoice.
- *Two-way rebillings*. If a company is going to insist on billing for its exchange rate losses, it is only fair that it pay back its business partners when exchange rates shift in its favor.
- *Purchase order limitations*. Customers routinely place orders using a purchase order than only authorizes a certain spending level. If the company later issues an incremental billing that exceeds the total amount authorized for a purchase, the customer will probably not pay the company.

To mitigate these issues, billing a business partner for a change in exchange rates should only be enacted if the change is sufficiently large to breach a contractually-agreed minimum level. The minimum level should be set so that this additional billing is a rare event.

EXAMPLE

An outsourcing company enters into long-term services contracts with its customers, and so is at considerable foreign exchange risk. It offers customers a fixed price contract within a 5% currency trading band, outside of which customers share the risk with the company. If the company gains from a currency shift outside of the trading band, it discounts the contract price.

The conditions under which currency risk can be shifted elsewhere are not common ones. Most companies will find that if they insist on only dealing in their home currencies, such behavior will either annoy suppliers or drive away customers. Thus, we will continue with other risk management actions that will be more palatable to a company's business partners.

Time Compression

Large variations in exchange rates are more likely to occur over longer periods of time than over shorter periods of time. Thus, it may be possible to reduce the risk of exchange rate fluctuations by reducing the contractually-mandated payment period. For example, 30 day payment terms could be compressed to 10 or 15 days. However, delays in shipping, customs inspections, and resistance from business partners can make it difficult to achieve a compressed payment schedule. Also, a customer being asked to accept a shorter payment schedule may attempt to push back with lower prices or other benefits, which increases the cost of this option.

The time compression concept can take the form of a company policy that does not allow standard credit terms to foreign customers that exceed a certain number of days. By doing so, a company can at least minimize the number of days during which exchange rates can fluctuate.

Payment Leading and Lagging

If there is a pronounced trend in exchange rates over the short term, the accounts payable manager can be encouraged to alter the timing normally associated with payables payments to take advantage of expected changes in exchange rates. For example, if a foreign currency is becoming more expensive, it may make sense to pay those payables denominated in it as soon as possible, rather than waiting until the normal payment date to pay in a more expensive currency. Similarly, if a foreign currency is declining in value, there may be an opportunity to delay payments by a few days to take advantage of the ongoing decline in the exchange rate. The latter case may be too much trouble, since suppliers do not appreciate late payments.

Build Reserves

If company management believes that there is just as great a risk of a gain as a loss on a currency fluctuation, it may be willing to accept the downside risk in hopes of attaining an upside profit. If so, it is possible to build cash and debt reserves greater than what would normally be needed, against the possibility of an outsized loss. This may entail investing a large amount of cash in very liquid investments, or retaining extra cash that might otherwise be paid out in dividends or used for capital expenditures. Other options are to obtain an unusually large line of credit that can be called upon in the event of a loss, or selling more stock than would typically be needed for operational purposes.

Building reserves will protect a business from foreign exchange risk, but the cost of acquiring and maintaining those reserves is substantial. Cash that is kept on hand could have earned an investment, while a commitment fee must be paid for a line of credit, even if the line is never used. Similarly, investors who buy a company's stock expect to earn a return. Thus, there is a noticeable cost associated with building reserves. A less-expensive option is hedging, which we will address shortly.

Maintain Local Reserves

If the company is routinely engaging in the purchase and sale of goods and services within another country, the answer may be to maintain a cash reserve within that country, which is denominated in the local currency. Doing so eliminates the cost of repeatedly buying and selling currencies and paying the related conversion commissions. The downside of maintaining local reserves is that a company is still subject to translation risk, where it must periodically translate its local cash reserves into its home currency for financial reporting purposes – which carries with it the risk of recording a translation loss.

Hedging

When all operational and strategic alternatives have been exhausted, it is time to consider buying hedging instruments that offset the risk posed by specific foreign exchange positions. Hedging is accomplished by purchasing an offsetting currency exposure. For example, if a company has a liability to deliver 1 million euros in six months, it can hedge this risk by entering into a contract to purchase 1 million euros on the same date, so that it can buy and sell in the same currency on the same date. The ideal outcome of a hedge is when the distribution of probable outcomes is reduced, so that the size of any potential loss is reduced. The following exhibit shows the effect of hedging on the range of possible outcomes.

Impact of Hedging on Risk Outcome

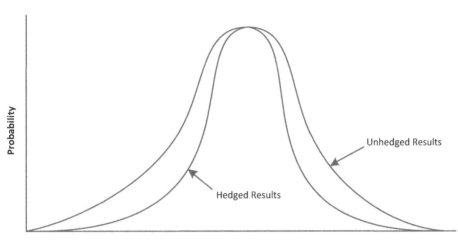

When a company has a multi-year contract with a customer, it may be necessary to create a long-term hedge to offset the related risk of currency fluctuations. If the customer subsequently terminates the contract early, the company may have to incur a significant cost to unwind the related hedge before its planned termination date. If this scenario appears possible, or if a business has experienced such events in the past, it may make sense to include in the contract a clause stating that the customer bears the cost of unwinding the hedge if there is an early contract termination.

> **Tip:** When entering into a long-term contract for which a hedge is anticipated, be sure to estimate the cost of the hedge in advance, and include it in the formulation of the price quoted to the customer.

Summary

Clearly, there are many risk management alternatives available to a company that must deal with foreign exchange situations. We recommend avoiding active hedging strategies as long as possible, in favor of more passive methods that are easier to understand, implement, and monitor. If the risk situation is too extreme to be completely addressed by passive means, then an active hedging strategy is probably the answer. In the next section, we address several types of active hedging transactions.

Types of Foreign Exchange Hedges

This section describes a number of methods for hedging foreign currency transactions. The first type of hedge, which is a loan denominated in a foreign currency, is designed to offset translation risk. The remaining hedges target the transaction risk related to the currency fluctuations associated with either specific or aggregated business transactions.

Loan Denominated in a Foreign Currency

When a company is at risk of recording a loss from the translation of assets and liabilities into its home currency, it can hedge the risk by obtaining a loan denominated in the functional currency in which the assets and liabilities are recorded. The effect of this hedge is to neutralize any loss on translation of the subsidiary's net assets with a gain on translation of the loan, or vice versa.

EXAMPLE

Hammer Industries has a subsidiary located in London, and which does business entirely within England. Accordingly, the subsidiary's net assets are denominated in pounds. The net assets of the subsidiary are currently recorded at £10 million. To hedge the translation risk associated with these assets, Hammer acquires a £10 million loan from a bank in London.

One month later, a change in the dollar/pound exchange rate results in a translation loss of $15,000 on the translation of the subsidiary's net assets into U.S. dollars. This amount is exactly offset by the translation gain of $15,000 on the liability associated with the £10 million loan.

Tip: An ideal way to create an offsetting loan is to fund the purchase or expansion of a foreign subsidiary largely through the proceeds of a long-term loan obtained within the same country, so that the subsidiary's assets are approximately cancelled out by the amount of the loan.

There are two problems with this type of hedge. First, it can be difficult to obtain a loan in the country in which the net assets are located. Second, the company will incur an interest expense on a loan that it would otherwise not need, though the borrowed funds could be invested to offset the interest expense.

The Forward Contract

A forward contract is an agreement under which a business agrees to buy a certain amount of foreign currency on a specific future date, and at a predetermined exchange rate. Forward exchange rates can be obtained for twelve months into the future; quotes for major currency pairs can be obtained for as much as five to ten years in the future. The exchange rate is comprised of the following elements:

- The spot price of the currency
- The bank's transaction fee
- An adjustment (up or down) for the interest rate differential between the two currencies. In essence, the currency of the country having a lower interest rate will trade at a premium, while the currency of the country having a

higher interest rate will trade at a discount. For example, if the domestic interest rate is lower than the rate in the other country, the bank acting as the counterparty adds points to the spot rate, which increases the cost of the foreign currency in the forward contract.

The calculation of the number of discount or premium points to subtract from or add to a forward contract is based on the following formula:

$$\text{Exchange rate} \quad \times \quad \text{Interest rate differential} \quad \times \quad \frac{\text{Days in contract}}{360} \quad = \quad \text{Premium or discount}$$

Thus, if the spot price of pounds per dollar were 1.5459 and there were a premium of 15 points for a forward contract with a 360-day maturity, the forward rate (not including a transaction fee) would be 1.5474.

By entering into a forward contract, a company can ensure that a definite future liability can be settled at a specific exchange rate. Forward contracts are typically customized, and arranged between a company and its bank. The bank will require a partial payment to initiate a forward contract, as well as final payment shortly before the settlement date.

EXAMPLE

Hammer Industries has acquired equipment from a company in the United Kingdom, which Hammer must pay for in 60 days in the amount of £150,000. To hedge against the risk of an unfavorable change in exchange rates during the intervening 60 days, Hammer enters into a forward contract with its bank to buy £150,000 in 60 days, at the current exchange rate.

60 days later, the exchange rate has indeed taken a turn for the worse, but Hammer's treasurer is indifferent, since he obtains the £150,000 needed for the purchase transaction based on the exchange rate in existence when the contract with the supplier was originally signed.

A forward contract is designed to have a specific settlement date, but the business transaction to which it relates may not be so timely. For example, a business has a contract to sell £10,000 in 60 days, but may not be able to do so if it has not yet received funds from a customer. A *forward window contract* is designed to work around this variability in the timing of receipts from customers by incorporating a range of settlement dates. One can then wait for a cash receipt and trigger settlement of the forward contract immediately thereafter.

The primary difficulties with forward contracts relate to their being customized transactions that are designed specifically for two parties. Because of this level of customization, it is difficult for either party to offload the contract to a third party. Also, the level of customization makes it difficult to compare offerings from different banks, so there is a tendency for banks to build unusually large fees into these contracts. Finally, a company may find that the underlying transaction for which a forward contract was created has been cancelled, leaving the contract still to be settled. If so, one can enter into a second forward contract, whose net effect is to offset the first forward contract. Though the bank will charge fees for both contracts, this arrangement will settle the company's obligations.

The Futures Contract

A futures contract is similar in concept to a forward contract, in that a business can enter into a contract to buy or sell currency at a specific price on a future date. The difference is that futures contracts are traded on an exchange, so these contracts are for standard amounts and durations. An initial deposit into a margin account is required to initiate a futures contract. The contract is then repriced each day, and if cumulative losses drain the margin account, a company is required to add more funds to the margin account. If the company does not respond to a margin call, the exchange closes out the contract.

Given that futures contracts are standardized, they may not exactly match the timing and amounts of an underlying transaction that is being hedged, which can lead to over- or under-hedging. However, since these contracts are traded on an exchange, it is easier to trade them than forward contracts, which allows for the easy unwinding of a hedge position earlier than its normal settlement date.

In a forward contract, the bank includes a transaction fee in the contract. In a futures contract, a broker charges a commission to execute the deal.

The Currency Option

An option gives its owner the right, but not the obligation, to buy or sell an asset at a certain price (known as the *strike price*), either on or before a specific date. In exchange for this right, the buyer pays an up-front premium to the seller. The income earned by the seller is restricted to the premium payment received, while the buyer has a theoretically unlimited profit potential, depending upon the future direction of the relevant exchange rate.

Currency options are available for the purchase or sale of currencies within a certain future date range, with the following variations available for the option contract:

- *American option.* The option can be exercised on any date within the option period, so that delivery is two business days after the exercise date.
- *European option.* The option can only be exercised on the expiry date, which means that delivery will be two business days after the expiry date.
- *Burmudan option.* The option can only be exercised on certain predetermined dates.

The holder of an option will exercise it when the strike price is more favorable than the current market rate, which is called being *in-the-money*. If the strike price is less favorable than the current market rate, this is called being *out-of-the-money*, in which case the option holder will not exercise the option. If the option holder is inattentive, it is possible that an in-the-money option will not be exercised prior to its expiry date. Notice of option exercise must be given to the counterparty by the notification date stated in the option contract.

A currency option provides two key benefits:

- *Loss prevention.* An option can be exercised to hedge the risk of loss, while still leaving open the possibility of benefiting from a favorable change in exchange rates.
- *Date variability.* The holder can exercise an option within a predetermined date range, which is useful when there is uncertainty about the exact timing of the underlying exposure.

There are a number of factors that enter into the price of a currency option, which can make it difficult to ascertain whether a quoted option price is reasonable. These factors are:

- The difference between the designated strike price and the current spot price. The buyer of an option can choose a strike price that suits his specific circumstances. A strike price that is well away from the current spot price will cost less, since the likelihood of exercising the option is low. However, setting such a strike price means that the buyer is willing to absorb the loss associated with a significant change in the exchange rate before seeking cover behind an option.
- The current interest rates for the two currencies during the option period.
- The duration of the option.
- The volatility of the market. This is the expected amount by which the currency is expected to fluctuate during the option period, with higher volatility making it more likely that an option will be exercised. Volatility is a guesstimate, since there is no quantifiable way to predict it.
- The willingness of counterparties to issue options.

Banks generally allow an option exercise period of no more than three months. Multiple partial currency deliveries within a currency option can be arranged.

Exchange traded options for standard quantities are available. This type of option eliminates the risk of counterparty failure, since the clearing house operating the exchange guarantees the performance of all options traded on the exchange.

EXAMPLE

Hammer Industries has an obligation to buy £250,000 in three months. Currently, the forward rate for the British pound is 1.5000 U.S. dollars, so that it should require $375,000 to buy the £250,000 in 90 days. If the pound depreciates, Hammer will be able to buy pounds for less than the $375,000 that it currently anticipates spending, but if the pound appreciates, Hammer will have to spend more to acquire the £250,000.

Hammer's treasurer elects to buy an option, so that he can hedge against the appreciation of the pound, while leaving open the prospect of profits to be gained from any depreciation in the pound. The cost of an option with a strike price of 1.6000 U.S. dollars per pound is $3,000.

Three months later, the pound has appreciated against the dollar, with the price having changed to 1.75 U.S. dollars per pound. The treasurer exercises the option, and spends $400,000 for the requisite number of pounds (calculated as £250,000 × 1.6000). If he had not purchased the option, the purchase would instead have cost $437,500 (calculated as £250,000 × 1.7500). Thus, Hammer saved $34,500 by using a currency option (calculated as the savings of $37,500, less the $3,000 cost of the option).

Currency options are particularly valuable during periods of high currency price volatility. Unfortunately from the perspective of the buyer, high volatility equates to higher option prices, since there is a higher probability that the counterparty will have to make a payment to the option buyer.

The Cylinder Option

Two options can be combined to create a *cylinder option*. One option is priced above the current spot price of the target currency, while the other option is priced below the spot price. The gain from exercising one option is used to partially offset the cost of the other option, thereby reducing the overall cost of the hedge. In effect, the upside potential offered by one option is being sold for a premium payment in order to finance the protection afforded by the opposing option.

The cylinder option is configured so that a company can acquire the right to buy currency at a specified price (a call option) and sell an option to a counterparty to buy currency from the company at a specified price (a put option), usually as of the expiry date. The premium the company pays for the purchased call is partially offset by the premium payable to the company for the put option that it sold.

If the market exchange rate remains between the boundaries established by the two currency options, the company never uses its options and instead buys or sells currency on the open market to fulfill its currency needs. If the market price breaches the strike price of the call option, the company exercises the call option and buys currency at the designated strike price. Conversely, if the market price breaches the strike price of the put option, the counterparty exercises its option to sell the currency to the company.

A variation on the cylinder option is to construct call and put options that are very close together, so that the premium cost of the call is very close to the premium income generated by the put, resulting in a near-zero net hedging cost to the company. The two options have to be very close together for the zero cost option to work, which means that the effective currency price range being hedged is quite small.

Swaps

If a company has or expects to have an obligation to make a payment in a foreign currency, it can arrange to swap currency holdings with a third party that already has the required currency. The two entities engage in a swap transaction by agreeing upon an initial swap date, the date when the cash positions will be reversed back to their original positions, and an interest rate that reflects the comparative differences in interest rates between the two countries in which the entities are located.

Another use for a currency swap is when a forward exchange contract has been delayed. In this situation, one would normally sell to a counterparty the currency that it has just obtained through the receipt of an account receivable. If, however, the receivable has not yet been paid, the company can enter into a swap agreement to obtain the required currency and meet its immediate obligation under the forward exchange contract. Later, when the receivable is eventually paid, the company can reverse the swap, returning funds to the counterparty.

A swap arrangement may be for just a one-day period, or extend out for several years into the future. Swap transactions generally do not occur in amounts of less than $5 million, so this technique is not available to smaller businesses.

A potentially serious problem with swaps is the prospect of a default by the counterparty. If there is a default, the company once again assumes its foreign currency liability, and must now scramble to find an alternative hedge.

Netting

There are circumstances where a company has subsidiaries in multiple countries that actively trade with each other. If so, they should have accounts receivable and payable with each other, which could give rise to a flurry of foreign exchange transactions in multiple currencies that could trigger any number of hedging activities. Examples of these receivables and payables are noted in the following table.

Receivables and Payables that may be Netted

Debt payments	Intercompany funding	Management fees
Dividends	Investments	Royalty and licensing payments
Hedging contracts		Trade payables

However, salary and wage payments are not included in netting, nor are tax payments.

It may be possible to reduce the amount of hedging activity through *payment netting*, where the corporate parent offsets all accounts receivable and payable against each other to determine the net amount of foreign exchange transactions that actually require hedges. A centralized netting function may be used, which means that each subsidiary either receives a single payment from the netting center, or makes a single payment to the netting center. Netting results in the following benefits:

- Foreign exchange exposure is no longer tracked at the subsidiary level
- The total amount of foreign exchange purchased and sold declines, which reduces the amount of foreign exchange commissions paid out
- The total amount of cash in transit (and therefore not available for investment) between subsidiaries declines

This may require modeling of the number of netting cycles per month. If there are many transactions to be netted, then a netting cycle could be as frequent as once a week. A lower volume of transactions could call for a correspondingly longer time period over which to let transactions accumulate, perhaps resulting in a monthly netting cycle.

Tip: It is easier to create an intracompany netting system when there is already a centralized accounts payable function for the entire business, which is called a *payment factory*.

Intracompany netting will still result in some payments between subsidiaries located in different countries. Since each subsidiary may be operating its own cash concentration system, this means that cash must be physically shifted from one cash pool to another, which is inefficient. Where possible, the treasury staff should consider creating cash pools that span international boundaries, so that there is no need for cross-border transfers between cash pools. The result is essentially free cash transfers within the company.

The same concept can be applied to payables and receivables with outside entities, though a considerable amount of information sharing is needed to make the concept work. In some industries where there is a high level of trade between companies, industry-wide netting programs have been established that routinely offset a large proportion of the payables and receivables within the industry. The net result is that all offsetting obligations are reduced to a single payment per currency per value date between counterparties.

A related concept is *close-out netting*, where counterparties having forward contracts with each other can agree to net the obligations, rather than engaging in a large number of individual contract settlements. Before engaging in close-out netting, discuss the concept with corporate counsel. A case has been made in some jurisdictions that close-out netting runs counter to the interests of other creditors in the event of a bankruptcy by one of the counterparties.

A downside of netting is that the accounting departments of the participating companies must sort out how their various transactions are settled. This requires a procedure for splitting a group of netted transactions into individual payments and receipts in the cash receipts and accounts payable modules of their accounting systems. This can require significant coordination effort, as well as systems development time. Here are several other concerns to address when deciding whether to engage in a netting program:

- *Bank holidays*. There are different bank holidays in different countries, so factor these non-processing days into the consideration of when payments are to be processed through the system.
- *Costs*. Only engage in netting after conducting a complete cost-benefit analysis to determine whether such an arrangement can indeed provide a net benefit to the organization. If there are few applicable transactions, the overhead cost associated with maintaining a netting program could overwhelm any possible benefits to be gained.
- *Tax withholdings*. Some taxing authorities levy a withholding on certain payments, which must still be made, irrespective of other netting arrangements. This can be a particularly difficult area to integrate into a netting system.
- *Transaction accuracy*. If transactions are not input to the system correctly, there is a risk of diverting a significant amount of cash into the wrong currency. Another concern is the timeliness of data entry, since a late entry may not be addressed until the following netting cycle.

If there are areas of particular netting complexity, it could make sense to avoid these transactions until a later date, and initially roll out the system using the simplest set of transactions. After all bugs are eliminated from the system, including additional and more complex transactions could then be contemplated.

Interest Risk Overview

Interest rate risk involves the risk of increases in interest rates on debt, as well as reductions in interest rates for investment instruments, with the attendant negative impact on profitability. This risk can take the following forms:

- *Absolute rate changes*. The market rate of interest will move up or down over time, resulting in immediate variances from the interest rates paid or earned by a company. This rate change is easily monitored.
- *Reinvestment risk*. Investments must be periodically re-invested and debt re-issued. If interest rates happen to be unfavorable during one of these rollover periods, a company will be forced to accept whatever interest rate is available.
- *Yield curve risk*. The yield curve shows the relationship between short-term and long-term interest rates, and typically slopes upward to indicate that long-term debt carries a higher interest rate to reflect the risk to the lender

associated with such debt. If the yield curve steepens, flattens, or declines, these relationships change the debt duration that a company should use in its borrowing and investing strategies.

Interest risk is a particular concern for those businesses using large amounts of debt to fund their operations, since even a small increase in the interest rate could have a profound impact on profits, when multiplied by the volume of debt employed. Further, a sudden boost in interest expense could worsen a company's interest coverage ratio, which is a common covenant in loan agreements, and which could trigger a loan termination if the minimum ratio covenant is not met.

Interest Rate Risk Management

The primary objective of interest risk management is to keep fluctuations in interest rates from impacting company earnings. Management can respond to this objective in many ways, ranging from a conscious decision to take no action, passing through a number of relatively passive alternatives, and culminating in several active techniques for risk mitigation. We provide an overview of each option in this section.

Take No Action

There may be situations where a company has minimal investments that earn interest, or issues only minor amounts of debt. If so, it is certainly acceptable to not implement an aggressive risk management campaign related to interest rates. However, this state of affairs does not typically last for long, after which there will be some degree of risk related to interest rates. In anticipation of such an event, it is useful to model the amount of interest rate change that must occur before there will be a serious impact on company finances. Once that trigger point is known, the treasurer can begin to prepare any of the risk mitigation alternatives noted later in this section.

Avoid Risk

The risk associated with interest rates arises between external entities and a business; it does not arise between the subsidiaries of the same business. Thus, a company can act as its own bank to some extent, by providing intercompany lending arrangements at interest rates that are not subject to fluctuations. This is particularly useful in a multi-national corporation, where cash reserves in different currencies may be scattered throughout the business, and can be lent back and forth to cover immediate cash needs.

Another way to avoid risk is to operate the business in such a conservative manner that the company has no debt, thereby eliminating the risk associated with interest rates on debt. The same result can be achieved by using invested funds to pay off any outstanding debt. The main downside of the low-debt method is that a company may be constraining its growth by not taking advantage of a low-cost source of funds (i.e., debt).

Asset and Liability Matching

A key trigger for interest rate risk is when short-term debt is used to fund an asset that is expected to be held for a long period of time. In this situation, the short-term debt must be rolled over multiple times during the life span of the asset or until the debt is paid off, introducing the risk that each successive debt rollover will result in an increased interest rate. To avoid this risk, arrange for financing that approximately matches the useful life of the underlying asset. Thus, spending $1 million for a machine that is expected to have a useful life of 10 years should be funded with a loan that also has a 10-year life.

Hedging

Interest rate hedging is the practice of acquiring financial instruments whose effects offset those of the underlying scenario causing interest rate fluctuations, so that the net effect is minimized rate fluctuations. Hedges fall into two categories:

- *Forward rate agreements and futures.* These financial instruments are designed to lock in an interest rate, so that changes in the actual interest rate above or below the baseline interest rate do not impact a business. These instruments do not provide any flexibility for taking advantage of favorable changes in interest rates.
- *Options.* These financial instruments only lock in an interest rate if the holder wants to do so, thereby presenting the possibility of benefiting from a favorable change in an interest rate.

The various types of interest rate hedges are discussed next.

Types of Interest Rate Hedges

This section describes a number of methods for hedging the variability in interest rates. These options are mostly designed for high-value transactions, and so are not available to smaller companies.

The Forward Rate Agreement

A forward rate agreement (FRA) is an agreement between two parties to lock in a specific interest rate for a designated period of time, which usually spans just a few months. Under an FRA, the parties are protecting against opposing exposures: the FRA buyer wants to protect against an increase in the interest rate, while the FRA seller wants to protect against a decrease in the interest rate. Any payout under an FRA is based on a change in the reference interest rate from the interest rate stated in the contract (the FRA rate). An FRA is not related to a specific loan or investment – it simply provides interest rate protection.

The FRA rate is based on the yield curve, where interest rates usually increase for instruments having longer maturities. This means that the FRA rate typically increases for periods further in the future.

Several date-specific terms are referred to in a forward rate agreement, and are crucial to understanding how the FRA concept works. These terms are:

1. *Contract date*. The date on which the FRA begins.
2. *Expiry date*. The date on which any variance between the market rate and the reference rate is calculated.
3. *Settlement date*. The date on which the interest variance is paid by one counterparty to the other.
4. *Maturity date*. The final date of the date range that underlies the FRA contract.

In essence, these four dates anchor the two time periods covered by an FRA. The first period, which begins with the contract date and ends with the expiry date, spans the term of the contract. The second period begins with the settlement date and ends with the maturity date, and spans the period that underlies the contract. This date range is shown graphically in the following example.

Relevant FRA Dates

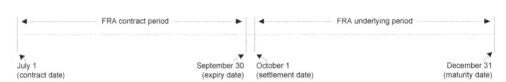

The FRA rate is based on a future period, such as the period starting in one month and ending in four months, which is said to have a "1 × 4" FRA term, and has an effective term of three months. Similarly, a contract starting in three months and ending in six months is said to have a "3 × 6" FRA term, and also has an effective term of three months.

At the *beginning* of the designated FRA period, the interest rate stated in the contract is compared to the reference rate. The reference rate is usually a well-known interest rate index, such as the London Interbank Offered Rate (LIBOR). If the reference rate is higher, the seller makes a payment to the FRA buyer, based on the incremental difference in interest rates and the notional amount of the contract. The payment calculation is shown in the following example. If the reference rate is lower than the interest rate stated in the contract, the buyer makes a payment to the FRA seller. The payment made between the counterparties must be discounted to its present value, since the payment is associated with the FRA underlying period that has not yet happened. Thus, the discount assumes that the money would actually be due on the maturity date, but is payable on the settlement date (which may be months before the maturity date). The calculation for discounting the payment between counterparties is:

$$\frac{\text{Settlement amount}}{1 + (\text{Days in FRA underlying period}/360 \text{ Days} \times \text{Reference rate})} = \frac{\text{Discounted}}{\text{Payment}}$$

The reason why the contract payment is calculated at the *beginning* of the designated FRA period is that the risk being hedged by the contract was from the initial contract date until the date on which the FRA buyer expects to borrow money and lock in an interest rate. For example, a company may enter into an FRA in January, because it is uncertain of what the market interest rate will be in April, when it intends to borrow funds; the period at risk is therefore from January through April. The following example illustrates the concept.

EXAMPLE

Hammer Industries has a legal commitment to borrow $50 million in two months, and for a period of three months. Hammer's treasurer is concerned that there may be an increase in the interest rate during the two-month period prior to borrowing the $50 million. The treasurer elects to hedge the risk of an increase in the interest rate by purchasing a three-month FRA, starting in two months. A broker quotes a rate of 5.50%. Hammer enters into an FRA at the 5.50% interest rate, with 3rd National Bank as the counterparty. The notional amount of the contract is for $50 million.

Two months later, the reference rate is 6.00%, so 3rd National pays Hammer the difference between the contract rate and reference rate, which is 0.50%. At the same time, Hammer borrows $50 million at the market rate (which happens to match the reference rate) of 6.00%. Because of the FRA, Hammer's effective borrowing rate is 5.50%.

The amount paid by 3rd National to Hammer is calculated as:

(Reference rate – FRA rate) × (FRA days/360 days) × Notional amount = Profit or loss

or

(6.00% - 5.50%) × (90 days/360 days) × $50 million = $62,500

Since the payment is made at the beginning of the borrowing period, rather than at its end, the $62,500 payment is discounted and its present value paid. The discounting calculation for the settlement amount is:

$$\frac{\$62,500}{1 + (90/360 \text{ Days} \times 6.00\%)} = \$61,576.35$$

What if the reference rate had fallen by 0.50%, instead of increasing? Then Hammer would have paid 3rd National the discounted amount of $62,500, rather than the reverse. Hammer would also end up borrowing the $50 million at the new market rate of 5.00%. When the payment to 3rd National is combined with the reduced 5.00% interest rate, Hammer will still be paying a 5.50% interest rate, which is what it wanted all along.

133

From the buyer's perspective, the result of an FRA is that it pays the expected interest rate – no higher, and no lower.

The Futures Contract

An interest rate futures contract is conceptually similar to a forward contract, except that it is traded on an exchange, which means that it is for a standard amount and duration. The standard size of a futures contract is $1 million, so multiple contracts may need to be purchased to create a hedge for a specific loan or investment amount. The pricing for futures contracts starts at a baseline figure of 100, and declines based on the implied interest rate in a contract. For example, if a futures contract has an implied interest rate of 5.00%, the price of that contract will be 95.00. The calculation of the profit or loss on a futures contract is derived as follows:

Notional contract amount × Contract duration/360 Days × (Ending price – Beginning price)

Most trading in interest rate futures is in Eurodollars (U.S. dollars held outside of the United States), and are traded on the Chicago Mercantile Exchange.

Hedging is not perfect, since the notional amount of a contract may vary from the actual amount of funding that a company wants to hedge, resulting in a modest amount of either over- or under-hedging. For example, hedging a $15.4 million position will require the purchase of either 15 or 16 $1 million contracts. There may also be differences between the time period required for a hedge and the actual hedge period as stated in a futures contract. For example, if there is a seven month exposure to be hedged, a treasurer could acquire two consecutive three-month contracts, and elect to have the seventh month be unhedged.

Tip: If the buyer wants to protect against interest rate variability for a longer period, such as for the next year, it is possible to buy a series of futures contracts covering consecutive periods, so that coverage is achieved for the entire time period.

EXAMPLE

The treasurer of Hammer Industries wants to hedge an investment of $10 million. To do so, he sells 10 three-month futures contracts with contract terms of three months. The current three-month LIBOR is 3.50% and the 3 × 6 forward rate is 3.75%. These contracts are currently listed on the Chicago Mercantile Exchange at 96.25, which is calculated as 100 minus the 3.75% forward rate.

When the futures contracts expire, the forward rate has declined to 3.65%, so that the contracts are now listed at 96.35 (calculated as 100 – the 3.65 percent forward rate). By engaging in this hedge, Hammer has earned a profit of $2,500, which is calculated as follows:

$$\$10,000,000 \times (90/360) \times (0.9635 \text{ Ending price} - 0.9625 \text{ Beginning price})$$

$$= \$2,500$$

When the buyer purchases a futures contract, a minimum amount must initially be posted in a margin account to ensure performance under the contract terms. It may be necessary to fund the margin account with additional cash (a *margin call*) if the market value of the contract declines over time (margin accounts are revised daily, based on the market closing price). If the buyer cannot provide additional funding in the event of a contract decline, the futures exchange closes out the contract prior to its normal termination date. Conversely, if the market value of the contract increases, the net gain is credited to the buyer's margin account. On the last day of the contract, the exchange marks the contract to market and settles the accounts of the buyer and seller. Thus, transfers between buyers and sellers over the life of a contract are essentially a zero-sum game, where one party directly benefits at the expense of the other.

It is also possible to enter into a bond futures contract, which can be used to hedge interest rate risk. For example, a business that has borrowed funds can hedge against rising interest rates by selling a bond futures contract. Then, if interest rates do in fact rise, the resulting gain on the contract will offset the higher interest rate that the borrower is paying. Conversely, if interest rates subsequently fall, the borrower will experience a loss on the contract, which will offset the lower interest rate now being paid. Thus, the net effect of the contract is that the borrower locks in the beginning interest rate through the period of the contract.

Tip: A bond futures contract is not a perfect hedge, for it is also impacted by changes in the credit rating of the bond issuer.

When a purchased futures contract expires, it is customary to settle it by selling a futures contract that has the same delivery date. Conversely, if the original contract was sold to a counterparty, then the seller can settle the contract by buying a futures contract that has the same delivery date.

The following table notes the key differences between forward rate agreements and futures contracts. Similarities between the two instruments are excluded from the table.

Differences between a Futures Contract and FRA

Feature	Futures Contract	Forward Rate Agreement
Trading platform	Exchange-based	Between two parties
Counterparty	The exchange	Single counterparty
Collateral	Margin account	None
Agreement	Standardized	Modified
Settlement	Daily mark to market	On expiry date

The preceding table reveals two key differences between a futures contract and an FRA. First, there can be significant counterparty risk in an FRA, since the contract period can be lengthy, and financial conditions can change markedly over that time. Second, a futures contract is settled every day, which can create pressure to fund a margin call if there are significant losses on the contract.

The Interest Rate Swap

An interest rate swap is a customized contract between two parties to swap two schedules of cash flows that could extend for anywhere from one to 25 years, and which represent interest payments. Only the interest rate obligations are swapped, not the underlying loans or investments from which the obligations are derived. The counterparties are usually a company and a bank. There are many types of rate swaps; we will confine this discussion to a swap arrangement where one schedule of cash flows is based on a floating interest rate, and the other is based on a fixed interest rate. For example, a five-year schedule of cash flows based on a fixed interest rate may be swapped for a five-year schedule of cash flows based on a floating interest rate that is tied to the London Interbank Offered Rate (LIBOR).

The most common reason to engage in an interest rate swap is to exchange a variable-rate payment for a fixed-rate payment, or vice versa. Thus, a company that has only been able to obtain a floating-rate loan can effectively convert the loan to a fixed-rate loan through an interest rate swap. This approach is especially attractive when a borrower is only able to obtain a fixed-rate loan by paying a premium, but can combine a variable-rate loan and an interest rate swap to achieve a fixed-rate loan at a lower price.

A company may want to take the reverse approach and swap its fixed interest payments for floating payments. This situation arises when the treasurer believes that interest rates will decline during the swap period, and wants to take advantage of the lower rates.

A swap contract is settled through a multi-step process, which is:

1. Calculate the payment obligation of each party, typically once every six months through the life of the swap arrangement.
2. Determine the variance between the two amounts.
3. The party whose position is improved by the swap arrangement pays the variance to the party whose position is degraded by the swap arrangement.

Thus, a company continues to pay interest to its banker under the original lending agreement, while the company either accepts a payment from the rate swap counterparty, or issues a payment to the counterparty, with the result being that the net amount of interest paid by the company is the amount planned by the business when it entered into the swap agreement.

EXAMPLE

Hammer Industries has a $15 million variable-rate loan outstanding that matures in two years. The current interest rate on the loan is 6.5%. Hammer enters into an interest rate swap agreement with Big Regional Bank for a fixed-rate 7.0% loan with a $15 million notional amount. The first scheduled payment swap date is in six months. On that date, the variable rate on Hammer's loan has increased to 7.25%. Thus, the total interest payments on the swap date are $543,750 for Hammer and $525,000 for Big Regional. Since the two parties have agreed to swap payments, Big Regional pays Hammer the difference between the two payments, which is $18,750.

Hammer issues an interest payment of $543,750 to its bank. When netted with the cash inflow of $18,750 from Big Regional, this means that the net interest rate being paid by Hammer is 7.0%.

Several larger banks have active trading groups that routinely deal with interest rate swaps. Most swaps involve sums in the millions of dollars, but some banks are willing to engage in swap arrangements involving amounts of less than $1 million. There is a counterparty risk with interest rate swaps, since one party could fail to make a contractually-mandated payment to the other party. This risk is of particular concern when a swap arrangement covers multiple years, since the financial condition of a counterparty could change dramatically during that time.

If there is general agreement in the marketplace that interest rates are headed in a certain direction, it will be more expensive to obtain a swap that protects against interest rate changes in the anticipated direction.

Interest Rate Options

An option gives its owner the right, but not the obligation, to trigger a contract. The contract can be either a call option or a put option. A *call option* related to interest rates protects the option owner from rising interest rates, while a *put option* protects the option owner from declining interest rates. The party selling an option does so in exchange for a one-time premium payment. The party buying an option is doing so to mitigate its risk related to a change in interest rates.

An interest rate option can be relatively inexpensive if there has been or is expected to be little volatility in interest rates, since the option seller does not expect interest rates to move enough for the option to be exercised. Conversely, if there has been or is expected to be considerable interest rate volatility, the option seller must assume that the option will be exercised, and so sets a higher price. Thus, periods of high interest rate volatility may make it cost-prohibitive to buy options.

Tip: An interest rate hedge using an option may not be entirely successful if the reference rate used for the option is not the same one used for the underlying loan. For example, the reference rate for an option may be LIBOR, while the rate used for the underlying loan may be a bank's prime rate. The result is a hedging mismatch that can create an unplanned gain or loss.

An interest rate option sets a *strike price*, which is a specific interest rate at which the option buyer can borrow or lend money. The contract also states the amount of funds that the option buyer can borrow or lend (the *notional amount*). Rate increases and declines are measured using a *reference rate*, which is typically a well-known interest rate index, such as LIBOR. There is also an option expiration date, or *expiry date*, after which the option is cancelled. The buyer can specify the exact terms needed to hedge an interest rate position with a customized option.

If an option buyer wants to be protected from increases in interest rates, a *cap* (or ceiling) is created. A cap is a consecutive series of options, all having the same strike price. The buyer of a cap is paid whenever the reference rate exceeds the cap strike price on an option expiry date. For example, if a company wants to hedge its interest risk for one year with a strike price of 6.50%, beginning on January 1, it can buy the following options:

Desired Coverage Period	Option Number	Expiry Date	Option Term	Strike Price
January - March	--	Not applicable*	Not available*	N/A*
April - June	1	April 1	4 to 6 months	6.50%
July – September	2	July 1	7 to 9 months	6.50%
October - December	3	October 1	10 to 12 months	6.50%

* There is no option available for the first three-month period, since the expiry date is at the beginning of the contract period, so the expiry date will be reached immediately.

With a cap arrangement, the buyer is only subject to interest rate changes up to the cap, and is protected from rate changes above the cap if the reference rate exceeds the cap strike price on predetermined dates. If the reference interest rate is below the cap at the option expiration, the option buyer lets the option expire. However, if the reference rate is above the cap, the buyer exercises the option, which means that the option seller must reimburse the buyer for the difference between the reference rate and the cap rate, multiplied by the notional amount of the contract.

A cap may be included in a loan agreement, such that the borrower is guaranteed not to pay more than a designated maximum interest rate over the term of the loan, or for a predetermined portion of the loan. In this case, the lender has paid for the cap, and will probably include its cost in the interest rate or fees associated with the loan.

If a treasurer wants to be protected from decreases in interest rates (for invested funds), a *floor* is structured into an option, so that the option buyer is paid if the reference rate declines below the floor strike rate.

EXAMPLE

Hammer Industries has a $25 million 3-month loan that currently carries a fixed interest rate of 7.00%. Hammer's bank refuses to grant a fixed-rate loan for a longer time period, so Hammer plans to continually roll over the loan every three months. Recently, short-term interest rates have been spiking, so the treasurer decided to purchase an interest rate cap that is set at 7.50%, and which is comprised of two consecutive options, each with a three-month term.

At the expiry date of the first option, the reference rate is 7.25%, which is below the cap strike rate. The treasurer lets the option expire unused and rolls over the short-term loan at the new 7.25% rate.

At the next option expiry date, the reference rate has risen to 7.75%, which is 0.25% above the cap strike rate. The treasurer exercises the option, which forces the counterparty to pay Hammer for the difference between the cap strike rate and the reference rate. The calculation of the amount to be reimbursed is:

(Reference rate – Strike rate) × (Lending period/360 days) × Notional amount = Profit or loss

or

(7.75% - 7.50%) × (90/360) × $25 million = $15,625

Of course, the cost of the option reduces the benefits gained from an interest rate option, but still is useful for providing protection from outsized changes in interest rates.

Tip: From an analysis perspective, it is useful to include the premium on an option with the amount of interest paid on a loan and any proceeds or payments associated with an exercised option, in order to derive the aggregate interest rate on any associated debt being hedged.

The cylinder option described earlier for foreign exchange risk can also be applied to interest rates. Under this concept, a company purchases a cap and sells a floor, with the current reference rate located between the two strike rates. The gain from exercising one option is used to partially offset the cost of the other option, which reduces the overall cost of the hedge. The three possible outcomes to this *collar* arrangement are:

1. The reference rate remains between the cap and floor, so neither option is exercised.
2. The reference rate rises above the cap, so the company is paid for the difference between the reference rate and the cap strike rate, multiplied by the notional amount of the contract.
3. The reference rate falls below the floor, so the company pays the option counterparty for the difference between the reference rate and the floor strike rate, multiplied by the notional amount of the contract.

The functioning of a collar arrangement is shown in the following exhibit, where the cap is set at 5% and the floor is set at 3%. No option is triggered until the reference rate drops to 2% in one of the later quarters, and again when it rises to 6%. In the first case, the company pays the 1% difference between the 3% floor and the 2% reference rate. In the latter case, the company is paid the 1% difference between the 5% cap and the 6% reference rate.

The Operation of an Interest Rate Collar

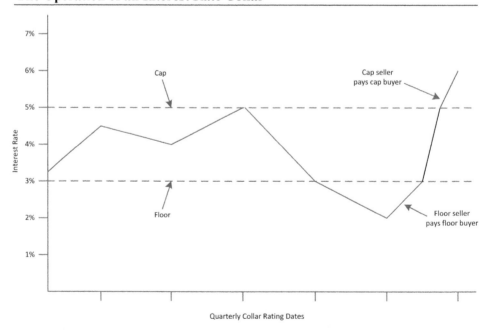

From the perspective of a company using a collar arrangement, the net effect is that interest rates will fluctuate only within the bounds set by the cap and floor strike rates.

A variation on the interest rate option concept is to include a call feature in a debt issuance. A call feature allows a company to buy back its debt from debt holders. The feature is quite useful in cases where the market interest rate has fallen since debt was issued, so a company can refinance its debt at a lower interest rate. However, the presence of the call option makes investors wary about buying it, which tends to increase the effective interest rate at which they will buy the debt. Investor concerns can be mitigated to some extent by providing for a fairly long time period before the issuing company can trigger the call option, and especially if the call price is set somewhat higher than the current market price.

Interest Rate Swaptions

A swaption is an option on an interest rate swap arrangement. The buyer of a swaption has the right, but not the obligation, to enter into an interest rate swap. In essence, a swaption presents the option of being able to lock in a fixed interest rate or a variable interest rate (depending on the terms of the underlying swap arrangement). Thus, a treasurer may suspect that interest rates will begin to rise in the near future, and so enters into a swaption to take over a fixed interest rate. If interest rates do indeed rise, the swaption holder can exercise the swaption. If interest rates hold steady or decline, the swaption is allowed to expire without being exercised.

The two types of swaption are the *payer swaption* and the *receiver swaption*, which are defined as follows:

- *Payer swaption.* The buyer can enter into a swap where it pays the fixed interest rate side of the transaction.
- *Receiver swaption.* The buyer can enter into a swap where it pays the floating interest rate side of the transaction.

There is no formal exchange for swaptions, so each agreement is between two counterparties. This means that each party is exposed to the potential failure of the counterparty to make scheduled payments on the underlying swap. Consequently, it is prudent to only enter into these arrangements with counterparties with high credit ratings or other evidence of financial stability.

Swaption market participants are primarily large corporations, banks, and hedge funds. The most likely counterparty for a corporation is a large bank that has a group specializing in swaption arrangements.

Summary

When reviewing the treasury risk management options outlined in this chapter, pay attention to the level of complexity involved in some of the alternatives. If the company does not have the expertise to engage in transactions involving the more complicated derivatives, do not attempt them; there is a risk of entering into an incorrect derivative transaction, which *increases* a risk rather than reducing it. Instead, work on the less convoluted risk management techniques first, and only enter into more difficult arrangements with proper counseling and oversight. It may be several years before management wants to take on certain derivative arrangements on a regular basis.

Chapter 11
Insurance

Introduction

The treasurer is sometimes tasked with the management of an organization's insurance policies. Insurance is a contractual arrangement in which an organization pays an insurance carrier in exchange for the assumption of risk by the carrier. The arrangement is used by a business when it wishes to offload risk that it does not want to or cannot retain internally.

Insurance is designed for events that are infrequent and high-loss. If events are too frequent, the cost of insurance coverage will be too expensive. If an event has small losses, there is no point in obtaining insurance coverage, since self-insurance is less expensive. Thus, insurance is intended for a very specific set of situations.

In this chapter, we address how insurers are rated, policy terms and conditions, the major types of business insurance, and how to manage the cost of insurance.

Insurance Distribution

There are several methods by which insurance is sold. *Direct writers* are insurance companies that sell insurance through their own distribution networks. Salespeople are only allowed to sell the insurance offerings of their employer. There is no option for a client to review quotes from other insurers, unless the clients also work with a broker. A variation on the direct writer concept is the *exclusive representative*, where the representative is required to first approach its designated insurer about a prospective insurance policy, which has the right of first refusal. If the request is denied, the representative can then offer the policy to other insurers. Direct writers also contact prospects through a variety of solicitations, such as the Internet, phone calls, and the mail. These latter approaches can be cost-effective for an insurer, because no commissions are paid.

Other insurance providers sell through a network of independent agents or brokers, who typically represent the insurance products of several insurance companies.

An *agent* is a legal representative of an insurance company, and may represent several insurers. An agent receives the rights to policy renewals for the agent's clients, along with the associated commissions. This renewal right allows an agent to build up a larger revenue stream over time. A variation on the agent concept is the *captive agent*, which only represents a single insurer. A captive agent may receive certain benefits, training, and even business leads in exchange for agreeing to this arrangement. The business leads appear when a policyholder moves into a captive agent's territory.

A *broker* represents the client, and assists the client in shopping for the best combination of coverage and price. Once a client accepts the recommendations of the broker, the broker must place the insurance contracts with the agents of the selected insurers.

If the treasurer decides to work with an agent or broker, the selection should be based on multiple possible criteria, such as:

- *Areas of expertise.* An agent or broker may have particular experience in certain industries, and provide advice in these areas. Evidence of expertise includes the resumes of its technical support staff and the types of clients represented.
- *Carriers represented.* The treasurer may have good experience with certain insurance carriers, and so will only work with an agent that represents those same carriers.
- *Services provided.* An agency or broker may offer an array of services, such as claims management, on-site inspections, policy analysis, and loss modeling.

An entirely different approach to insurance distribution is price comparison websites, which receive commissions when policies are sold through their sites. Alternatively, they may be paid a fee for each click-through from their sites.

Insurance Policy Terms and Conditions

When buying insurance, the treasurer must be cognizant of the related contract terms and conditions, since they can greatly restrict the amount of coverage that a carrier is actually agreeing to. The net result of the following terms and conditions is that a carrier is limiting the extent of its maximum payout, avoiding certain high-loss events, and forcing buyers to participate to varying degrees in any losses incurred.

Indemnity

The terms of an insurance contract may state that the insurer will indemnify the insured party if there is a loss. An indemnity refers to a payment by the insurer for the monetary value of a loss, as defined by the related insurance contract. The amount of an indemnity does not exceed the monetary loss experienced by the insured party, since an excessive payment would be akin to a gambling win by the insured.

Deductibles

The typical insurance policy contains a deductible, which is an initial loss amount that must be absorbed by the insured party. There are several reasons why insurance companies impose a deductible, which are:

- *Frivolous claims avoidance.* The bulk of all losses incurred by an organization are quite small, and they would inundate insurers with these claims if the insurers were solely responsible for losses. The cost to investigate and pay these claims would be excessive. The deductible keeps these smaller claims from ever being filed.

- *Ownership of losses.* If insured entities can pass the full amount of losses on to their insurers, they have no reason to take action to avoid losses. By making the insured parties responsible for smaller losses, there is a stronger incentive to avoid all types of losses.

Limit of Insurance

All insurance policies contain a limit of insurance, which is the maximum amount that the insurer will pay. This is needed by the insurer in order to avoid massive payouts due to catastrophic loss situations. Some of these limits of insurance are set quite low, so that the amounts paid out are inconsequential. If so, there may be little point in obtaining the insurance, since the amount of risk being passed off to the insurer is immaterial.

Coinsurance

There may be a coinsurance provision in an insurance policy. This provision is designed to penalize the insured party if it under-insures the value of property. Coinsurance is stated as a percentage. The following example illustrates the concept.

EXAMPLE

Hodgson Industrial Design owns its headquarters building, which has a replacement cost of $3,000,000. The company's property insurance contains an 80% coinsurance clause, which means that the insured amount must be at least 80% of the replacement cost of the building, or $2,400,000. The actual amount insured is for $2,000,000. Since the insured value is less than 80% of its replacement value, a loss payout under the policy will be subjected to an under-reporting penalty.

The building subsequently suffers $500,000 of property damage. The amount paid to Hodgson by the insurer is calculated as follows:

$2,000,000 insured amount ÷ (80% coinsurance percentage × $3,000,000 replacement cost) × $500,000 loss

= $416,667

In essence, Hodgson pays an $83,333 penalty because it did not insure the full value of the property.

The most commonly-used coinsurance percentage is 80%. If the percentage is higher, the insurer is imposing a stricter standard on the insured entity to insure the full value of property.

Given the negative impact of the coinsurance provision, a business must routinely examine the values of its insured property to verify that adequate amounts of insurance are being carried. Otherwise, a loss could result in a significantly reduced payout by the insurer.

Exclusions

Insurance policies typically contain a lengthy list of exclusions. If losses are caused by one of these events, they are not covered by the insurance. The exact exclusions will vary by insurance policy, but may include the items noted in the following table.

Sample Policy Exclusions

Earthquakes	Government seizure	War or sabotage
Flooding	Mold damage	Windstorm or hail
	Nuclear explosions or radiation	

Insurance Riders

An insurance rider is an adjustment to a basic insurance policy. A rider usually provides an additional benefit over what is described in the basic policy, in exchange for a fee payable to the insurer. A rider is not a standalone insurance product; it must be attached to a standard insurance policy. A rider is useful for tailoring an insurance policy to the precise needs of the insured entity. Examples of insurance riders are:

- *Life insurance.* An accelerated death benefit is added to the policy, so that a payout occurs when the policy holder is diagnosed with a terminal illness.
- *Directors and officers insurance.* A "tail" is added to the policy, so that the directors and officers receive coverage for several years following the normal termination of the policy.
- *Property insurance.* Additional coverage is provided for flooding, earthquakes, and fire damage, which may not be addressed by the basic policy.

Perils

Insurers may attempt to underwrite only a specific set of risks that they identify in the coverage; this is called *named perils* coverage. Since this type of coverage can exclude many types of risks, one should instead strive for *all-perils* coverage. Realistically, the cost of all-perils coverage may be so high that it is not attainable; if so, obtaining insurance devolves into an analysis of how to obtain the largest amount of named perils coverage for the lowest price.

Endorsements

Endorsements are attachments to a contract that either add to or restrict coverage. In essence, each endorsement is designed to adapt a boilerplate policy to the specific needs of the insured party.

Who is the Payee?

It is useful to understand which party is being paid by an insurer in the event of a claim. When the insurer is taking on a liability on behalf of an insured party, the insurer is paying the injured party, which is not the insured. For example, a company's customer sues in regard to an alleged product flaw that injured the customer. The insurer pays the customer the amount required to settle the claim, doing so on behalf of the insured party. Commercial general liability insurance and directors and officers insurance both feature this type of payment. Most other types of insurance provide for payments being made to the insured party.

Insurance Company Analysis

When purchasing insurance, be sure to review the credit rating of the insurer, to see if it has adequate reserves to pay claims if the company experiences a loss. The easiest way to do so is to look up the *financial strength rating* (FSR) of the insurer, which is formulated and published by A.M. Best. The FSR rating represents an assessment of an insurer's ability to meet its payment obligations to policy holders. The rating is based on numerous factors, including an insurer's balance sheet and financial performance and an assessment of its operating plans and management. The A.M. Best ratings are as noted in the following table.

A.M. Best Ratings

Secure Insurer Ratings		Vulnerable Insurer Ratings	
Rating	Description	Rating	Description
A++, A+	Superior	B, B-	Fair
A, A-	Excellent	C++, C+	Marginal
B++, B+	Good	C, C-	Weak
		D	Under
		E	Under regulatory supervision
		F	In liquidation
		S	Rating suspended

It is imperative to only do business with insurers that have secure ratings. In particular, the umbrella policy should be with an insurer that has been awarded an A+ or A++ rating, since this policy provides coverage for extremely large losses. If a business finds that the insurer backing its umbrella policy is bankrupt, a massive claim could then bankrupt the business, as well.

Insurer Financial Performance

How does an insurer make money? There are two ways to do so. First, an insurer receives insurance payments from its (presumably) many policyholders, from which it can then earn income by investing the funds. Second, it can generate a profit by charging premiums that will exceed all related administrative expenses and claims payments. Both tasks can be difficult, as noted next:

- *Profit from investments.* The insurer has a time period known as the float, during which it can invest premiums paid by policyholders. The float is the time period from the receipt of a premium to the date of a claim payment. The insurer matches the duration of its investments to the dates when its claims payments are expected. Thus, an insurer with predominantly short-term obligations would invest in highly liquid investments, such as commercial paper, while an insurer with longer-term obligations could afford to invest in real estate (or real estate investment trusts), bonds, and commercial mortgages. In general, investments must be made cautiously, in order to avoid a loss of invested funds. Also, state regulators prohibit risky investments.
- *Profit from underwriting.* Employees of an insurer must properly assess the risk associated with a potential policyholder, as well as the likelihood of any valid claims being received, and the amount of those claims. A bad decision in this area could lead to massive losses.

The amount of claims made against a policy may not be known for quite a long time, so insurers recognize an estimated reserve against future losses. These reserves can be impacted by a catastrophe, and so are not always good indicators of the financial performance of an insurer.

One method for determining the financial performance of an insurer is to calculate its combined ratio, which compares the total amount of incurred losses and expenses to insurance premiums earned. When this ratio is less than 1, an insurer is generating a profit from its underwriting activities. However, a key failing of the ratio is that it does not include any investment income that an insurer may generate, which could be a substantial amount. The combined ratio formula appears next.

$$\frac{\text{Claims incurred} + \text{Expenses}}{\text{Earned premiums}} = \text{Combined ratio}$$

EXAMPLE

In the past year, Gulf Coast Insurance has incurred claims of $15 million and other expenses of $3 million. During that time, its earned premiums totaled $16 million. The resulting combined ratio is:

$$\frac{\$15,000,000 \text{ Claims incurred} + \$3,000,000 \text{ Other expenses}}{\$16,000,000 \text{ Earned premiums}} = 1.125 \text{ Combined ratio}$$

The combined ratio for Gulf Coast is 1.125, which indicates a solid underwriting loss. However, the company has also generated $1.5 million of investment income. If investment income were to be added to the denominator of this calculation, the revised combined ratio would be 1.03. This more comprehensive calculation still indicates a loss, but a much smaller one.

Boiler and Machinery Insurance

Boiler and machinery insurance (also known as equipment breakdown insurance) was initially designed to provide coverage for boiler explosions, but has since expanded to include coverage against equipment breakdowns (depending on the exact coverage purchased). A key benefit of this type of insurance is that the insurer provides safety inspections and loss prevention advice as part of its coverage. Because of these inspections, an insurance company can also suspend its coverage if a reviewer determines that covered equipment is in a dangerous condition.

There is an insurance loss under this policy when there is an equipment breakdown. The definition of a breakdown will depend on the specific policy, but typically encompasses a mechanical or electrical failure, or the failure of pressure equipment. A covered event should be one in which there is a sudden and accidental breakdown that causes damage to the equipment. Certain issues are excluded from coverage. These exclusions include breakdowns caused by computer viruses, damage to support structures, defects, and leakages.

Payments made under this coverage include not just the damage to equipment, but also any damage to other property that is caused by the damage to the covered equipment. The cost of debris removal caused by the damage is also covered. Further, coverage is provided for those costs needed to make temporary repairs to equipment.

Quite a broad range of equipment may be covered by this policy, include heating and air conditioning systems, motors, telephone systems, office and computer equipment, compressors, and production machinery. Be sure to review the document carefully to determine which types of equipment are *not* covered, such as excavation equipment and equipment being manufactured for sale.

This type of insurance is most commonly purchased by manufacturers, since they own a large amount of the targeted equipment.

Business Interruption Insurance

Business interruption insurance is designed to provide compensation to an organization if a designated disaster shuts down its operations for a period of time. This policy covers lost profits from business interruption, as well as the reimbursement of actual expenses incurred during the period when a business cannot conduct its normal operations. Though the probability of a major business interruption is usually low, this coverage may be critical when a claim does occur, and may keep a business from being forced into bankruptcy. It can be expensive insurance for manufacturers, which have a larger base of fixed costs to cover during periods when they are inoperable.

Policy Inclusions

The amount of profit to be reimbursed by the insurer is based on the amount of lost sales or customer orders, which are estimated based on historical sales information. The calculation of compensation can be quite subjective, involving the roll-forward of historical performance into the period of loss. The company's lost profits are then estimated based on the amount of lost sales and its historical profit percentage.

The amount of reimbursement under this policy is based on its profit history. If an organization has a continuing history of sustaining losses, the insurer will not reimburse it for lost profits, since there were no profits to lose. However, the insurer may still issue payments to reimburse the entity for certain fixed costs.

The policy will also reimburse the insured party for normal operating costs incurred during the shutdown period, including payroll. Depending on the policy, this can include extra expenses incurred that would not have been incurred if there had been no property damage or suspension of operations. Examples of these extra expenses are relocation costs and the incremental increase in costs required to subcontract work to third parties.

The reimbursement of certain costs incurred by the insured party may be subject to debate, depending on the circumstances. Examples are:

- *Advertising.* When the operations of a business have been completely halted, a case can be made that there should be no ongoing advertising expenditures until operations have been re-started. However, if the insured party uses advertising to sell off goods damaged during the event, this can be considered a loss mitigation cost, and so should be reimbursed by the insurer.
- *Depreciation.* This expense will not be covered to the extent that it relates to destroyed property, but should be covered for any assets that continue in operation.
- *Insurance premiums.* Most types of insurance that benefit the business are considered a fixed cost of operating a business. As such, they should be covered by the insurer. Conversely, any insurance intended to benefit a third party would not be covered.

- *Interest expense.* If a business is obligated to pay interest on outstanding debt, this is considered a fixed cost of doing business, and so will be covered.
- *Rent.* If a business rents a facility, and the rental agreement contains a clause not requiring rent payments when the facility is unusable, then this is an avoidable cost, and is not covered by the insurance. If such an abatement clause is not present, then rent is considered a fixed cost through the business interruption period, and so is a covered expense.
- *Utilities.* Charges for electricity, phones, sewage, and Internet access will be covered when there is a contract that involves ongoing fixed charges.
- *Variable operating costs.* If certain activities of the insured party have been stopped, then so too should the expenses associated with those activities. For example, the use of warehouse vehicles and delivery trucks may cease, in which case there should be a substantially reduced amount of expenditure for fuel. Similarly, if there are no sales during a stoppage period, there should be no commission expense.

Additional Coverages

Several coverages can be added to the basic business interruption insurance, which may be attractive options under certain circumstances. These coverages include:

- *Civil authority.* This coverage pays for business interruption losses caused by order of the local government. This usually occurs when damage to a facility forces the government to prohibit access to it for a period of time, typically for safety reasons.
- *Extended business income.* As the name implies, this coverage extends the period during which business interruption coverage applies, up until operations return to normal. This coverage can be useful when there is a large fixed asset base that cannot easily be returned to its normal operating condition (such as an oil refinery).

Management Actions

The treasurer can take several steps to improve interactions with the insurer following the filing of a claim, including the following:

- *Mitigate insurance cost.* There are several actions that management can take to reduce the cost of business interruption insurance. For example, it can install sprinkler systems to suppress fires, adopt fire-resistant construction materials, and use safety procedures such as 24×7 patrols of the facility to detect in-process fires or flooding. Another option is to have multiple facilities among which capacity usage can be shifted, so that the shutdown of one facility will not have an undue impact on the entity as a whole. The same concept can be applied to the dispersed storage of inventory, so that the destruction of one warehouse will not completely eliminate all available stocks. All of these issues should be pointed out to the insurer when it formulates the insurance quote.

- *Maintain off-site records.* The impact of a disaster implies that an organization's records might be destroyed, which makes it quite difficult to calculate lost profits. To improve the situation, store financial records in the cloud or in a secure off-site location.

- *Return to full performance.* A requirement of this policy is that the insured entity must make its best efforts to reduce the amount of its losses from a disaster. This calls for active management of the situation to promptly protect damaged property from the elements, and to return to normal productive operations within a reasonable period of time. This may call for a detailed contingency plan to subcontract work elsewhere, sublease alternate working space, and so forth, run by a properly organized loss recovery team with members from all key areas of the business.

- *Documentation of mitigation costs.* When a business is actively engaged in mitigating its losses from a business interruption, the accounting staff must collect and organize all related billings. If internal company labor is used, the staff should keep track of the hours worked and the cost of this labor. The information is then forwarded to the insurer for reimbursement. If the documentation process is disorganized, it is quite likely that some expenditures will never be reimbursed, or that the insurer will question certain submitted items for which the associated documentation is poor or nonexistent.

Tip: Review the larger remediation expenses with the insurance adjuster before accepting supplier quotes, since the adjuster may disagree with the assertion that these expenses will be reimbursed. Doing so will prevent a company from incurring obligations and later finding that it does not have the cash to pay for them.

The best efforts clause just described also means that the insured party cannot simply abandon a property and effectively turn it over to the insurer.

Commercial Automobile Insurance

This policy covers damage to the vehicles used in a business, as well as injuries to third parties caused by those vehicles. This coverage may not be necessary if a company does not own vehicles or has employees use their own vehicles on company business.

The core coverage is comprehensive coverage, which (despite the name) does not provide protection from the collision of an auto with another object; that requires the additional purchase of collision coverage. It is also possible to acquire special perils coverage for such events as fire, explosion, theft, hail, flooding, and vandalism.

A truckers policy is available that is designed for long-haul truckers. It provides liability, physical damage, and medical payments coverage. Pricing is based on vehicle size, the intensity of usage, and the radius of operation.

Commercial Crime Insurance

This policy covers a business against losses arising from a number of criminal activities. The insured party can select from several possible coverages, each of which provides a specific type of loss protection. These coverages are:

- *Employee theft.* The theft of property by employees.
- *Forgery or alteration.* Losses due to the forgery or alteration of checks or similar documents.
- *Inside the premises.* The theft of money and securities held on the premises of the insured party. Also, the taking of money or other valuables on the premises by force; includes shoplifting and safe burglary.
- *Outside the premises.* The taking of money or other valuables outside the premises, such as from an armored car.
- *Computer fraud.* The fraudulent transfer of property by use of a computer.
- *Funds transfer fraud.* The loss of funds and securities from the account of the insured party at a bank, due to fraudulent transfer instructions.
- *Money orders and counterfeit money.* The loss of funds from money orders that are not paid, and from counterfeit money that was accepted in a commercial transaction.

In determining the amount of a loss, securities are valued at their market value on the date of loss discovery, while property is valued at the cost to replace it.

Commercial General Liability Insurance

The purpose of liability insurance is to protect the insured entity from losses if the entity is held liable for causing injuries to others or damage to property owned by a third party. Commercial general liability insurance provides coverage for a number of possible events, such as claims arising from bodily injury, personal injury, and damage to property that is caused by the operations or products of a business. When a claim is made, the insurer defends the insured. The main types of coverage that can be purchased are:

- *Bodily injury and property damage.* Pays for losses arising from bodily injury or property damage to a third party when the insured entity is legally liable.
- *Personal and advertising injury.* Pays for losses arising from the loss of reputation, humiliation, economic loss, and bodily injury that is caused by several actions by the insured party, including copyright infringement, libel, slander, and wrongful eviction.
- *Medical payments.* Pays for the medical expenses of third parties when an injury was caused by an accident on the premises of the insured party or as a result of the operations of the insured party.

General liability insurance may contain coverage exclusions, so be sure to review the proposed policy with care. A selection of these exclusions follows:

- Criminal acts
- Distribution of materials in violation of statutes
- Intended injuries
- Material published prior to policy period
- Use of electronic chatrooms or bulletin boards

Another consideration when buying this type of insurance is to determine whether it is a claims-made or occurrence policy. A *claims-made* policy only provides coverage for claims made during a specific date range. An *occurrence* policy provides coverage for events occurring within a specific date range. Thus, a claims-made policy focuses on the date of the claim, while an occurrence policy focuses on the date of the triggering event.

Some customers may require that their suppliers have commercial general liability insurance, especially when large contracts are involved, so this is usually considered a mandatory type of insurance.

Coverage Limitations

Liability limits will be set for each individual policy. For example, a policy may state that there is a $100,000 limit per personal injury occurrence and $250,000 per property damage occurrence. The insured party would be liable for any losses above these limits. When there is a per occurrence limit, this means that the amount paid by the insurer is limited to the designated amount for an occurrence, irrespective of the number of claims received from all affected parties that arose from that occurrence.

An alternative form of coverage limitation is for the insurer to set a single aggregate liability limit, irrespective of the number of occurrences. Once claims are paid up to this limit, the insurer will not pay out any additional amounts during the policy year.

Umbrella Coverage

Umbrella coverage is a separate policy that provides an extra tranche of coverage for a general liability policy. It is not activated unless a loss exceeds the per occurrence or aggregate limits on the underlying liability policy. The underlying coverage must be maintained for the umbrella coverage to take effect.

Credit Insurance

The treasurer may find that some of the risk associated with accounts receivable can be shifted to a firm that provides credit insurance. Under a credit insurance policy, the insurer protects the seller against customer nonpayment. The insurer should be willing to provide coverage against customer nonpayment if a proposed customer clears its internal review process. Credit insurance offers the following benefits:

- *Increased credit.* A company may be able to increase the credit levels offered to its customers, thereby potentially increasing revenue.
- *Faster international deals.* An international sale might normally be delayed while the parties arrange a letter of credit, but can be completed faster with credit insurance.
- *Custom product coverage.* The insurance can cover the shipment of custom-made products, in case customers cancel their orders prior to delivery.
- *Reduced credit staff.* Credit insurance essentially shifts risk away from a business, so it is especially beneficial in companies that have an under-staffed credit department that cannot adequately keep track of customer credit levels.
- *Knowledge.* A credit insurance firm specializes in the risk characteristics of various industries, and so may have deep knowledge about the risk profiles of individual customers, as well as aggregations of customers by region. This information is a useful supplement to other sources of information about customers.
- *Tax deductibility.* Credit insurance premiums are immediately deductible for tax purposes, whereas the allowance for doubtful accounts is only deductible when specific bad debts are recognized.

Be sure to examine the terms of a credit insurance agreement for exclusions, to see what the insurer will not cover. In particular, coverage should include the receivables of customers that file for bankruptcy protection or simply go out of business.

Insurers will only provide coverage for legally sustainable debts, which are those receivables that are not disputed by the customer. If there is a dispute, the insurer will only provide coverage after the company has won a court judgment against the customer. The issue of a legally sustainable debt can be a serious one if a company has a track record of disputes with its customers over product quality, damaged goods, returns, and so forth.

Tip: It may be possible to offload the cost of credit insurance to customers by adding it to customer invoices. This is most likely to be acceptable for international deals, where a customer would otherwise be forced to obtain a letter of credit to pay for a transaction.

Insurers are more willing to provide coverage of accounts receivable if the seller is willing to take on a small part of the bad debt risk itself. This typically means that a customer default will result in the insurer reimbursing the seller, minus the amount of a 5% to 20% deductible. There may also be an annual aggregate deductible that requires the company to absorb a certain fixed amount of losses in a year before the insurer begins to pay reimbursements. Requiring a deductible means that the company continues to have an interest in only selling to credit-worthy customers.

EXAMPLE

Micron Metallic sells stamping machines to a variety of industrial customers. The company's credit insurance policy states that Micron will absorb the first $200,000 of bad debt losses in each calendar year, after which the insurer will pay 85% of all bad debts incurred, other than for invoices related to international sales, which are not covered by the policy. The policy also specifically excludes receivables related to ABC Company, which the insurer considers to be at an excessively high risk of default.

For some customers, or geographic regions subject to considerable political risk, a credit insurer may consider the risk to be so great that it will not provide coverage, or only at a high premium. If so, the treasurer must decide whether it is better for the company to assume the risk of these sales, or to pay the cost of the insurance to obtain coverage. Also, if the insurer discovers that the company's historical loss experience with its customers has been excessively high, it may require such a large premium that the company may conclude that insurance coverage is not a cost-effective form of risk reduction.

Insurers may only be willing to insure a certain amount of receivables per year with some customers. If the company chooses to sell additional amounts on credit to these designated customers, the company will sustain the entire incremental amount of credit risk. To avoid the additional risk, it is necessary to track the cumulative amount of credit sales to these customers on an ongoing basis.

Directors and Officers Liability Insurance

Directors and officers (D&O) liability insurance covers claims made by third parties against directors and officers, alleging that the directors and officers have caused damages by violating their duty. Examples of such claims are as follows:

- A competitor claims that the company has improperly hired away several key employees
- A shareholder claims that the company has failed to properly disclose financial information related to irregular accounting practices
- A limited partner claims that the company has diverted assets to several related parties
- Company officials are held liable in a trademark infringement case

- The owner of a nearby business claims that the demolition of a structure on company property damaged his own property
- The government claims that a company is liable for the illegal dumping of hazardous materials

D&O coverage is essential, since the personal assets of directors and officers can be pursued by aggrieved shareholders, vendors, customers, employees, government agencies, and other parties. With this insurance, directors and officers are covered for acting within the scope and capacity of their positions. Coverage includes defense costs, as well as settlements and judgments. Typical exclusions from this policy include fraud, criminal acts, known liabilities, and punitive damages.

D&O insurance is underwritten on a *claims-made* basis. This means that the policy currently in effect absorbs the liability for claims made, rather than the year in which the alleged wrongdoing took place. This aspect of D&O coverage can be a major problem for directors and officers, who have a five-year statute of limitations on alleged wrongdoing, and yet may no longer be with the company during the latter part of that period, and so have no control over the quality of the D&O coverage in subsequent years. It is possible to purchase insurance for retired directors and officers that addresses this problem. Realistically, most claims are filed against directors and officers immediately after the triggering event, so this risk may not be considered an especially large one.

Management Actions

An excellent supplement to D&O insurance is for a company to indemnify directors and officers in its charter or bylaws, thereby limiting their personal liability from the assertion that they acted negligently. This approach helps to retain directors and officers when a business is in difficult financial circumstances for various reasons, and is therefore more likely to be sued.

Additional Coverages

Coverage against the employment practices liability (EPL) can be added to D&O insurance. EPL coverage protects against damages related to wrongful termination, sexual harassment, emotional distress, and similar issues. If EPL is added to D&O coverage, the aggregate limit of the D&O coverage will be shared with the EPL coverage, which effectively weakens the total amount of D&O coverage. A reasonable solution is to pay for an increase in the aggregate D&O coverage limit.

Inland Marine Insurance

This policy covers damage to commercial goods while in transit on dry land, as well as when the goods are in storage. This coverage may not be necessary if a company uses third-party carriers that also have the insurance.

The policy coverage has gradually expanded from goods being transported on ships to a large number of coverages that may not appear to have any connection to the concept of "marine." The following table contains examples of what may be covered by an inland marine policy.

Samples of Inland Marine Coverage

Accounts receivable	Fine arts	Mobile medical equipment
Camera equipment	Furriers	Motor truck cargo
Communications towers	Guns	Museums
Contractor's equipment	Jewelry	Musical instruments
Exhibitions	Leased property	Valuable papers

Coverage under this type of policy is generally worldwide.

There may be several exclusions from an inland marine policy, such as pilferage from a shipment, securities, and currency. There may also be exclusions for goods transported by air, or outside of a specific geographic region.

It is possible to buy additional coverage for the loss of samples carried by salespersons, equipment used by contractors, livestock, and goods sold on an installment plan or rented.

Life Insurance

Life insurance pays the beneficiary if the insured person dies. This can be useful in a business under two circumstances. The first is when there will be a serious financial impact if an employee dies. For example, if a highly-experienced salesperson dies, the organization could see a major drop in its order volume. Life insurance can be used to keep a business afloat while it searches for a replacement hire. The second situation is to protect against the death of a sole proprietor. In this case, the heirs may need to pay estate taxes or the liabilities of the business, or both, and need cash from a life insurance policy to do so. A partnership might consider having life insurance on a partner, so that the proceeds from the policy can be used to buy out this person's heirs. For example, there could be a cross-purchase plan under which each partner buys insurance on the other partners, so that each partner can pay for his or her share of the buyout of the interest of a deceased partner.

Key man (or key person) life insurance is designed for use by businesses, where the insured person is an employee of a business and the beneficiary is the business. The term of the policy does not extend past the key person's employment period with the business.

The two main types of life insurance are term life and whole life. The characteristics of each one are as follows:

- *Whole life insurance.* This policy pays a death benefit and accumulated a cash value. Coverage extends over the life of the insured party, and premium payments remain level over time. Some variations on the concept require periodic payments only over a specific period of time, after which coverage continues.

- *Term life insurance.* This policy pays a death benefit. The coverage terminates at the end of the policy term, and there is no savings element to the insurance. The amount of premium paid increases as the insured individual ages, thereby reflecting the increased risk of death. It is intended to provide financial protection to the beneficiary for a set period of time.

Property Insurance

This policy protects against the loss of physical assets. The cost ranges from minimal for a services business with few assets to a substantial sum for an asset-intensive manufacturing facility. If a business has used mortgages to acquire assets, the lienholders will require that property insurance be purchased in order to protect their interests in the assets. This is usually considered essential insurance, since it provides coverage of what may be the largest assets of a business.

Types of Property

The coverage given by property insurance applies to two types of property, which are real property and personal property. *Real property* is defined as any property that is directly attached to the land, plus land itself. Examples are buildings and storage units, as well as improvements to these structures. *Personal property* is defined as being movable, and so may include furniture and fixtures, vehicles, and collectibles. Inventory is considered personal property, and includes raw materials, work-in-process, and finished goods.

Policy Inclusions

There are three different classifications of damage to property that may be covered by property insurance, depending on the type of coverage purchased. The three classifications are as follows:

- *Causes of loss – basic form.* Coverage is provided when the causes of loss include fire, lightning, windstorms, hail, riots, damage by aircraft or vehicles, smoke, explosion, vandalism, volcanism, a sinkhole collapse, or discharge from an automatic sprinkler system.
- *Causes of loss – broad form.* Coverage is provided for all of the perils just noted for the basic form, as well as for falling objects, weight of snow, ice, or sleet, and water damage.
- *Causes of loss – special form.* Coverage is provided for all types of accidental loss, unless there is a specific exclusion.

Damage due to flooding and earthquakes is typically excluded from all property insurance policies, but can be added back as a separate endorsement to a policy.

Property is covered if it is located within 100 feet of the insured premises. Additional coverage can be obtained that provides coverage at other locations, as well as for newly acquired or constructed property that is obtained after the effective date of the policy.

Finished goods can be insured at their cost or their selling price. In the latter case, this means that a profit component is included in the coverage, which is similar to business interruption insurance. If the insured entity also has business interruption insurance, the value of this profit component will be subtracted from any business interruption insurance payments, to avoid double payments.

Personal property owned by third parties is also included in the insurance coverage, if this property is in the custody of the insured party and is located on the premises.

Policy Exclusions

A number of items are specifically excluded from a property insurance policy. Depending on the policy, exclusions may encompass the following:

- *Animals.* This depends on who owns the animals and how they are being stored. For example, horses boarded by the insured entity may be covered if they are kept in a stable.
- *Cash and securities.* This includes bills and coins, bonds, and equity securities.
- *Land and land improvements.* This includes roadways, lawns, bridges, underground pipes, patios, roadways, pilings, and parking lots.
- *Plants and outdoor property.* This includes crops, lawns, shrubs, trees, antennas and signs.
- *Vehicles.* This exclusion applies except when the vehicles are being manufactured, held for sale, or stored.
- *Covered elsewhere.* This includes property that is more specifically addressed under another insurance policy.

Additional Coverages

There are a number of additional coverages that can be added to property insurance. They only apply to specific circumstances, and so may only be needed for shorter periods of time. If so, be sure to remove them during the next coverage period, so that the company is not needlessly paying for inapplicable coverage. Several additional coverages are:

- *Buildings under construction.* A building that is under construction may not be covered by property insurance. This situation can be remedied by adding an endorsement to the standard property insurance policy. The endorsement should cover materials, equipment, and temporary structures adjacent to the work site. For example, a general conflagration could consume nearby building materials and the on-site trailer used by the construction staff.
- *Debris removal.* This coverage pays for the cost of removing debris from a damaged or destroyed facility, up to a maximum cap. This typically does not include the cost to remediate pollution caused by whatever caused the property damage. This can be useful coverage when property is extensive, such as a large warehouse facility.

- *Fire department charges.* This coverage reimburses the insured entity for the amount of any service charges imposed by the local fire department for sending its equipment to a covered location. This coverage can be useful when local ordinances require such charges to property holders by the fire department.
- *Pollutant clean-up.* This coverage pays for the cost to remove pollutants from the premises if the pollution was caused by the event that damaged the property. This coverage can be useful when a business stores pollutants on its premises. There is a cap on this coverage.
- *Property preservation.* This coverage addresses any damage to property while it is being transported to a safe location or being stored there. This coverage can make sense if high-value items are being insured, such as art-work.

Coverage Limitations

Depending on the policy, the insurance limitation applies to each individual loss occurrence, with no aggregate limit. However, an aggregate limit *does* apply to any pollution cleanup or debris removal losses.

A coinsurance clause will likely be applied to this type of insurance. As described earlier in the Insurance Policy Terms and Conditions section, coinsurance is designed to penalize the insured party if it under-insures the value of property.

Valuation Issues

The insurance pays for the rebuilding of damaged or destroyed real property. Further, it pays for the value or replacement cost of any lost or damaged personal property. If a policy is paying for the value of an asset, this means the replacement cost of the asset, less depreciation. Thus, an older asset will have a significantly lower replacement value than a new asset. The amount paid may be based on the production capacity of equipment. For example, if a fire destroys several identical machines, the insurer might decide to reimburse based on a single machine that has the same production capacity as the group of destroyed machines.

The depreciation concept can seriously reduce the amount of a payment related to a loss, since the insurer reduces the value of the damaged asset by an estimate of its prior use. The following example explains the concept.

EXAMPLE

Grissom Granaries owns a grain storage facility near the Mississippi River. The facility is pummeled by a hailstorm, and must be replaced. The insurer notes that the facility had a useful life of 30 years, of which 10 years had already passed prior to the loss event. This means the value of the facility is depreciated by one-third when calculating the amount of the claim payout.

Management Actions

There can be arguments over the number and types of assets for which reimbursement is claimed. To bolster the organization's case, it is useful to take the following steps:

- *Record contents.* Create a record of the contents of the business' offices, including digital photos, which can be used to substantiate a claim. This record will soon be out of date, so schedule an annual update of the report. A variation on the concept is to take a video of the offices, to which can be appended an audio commentary. A video takes less time to complete than a formal written record.
- *Store records safely.* Maintain all documentation pertaining to the purchase cost of assets in a fire-proof safe, or in a secure off-site location. It may make sense to maintain a duplicate set of records in an alternate location.

Management should be made aware of situations in which insured equipment is old, and needs to be replaced with more modern equipment. In these cases, an insured loss will only result in a payment that covers the old equipment, leaving the business with a potentially large funding shortfall to pay for the latest equipment. It is useful to periodically summarize this potential shortfall and recommend that a cash reserve or line of credit be maintained that can be used to cover the difference.

In addition, one should take action to prevent further damage to property, once a loss event has occurred. For example, if a building's roof is destroyed, the insured should take prompt action to protect the contents of the building from further weather-related damage. If not, the insurer may deny claims related to subsequent damage to the building contents.

Surety Bonds

A surety bond is a contract that involves a guarantee that a legal agreement will be completed. It is commonly used to ensure that performance is completed under the terms of a contract. A bond agreement involves the participation of the following three entities:

- *The principal.* This is the party that is supposed to perform in accordance with the requirements of a contract.
- *The obligee.* This is the party receiving the obligation; typically the counterparty to the contract with the principal.
- *The surety.* This is a third party that does not directly perform the requirements of the contract, but rather who guarantees the performance of the principal under the contract.

Thus, a surety bond is a promise to pay the obligee if the principal does not perform under the contract. The surety makes the payment to the obligee. In exchange for this service, the principal pays a fee to the surety for as long as the surety bond is outstanding. In cases where the financial resources of the principal are in doubt, the fee will be quite high, or the surety will insist that all or most of the bond be kept in escrow during the term of the bond.

If there is a claim by the obligee for reimbursement under the surety bond, the surety will investigate the claim, pay it if the claim is valid, and then turn to the principal for reimbursement.

There are a number of types of surety bonds, including the following:

- *Bail bond.* The bail bondsman guarantees that an individual will appear in court.
- *Bid bond.* The principal guarantees that it will enter into an agreement with the obligee if awarded the contract.
- *Performance bond.* The principal guarantees that it will perform the services specified in the contract.

The principal agrees to enter into a surety bond arrangement in order to mitigate the risk to the obligee that the contract between the two parties will not be fulfilled. Also, it is common practice in some industries (particularly the government and construction sectors) to always require a surety bond of any party that does a certain minimum amount of contractual business with an entity.

While a surety bond does show that a business has a certain amount of capital, it also acts to block smaller competitors unable to obtain a surety bond from bidding against them. Thus, a surety bond tends to reduce competition.

Surplus Lines Insurance

A surplus lines policy is one that protects against a financial risk that a normal insurer is incapable of accepting, for any of the following reasons:

- A very high insurance limit is needed
- The risk is extremely specialized
- The risk has such unfavorable attributes that normal insurers will not accept it

Given the one-off nature of these risks, a surplus lines policy is more likely to be a unique one that is constructed for a specific policyholder. Since there is more administrative overhead associated with this type of coverage and there is little competition, insurance premiums are usually higher.

An insurer that takes on this type of risk is usually one that has not been licensed by the state in which the insured entity is located; as nonadmitted carriers, these insurers have fewer restrictions on certain types of coverage and pricing requirements. Also, the insurance agent handling the transaction must have a surplus lines license in order to offer this type of insurance.

A concern when making use of surplus lines insurance is that there is no state guaranty fund from which a claim payment can be obtained if the surplus lines insurer is unable to make a payment. This is because the insurer has not been licensed by the state, so the state's guaranty fund does not apply to it.

Managing the Cost of Insurance

Depending on the risk profile of a business and the types of risks being transferred to insurers, the cost of insurance can be quite high. If so, there are a number of steps that can be taken to keep this cost as low as possible, as described in the following sub-sections.

Broker Training

The company's insurance broker should have an excellent knowledge of the entity's operations, which should result in the best possible tailoring of insurance products to the needs of the firm. Otherwise, there is a possibility that some insurance will be purchased that is not necessary. A high level of broker knowledge can be achieved when there is a long-term relationship between the broker and the business. This may mean sticking with a specific broker who knows the business, even if that broker switches to a different employer.

> **Tip:** Do not switch brokers too frequently, as the business will build a reputation for skipping around, which could make it difficult to obtain reasonable coverage at a good price.

Odds Analysis

Review coverage to see if certain risks being covered are highly unlikely to occur, not only historically for the company, but also for the industry as a whole. If the amount of loss associated with these risks is relatively low, it may not make sense to continue obtaining insurance coverage. Instead, such items would be good targets for self-insurance. An analysis of the odds of occurrence is particularly effective when an entity has changed its location or there has been some other major change to its business.

EXAMPLE

A business had previously been located in a flood plain, and paid for quite expensive flood insurance for many years. It has recently relocated to an area for which there is no record of a flood ever having occurred. Given the reduced odds of flooding, the company might consider eliminating its flood coverage.

Insurer Messaging

If the cost of a particular type of insurance continues to rise over a period of time, this means that the insurer believes there is a high probability of loss and resultant payouts to policy holders. If so, and rather than continuing to pay the insurance, consider whether the company should restructure its business to mitigate the risk. After all, the insurer is using its pricing to tell management that a business activity is excessively risky. For example, if flood insurance rises to absurd levels, take this as a warning that the company needs to move its operations to a safer location.

Covered Items Analysis

Review existing insurance contracts to see if the company is still paying for the coverage of assets that no longer exist, or for inconsequential risks. Of course, a result of this review could well be an increase in insurance costs, if it is found that some assets are not being covered, or major risks are not being addressed.

Double Coverage Analysis

Compare the coverage of all insurance policies to see if the company is paying for different insurance contracts that provide overlapping coverage of the same asset or risk. If so, eliminate the overlap when the contracts are up for renewal.

A concern with insurance riders is that they can provide duplicate coverage, so be sure to examine the terms of the basic policy to see if each rider is really needed.

Split Limits Elimination

When providing coverage, an insurer may provide different levels of coverage for certain sub-categories of incidents. The insurer tries to maintain lower levels of coverage for those categories most likely to occur, so that its payout is reduced. This exposes the insured party to a greater risk of loss. Consequently, try to impose a single limit on all categories of incidents listed in a policy. For example, a commercial automobile insurance policy might provide for $300,000 of coverage per accident, and a $100,000 injury limit per person. The real cap on the coverage is $100,000, since injury awards to individuals can vastly exceed $100,000.

EXAMPLE

A business has a commercial automobile insurance policy that contains an injury limit of $100,000 per person and an accident limit of $300,000. An employee driving a company delivery van rear-ends a passenger car, sending its two occupants to the hospital. A jury awards $125,000 to each of the occupants. Though the total of this award is $250,000, the overriding limit is the $100,000 injury limit imposed by the insurer. In this case, the insurer only pays out $100,000 per occupant, leaving the business to pay for the remaining $50,000.

Continual Policy Updates

The risk profile of a business changes throughout the year, so the accompanying insurance policies should change, too. This means establishing a clear line of communication from the business unit managers to the treasurer, and from there to the insurer. This may result in selective increases and decreases in coverage. In cases where coverage is increased, the net cost to the business may still decline, since the intent of the coverage is to guard against unintended losses.

Unlikely Rider Payouts

Many policy riders cover events that are very unlikely to happen. Consequently, make a reasonable estimation of the actual need for a rider before paying additional cash for it.

Non-Comparability

The terms and fees associated with riders are customized to the specific needs of the insured entity, so it can be difficult to compare competing insurance offers. Insurers can use the non-comparability of policy terms to build additional profits into their offerings, so be certain that riders are really needed before adding them to a basic policy.

Deductibles Analysis

An insurance provider may offer different prices, depending on the amount of the deductible that an organization is willing to absorb. The correct deductible to select can be calculated in a two-step process, which is:

1. Determine the historical average loss experience of the business, and multiply this amount by the proposed deductible to arrive at the amount of the loss that the business is likely to absorb at the designated deductible level.
2. Compare the estimated loss to the premium savings associated with the deductible. If the loss is less than the premium savings, then the proposed deductible is a good deal for the organization.

EXAMPLE

The insurance provider for Horton Corporation is proposing that the deductible on the company's commercial vehicle insurance policy be raised from the current $250 level to $500. In exchange, the provider proposes to drop the per-vehicle annual insurance cost by $50. Horton currently insures 30 vehicles.

To see if this is a good deal, a company analyst notes that Horton has had an average of five vehicle-related claims per year for the past decade. In all cases, the amount of the claim exceeded $500, so the full amount of the deductible would always be applicable. The increase in deductible would cost the company an additional $1,250 per year (calculated as five claims × $250 additional deductible/each). The cost savings from a reduced insurance premium will be $1,500 (calculated as 30 vehicles × $50 premium savings/each). Since the savings exceed the projected loss by $250, Horton should accept the proposed deal.

Small Claims Avoidance

When a business continually files claims for small amounts, the insurer may not have to pay out much for actual claims, but will need to incur a significant amount of administrative costs to investigate each claim. The administrative cost may exceed the cost of the claims paid. When a policy comes up for renewal, an insurer may increase the price of coverage, either to offset the expected future administrative cost of the multitude of small claims, or to send a message to the insured entity that it no longer wants to do business. Thus, it can make sense for the insured party to avoid a continuing series of minor claims. The company's agent can provide advice regarding the minimum threshold below which many claims could trigger a subsequent rate increase.

Tip: If the decision is made to avoid filing small claims, it makes sense to have higher deductibles. The increase in deductibles reduces the total cost of insurance.

Self-Funded Insurance

A very large business is likely to have many more insurance claims than a smaller organization. With a larger number of losses, such a large enterprise has enough information to statistically predict its losses. When these losses occur with high frequency and a low cost per claim, there is an opportunity to reduce costs by self-funding claims from an established reserve. The cost savings arises from the elimination of the selling costs and profits that an independent insurer must build into its prices. However, the organization must now pay for the administrative cost of settling claims, and may also need to pay for legal representation to defend it against spurious claims. An additional concern is that the business may be placed in the potentially uncomfortable position of denying claims from its own employees, depending on the type of insurance.

In situations where self-funded insurance is used, there may be a low risk of large claims. If so, the treasurer can purchase stop loss insurance that provides coverage once an employee's annual claims experience exceeds a certain predetermined amount.

An added benefit of self-insurance is the detailed level of information available to the company concerning the types of claims being filed. With this information, it may be possible to create risk reduction programs that target the types of claims being filed.

Captive Insurance Company

A variation on the self-funding concept is to create and fund a captive insurance company. The captive insurance concept involves purchasing insurance coverage from an insurance company that is owned and controlled by the insured entity. The insurance premiums paid by the insured entity are tax deductible. In addition, the premiums collected by the captive are tax-free. This approach is less expensive than buying insurance from an independent insurance entity, which must include a provision in its pricing for sales costs and an adequate profit.

The tax effects associated with a captive are important. From the perspective of the insured entity, all of its premiums paid to the captive are tax deductible. Thus, if it pays $100,000 in premiums to the captive and its tax rate is 35%, it has just reduced its tax liability by $35,000. In addition, the U.S. Internal Revenue Code, section 831(b) states that the first $1.2 million of premium income received by the captive in each year is tax exempt. In essence, this means that an insured entity can take a tax deduction on an insurance premium that it has paid to itself (the captive), while not owing any income tax on those funds – and this tax advantage continues to accrue, year after year.

Because of this tax advantage, it is possible for a business owner to buy more insurance coverage than it normally would from a third-party insurer, on the grounds that it can take a tax deduction on these premiums, while still retaining the funds within the captive (to the extent that there are no offsetting claims). Since the insured entity owns the captive, this represents a net profit increase for the insured entity.

The captive processes all claims forwarded from the insured entity, so that no administrative issues need to be handed off to a regular insurance company. In addition, the captive participates in a reinsurance pool with other captives to reinsure each other's risks. Doing so protects it from bankruptcy if it were to receive a catastrophic claim that would otherwise wipe out its reserves. In addition, participating in a reinsurance pool is part of the qualifications required of a captive, so that it meets the risk distribution requirements for an insurance company.

Captive insurance companies are set up within governmental jurisdictions that have provided favorable captive insurance laws, and which have a favorable business climate. Historically, several Caribbean and nearby island governments have been the best locations for captives, including Grand Cayman, the British Virgin Islands, St. Lucia, Anguilla, and the Bahamas. Several state governments have created favorable laws for captives as well, but operating costs in these states are higher than the island-based alternatives (partially because the states also impose state income taxes on the earnings of captives). Examples of states with captive-friendly laws are Delaware, Tennessee, and Vermont. There are advisors in these locations that provide complete packages to start up a captive, including an actuarial assessment of the business, licensing a captive, arranging reinsurance for it, preparing an operations manual, arranging for annual audits, and maintaining the captive over time. They can also invest any funds held by a captive, though investment management can also be handled by a third party.

If a captive accumulates a large amount of profits over a period of time, one of the more tax-efficient ways for the insured entity to gain access to those profits is to liquidate the captive, which qualifies the insured entity to recognize a long-term capital gain on the captive's profits.

Given the costs to set up and manage a captive insurance company, as well as the cost to obtain an insurance license, this approach is usually only cost-effective for mid-sized or larger organizations, or entities engaged in high-risk activities, and which therefore pay significant premiums. A variation is the rent-a-captive approach, where several medium-sized organizations share a captive and centrally manage funds in order to reduce the total administrative cost per business.

Insurance Claims Administration

The administration of insurance claims is important, since the response time to these claims can be lengthy, and there is a high risk of claim rejection if the paperwork is not filled out properly. This issue can be mitigated by adhering to a specific claims administration process.

The core of this process flow is a checklist of activities that must be completed before any claim can be filed. The presence of a checklist keeps the treasury staff from missing a key step that could interfere with claim settlement. Other steps should also be included to record the associated transaction and to mitigate the risk of future losses of a similar type. The checklist should include the following items:

- *Itemizations.* List the estimated cost, replacement cost, and appraised cost of each item to be included in the claim, as well as the sources of this information.
- *Cost buildup.* Aggregate all of the related costs sustained by the company during the event, for which it may be possible to claim reimbursement.
- *Adjuster contact information.* Pull from the records the name of the claims adjuster to be contacted, and verify that this information is still correct.
- *Internal notifications.* Notify those people inside the company who may need to record the associated loss, and/or notify investors or senior management of the situation.
- *Problem analysis.* Review the cause of the claim and investigate whether steps can be taken to keep this type of loss from arising again.
- *Asset protection.* Ensure that no further damage to the damaged asset can occur. For example, move a water-damaged asset to a dry location. Otherwise, the insurer will only pay for the amount of damage initially sustained.

To ensure that these steps are followed, institute an occasional internal audit to review compliance with the checklist.

It is possible that a treasury group focusing on other issues will have a third party administer its insurance claims. If so, be sure to have a monitoring process to verify that claims are submitted accurately and on time, and that a high proportion of the submissions are paid out.

Summary

A business may find itself having to obtain insurance from a number of insurers in order to obtain full insurance coverage. To keep from being confused by a plethora of policies from different insurers, it is useful to work with an agent or broker, who can keep track of all coverages and identify where there may be a "hole" in the coverage. This individual is especially useful in explaining the meanings of the many policy terms and conditions, highlighting those that are of particular concern to an organization.

The blend of insurance policies that a business uses is constantly in flux, as some policies are added or terminated to reflect changing business conditions. Further, coverage amounts and riders may be altered. This means there is an ongoing need to review policies to ensure that the risk profile of a business is properly reflected in outstanding policies, and that there is no coverage overlap. A likely outcome of this ongoing analysis is that an organization will achieve a highly cost-beneficial insurance profile, with no money wasted on unnecessary insurance.

Chapter 12
Credit Management

Introduction

The treasurer is frequently put in charge of the credit function. The credit department is essentially in the business of lending funds to customers – albeit on a very short-term basis and without an interest charge. This lending function is based on four core activities, which are the development of a guiding credit policy, the use of a credit application, the calculation of credit ratings to measure the ability of customers to pay, and ongoing monitoring to ensure that the correct credit terms and limits are applied to each customer. All of these activities are addressed in the following pages.

Overview of the Credit Policy

The credit department must deal with a continuing stream of requests from customers for credit terms. Each customer has a different set of characteristics, such as their financial position, years in business, and payment history that must be sorted through and used to make a credit decision. In the absence of any sort of structure to this decision-making process, it is entirely likely that the resulting credit decisions will vary widely, even for customers with relatively similar characteristics.

The credit policy is used to bring a high level of consistency to the credit granting process. To do so, the policy should be constructed with a sufficient level of detail to clarify the following topics:

- The mission of the credit department
- Who is allowed to make credit decisions
- What rules to use for the derivation of credit
- The terms of sale to be used, other than the amount of credit granted

The credit policy should show how to deal with the most common credit decisions that the staff will encounter. If a company expands into multiple lines of business, the credit policy will likely have to expand too, to keep pace with the variety of credit scenarios that will arise in this expanded environment.

The credit policy is also an excellent training tool for new employees, since it sets guidelines for their activities. Not only does it ensure that they are aware of the policy from their first day on the job, it also sends the message that the company is serious about following the policy.

Credit Policy: Mission

The mission of the credit department sets the tone of the entire credit policy, for it describes the overarching reason why the company grants credit. The mission statement can lie anywhere along a continuum, where one end allows cheap and easy credit (therefore focusing on higher revenues) and the other end dwells on credit risk reduction (therefore focusing on fewer bad debts). Where the company positions itself on this continuum depends on senior management's propensity to expand sales or maintain a prudent financial position. The following factors should be considered when making the decision:

- *Product margins.* If the company sells products that have relatively low margins, then it cannot afford an excess amount of bad debt. Consequently, it has no choice other than to follow a tight credit policy. Conversely, ample profit margins allow management the alternative of granting easier credit in order to expand sales.
- *Economic trends.* The credit policy can fluctuate in accordance with economic trends. If the economy is expanding and customers therefore have more money, it may be acceptable to adopt a looser credit policy, and vice versa. However, adjusting the policy to match the economy also means that the company must follow leading indicators closely to ensure that the policy is modified at regular intervals.
- *Product obsolescence.* If a company has a significant volume of products on the shelf that are approaching obsolescence, it may make sense to grant much looser credit when doing so will sell off these items. Since the company would otherwise take a hefty loss to dispose of these goods, taking a risk granting credit to a lower-quality customer may not really be a risk at all.

Examples of mission statements that encompass the preceding issues are:

[Loose credit version] The credit department exists to facilitate sales. Accordingly, the department shall offer credit to all customers that have been in business for a reasonable period of time, except in those cases where there is a strong indication of probable bad debt losses. Every option will be considered before a customer is denied credit. Consequently, a certain amount of bad debt losses are expected.

[Tight credit version] The credit department exists to maximize company profits. Accordingly, the company shall only offer credit to those customers with verifiable credit histories that indicate on-time payments and no risk of default. All other customers will have mandatory cash on delivery terms until a payment history has been established. Bad debt losses are to be minimized at all times.

[Adjustable credit version] The credit department strikes a balance between the expansion of sales and profits. Accordingly, the department shall regularly examine its margins and liquidity, economic conditions, and other factors in order to set credit levels that yield prudent financial returns.

Credit Policy: Goals

There should be a goals section in the credit policy that states the targets against which the credit department will be judged. Examples of possible goals are:

- *Processing speed.* The department will process 95% of all credit applications within one business day of receipt.
- *Efficiency.* The department will operate with one credit full time equivalent per 500 customers.
- *Results.* The company's average days outstanding (DSO) figure will not exceed 50 days at any time.

Credit Policy: Responsibilities

The ultimate responsibility for making credit decisions should be clearly stated. Otherwise, the credit manager may be involved in ongoing quarrels with the sales manager over the amount of credit that will be granted.

In addition, the policy should clarify who is entitled to place a customer on credit hold status. Once again, the sales manager will want control over this function, even though the responsibility should lie with the credit manager.

A possible variation on this portion of the credit policy is to include an automatic approval escalation in the policy when the amount of money involved surpasses a predefined threshold level. For example, granting credit above $1,000,000 might call for the approval of the treasurer or CFO. A variation on this concept is for the sales manager to define a small group of "key customers," who cannot be placed on credit hold status without the prior approval of a senior manager; doing so may be needed if the company has a strategy of pursuing increased market penetration in certain areas.

An example of a credit policy clause concerning responsibilities is:

> All credit decisions for the issuance of credit must be approved by the credit manager. When the amount of credit exceeds $50,000, the approval of the treasurer must also be obtained.

> Credit hold decisions must be approved by the credit manager. If the credit line to be placed on hold exceeds $50,000, the approval of the treasurer must be obtained.

An additional factor to consider is stating in the credit policy that the credit function cannot report to anyone within the sales function; or alternatively, to state the position(s) to which these functions report. Doing so keeps the sales manager from gaining direct control over areas that should act as counterbalances to sales. An example of such a credit policy clause is:

> The credit manager reports to the treasurer. Under no circumstances may this position report to anyone who also supervises the sales function.

Credit Policy: Required Documentation

The credit policy can state the types of information required before a credit judgment can be made about a new customer or a credit revision for an existing customer. The following table contains samples of the documentation that may be required.

Sample Documentation by Credit Situation

Customer Type	Documentation Required
Individual – new customer	Credit application, credit report, credit references
Individual – existing customer, small increase request	Payment history
Individual – existing customer, large increase request	Credit application, credit report, payment history
Commercial – new customer	Credit application, credit report, financial statements
Commercial – existing customer, small increase request	Payment history
Commercial – existing customer, large increase request	Credit application, credit report, credit references, financial statements, payment history

Particular attention should be paid to the credit application, which is the form upon which the bulk of smaller credit decisions are made. The policy can state the primary responsibility for having applications completed, and note the importance of certain elements of the application. For example:

> The salesperson is responsible for delivering credit applications to customers, discussing its contents with them, and ensuring that the forms are completed. No credit application will be accepted for review that has not been signed by the customer. All credit applications will be rejected if the customer has crossed out any portions of the application.

The policy can address the periodic elimination of customer credit records, if the company is no longer doing business with them. For example:

> After the company has not done business with a customer for at least one year, its credit file is to be archived. After an additional period of ___ years, and with the prior approval of the credit manager, the credit files associated with inactive customer accounts are to be shredded.

The policy can also itemize the intervals at which selected information in a customer's credit file should be updated. Rather than being required for every customer at certain intervals, updates could instead be triggered in other ways, such as:

- New credit report when customer renews orders after at least a one-year lapse.
- New credit report whenever a not sufficient funds check is processed.
- Financial statements at annual intervals when the total amount of credit outstanding exceeds $___.
- Financial statements when the credit report indicates a score of less than ___.
- New credit application when there has been a change of control.

Credit Policy: Review Frequency

The policy should note the events that can trigger a review of an account by the credit department, or the intervals at which reviews should take place. Indicators of when these reviews might take place were just noted for the accumulation of required documentation. The following sample policy reveals the level of detail at which the policy can enforce the use of these reviews:

The credit department shall conduct a review of the credit extended to its customers using the following triggering mechanisms:

- Annually for those customers comprising the top 20% of company sales
- Annually for those customers whose average days to pay exceeds 20 days past terms
- Immediately when a not sufficient funds check is processed
- Immediately when a payment commitment is broken
- Immediately when there has been a change of control
- Quarterly for those customers whose average days to pay has increased by 10 or more days in the past year

In addition, when examining the reasons for bad debts, determine whether a change in the credit policy could have prevented a bad debt; this is possible if the company had evidence of a decline in credit quality, but did not act upon the information.

The policy can include mandates to completely cut off all credit in certain situations where there are strong indicators of looming customer failure. For example, a credit score below a predetermined threshold level could trigger a credit stoppage, as could the receipt of two not sufficient funds checks within a one-year period.

Credit Policy: Credit Calculation

The policy can clarify the amount of time that the credit staff is allowed in which to make a credit decision. For example:

> Assuming a normal backlog of credit applications, the credit department is expected to reach a decision on every submitted application within one business day of receipt. If there is not sufficient information available to make a decision, the sales manager shall be notified of the issue within two business days of receipt of a credit application.

The policy can include the detailed methodology for determining the amount of credit to be granted to customers, including the sources of information to be used and how decisions are to be made.

The credit calculation section should also address a number of common exception conditions that routinely arise in the credit function. For example, what action(s) should be taken if:

- A credit application is not signed by a customer
- A credit decision must be made without certain information
- A trade or bank reference does not respond
- A customer refuses to provide a personal guarantee

The policy can state the forms of payment that a customer is allowed if credit is not granted, or if the amount requested is greater than the credit granted. For example:

> If the amount of credit requested exceeds the amount granted, or if no credit is granted, the customer may still pay using any of the following methods: letter of credit, cash in advance, cash on delivery, or lease financing.

Credit Policy: Terms of Sale

The terms of sale granted to customers are usually kept the same for each business unit, so that each one can provide terms competitive to those found among their competitors. Thus, one business unit may offer net 30 day terms, while another may be compelled to offer 60 day terms.

Within the business unit level, it is best to adopt the same terms of sale for all customers, which makes it easier for the collections department to keep track of when customers are supposed to pay. Otherwise, special dispensations for longer payment terms may mistakenly lead to collection activity before a customer is required to pay. If there is to be an exception to this rule, codify it within the credit policy. An example is:

> Any requests for extended dating beyond normal credit terms must be approved by the credit manager. Extended dating is only granted when doing so is required to meet the terms of a competing sale. Extended dating is not to be granted when it is apparent that the company is simply providing longer-term financing to a customer.

Examples of the terms of sale that may be issued by a business unit are noted in the following table.

Sample Terms of Sale

Business Unit	Payment Terms	Volume Discounts
Book publishing	Net 60 days	20% over 100 units
Magazine publishing	20% on order placement, 80% in 30 days	15% over $10,000
Website construction	50% in advance, 50% when complete	None
App store	In advance by credit card	None

Credit Policy: Revision Frequency

It is a rare industry that is staid enough to have little customer turnover and minimal fluctuation in the ability of customers to pay. More commonly, there are ongoing cyclical changes in the economy that may trigger significant changes in how quickly customers are able to pay (if at all). The credit policy should reflect these changes, which means that it should be reviewed and revised at regular intervals. This could mean a mandatory review on set dates, or allowing the credit manager to conduct a review when necessary.

The most common update to the credit policy is a decision to either loosen or tighten the amount of credit issued by the company. It is also possible that changes in the competitive environment may allow (or require) the business to alter its terms of sale, such as lengthening the days over which customers are allowed to pay. However, such changes arise at much longer intervals, since they are triggered by industry trends that tend to become apparent only over long periods of time.

When altering the amount of credit issued, consider the impact of the following issues on the decision:

Has a seasonal pattern emerged?	It is possible that customers, in aggregate, are taking longer to pay at certain times of the year, which may call for credit restrictions to match the seasonal pattern.
What is the competition offering?	If the larger players in the industry are altering their credit terms, this may impact the company's ability to compete, and so may require a reactive change in the credit policy.
How is the economy impacting customers?	It is not sufficient to automatically alter the credit policy if there is a change in economic conditions. Customers may be insulated from these changes or more exposed to them, so the response may vary. For example, a company that caters to high net-worth individuals may not worry much about changes in the economy.
Is the customer profile changing?	The company may have created its credit policy based on a certain customer profile, which may no longer match the types of customers doing business with the company. A review of credit scores and historical profiles may reveal that credit is under- or over-extended in comparison to the actual customer base.
Have company gross margins changed?	The company may be allowing a certain amount of credit on the assumption that its gross margins are sufficiently high to offset projected bad debt losses. If gross margins have changed, the amount of credit granted may also need to change.

The need for a credit policy revision may be indicated when a series of related credit problems arise, such as a sudden spike in a certain class of customer. If so, it may make sense to create a reporting mechanism that tracks a variety of credit measurements on a trend line, and which can be used to trigger a credit policy review if there is a jump in one of these measurements.

Tip: If the credit environment can change quickly, consider running the trend line report as frequently as once a week, to gain early warning of conditions that may require a change in the credit policy.

The Credit Application

The credit application is intended to accumulate as much information about a prospective customer as possible, not only to serve as the basis for granting credit, but also to provide information for possible collection efforts in the future. A simplified credit application can be purchased from an office supply store, or can be constructed for the specific needs of a business. A sample credit application appears next.

Sample Credit Application

Credit Application

Customer Address Block	Date Started	For Company Use
	Business Type	Credit Amount
	Incorporation State	Date
	Corporate Parent	Approved By

Customer Financial Information

Last Year Sales	Current Cash	Current Debt Level
Last Year Profits/Losses	Current Working Capital	Current Retained Earnings

☐ Financial Statements Attached

References

Supplier Reference #1	Contact Information
Supplier Reference #2	Contact Information
Supplier Reference #3	Contact Information
Bank Reference	Checking Account Number
	Savings Account Number

I authorize the above suppliers and bank to release credit information to the Company for its evaluation of this credit application.

Customer Officer: [signature]	Date

The preceding sample only contains a basic set of information. In addition, consider including some or all of the following additional items in a more customized application form:

- *Contacts.* It is useful to obtain a list of the contact information for all of the people working for the applicant who may be able to assist with payment issues at a later date, such as the accounts payable clerk, accounts payable supervisor, and controller.
- *Credit request.* Allow the applicant to request a certain amount of credit. The credit staff is certainly entitled to ignore the amount requested, but at least should be aware of the expectations of the applicant.
- *DUNS number.* The DUNS number makes it easier for the credit staff to access the correct credit report for the applicant.
- *Trade names.* Have the applicant list all trade names under which it does business, which is useful for researching the entity.

- *Type of entity*. The application (if a business) can state the type of business entity. The company will have access to more assets in the event of an account delinquency if the business entity is a sole proprietorship and less if the entity is a corporation. Consequently, knowing that the entity is a corporation could trigger a request for a guarantee of funds owed, since the payment claims of the seller will otherwise be limited to the assets of the corporation.
- *Years in business*. Year in existence is considered a key determinant of the ability to pay by many credit managers.

Adjustments to the Credit Application

The credit application can be considered a legal document, since it may be signed by the applicant. If customers can be persuaded to sign the application, then consider adding a number of clauses to the document to give the company a variety of legal rights. For example:

- *Arbitration*. Both parties agree to arbitration of any payment disputes. By doing so, more expensive litigation is avoided. Include in the clause the exact arbitration steps to be followed, so there are no delays associated with later negotiation of these steps.
- *Binding signature*. The applicant could claim that the person signing the application does not have the authority to do so. A clause could state that the person signing the application *does* have the authority to agree to the terms and conditions stated in the application.
- *Early payment terms affirmation*. The applicant acknowledges that the company will charge back any early payment discounts that are taken too late, possibly including an additional processing fee.
- *Fee reimbursement*. If the company needs to pay a third party, such as a collection agency or attorney, to collect from the applicant, the applicant agrees to pay these fees. It is not likely that the fees will actually be collected, but it may be worthwhile to insert the clause just to provide the company with extra collection leverage.
- *Inspection*. The customer agrees to inspect goods from the company upon their arrival and issue a complaint about any problems found within a specific period of time. After that time period has expired, the customer revokes the right to continue to claim product damage. This clause reduces the number of options that a customer has for delaying payment.
- *Interest payments*. The applicant agrees to pay a stated rate of interest on any past due balances. The company then has the choice of activating this clause or ignoring it, depending on the circumstances.
- *Legal venue*. The parties agree that, if a legal outcome is necessary, the litigation will be addressed in the state of residence of the company, not the applicant. This reduces the cost of travel for the company.

- *Ownership change notice*. If there is a change in control of the applicant on a future date, it must provide written notice of the change in ownership to the company.
- *Personal guarantee*. The person signing the application agrees to personally guarantee the debts owed by the applicant. This clause is the most frequently objected to by applicants, but is worth attempting in order to establish a legal claim.
- *Returned check fees*. If the applicant pays the company with a check for which there are not sufficient funds, the company is entitled to charge the applicant the amount of the associated bank fees. This results in a minor expense reduction for the company, but can be useful for convincing customers to pay attention to the amount of available cash in their checking accounts.
- *Security interest*. The applicant grants the customer a security interest in any goods sold to the customer. Assuming the company follows up on this right by filing the appropriate paperwork, it will then have a right to those goods that has priority over the claims of unsecured creditors.

It is likely that a large number of additional clauses will spill over to the back side of the credit application. If so, include extra lines on the back for signatures or initials. Having these lines filled out provides legal evidence that the applicant has read and agreed to the additional provisions.

Some of these clauses will not be applicable, depending on the circumstances. For example, the security interest clause is of no use when the company sells services, rather than goods. Similarly, no one in a publicly-held company is likely to agree to a personal guarantee. In these cases, it is acceptable to either tailor the application to the circumstances, or accept the fact that certain clauses have been crossed out by the applicant.

Trade References

The trade references that a credit applicant submits on a credit application will have been carefully cultivated by the applicant. This may include paying the trade references well before any of its other suppliers. A particularly weak reference is a landlord or utility, since these entities must be paid on time by the applicant to avoid negative consequences. One way to sidestep this issue is to refuse to accept landlords, utilities, or similar entities as trade references, which forces the applicant to come up with more realistic references. Also, reject all trade references that have been doing business with the applicant for less than one year, on the grounds that it is preferable to obtain references that have an extensive record of payments from the applicant.

> **Tip:** When searching for additional trade references for an applicant, ask the salesperson who deals with the applicant. The salesperson may know which competitors have been selling to it. A trade reference from a competitor is especially valuable, since the applicant may have already been turned away by the competitor because of late payments.

The person making inquiries with trade references should ask the same questions of every reference, using a standard checklist. By doing so, the same information is consistently collected every time, and no information is missed. The following is a sample list of inquiries:

- How long the applicant has had an account with the trade reference
- The account balance with the applicant at the current date
- The amount of any past due balance at the current date
- The average number of days that the applicant normally takes to pay
- The highest account balance with the applicant in the past 12 months
- The last date on which the trade reference sold to the applicant
- The terms of sale with the applicant, as well as any guarantees

It is useful to ask for a new set of trade references whenever a customer is asked to supply the company with a new credit application (see the Updating the Credit Application section). Specifically, ask for a different set of trade references with each update, rather than the same set of references. Over time, this means that the credit staff will gain access to a larger pool of references.

If it proves difficult to contact trade references, it is possible to simply rely upon the payment information contained within a third party credit report. However, the identities of the reporting organizations on these reports are masked, so it is not possible to tell who has submitted payment experience information.

Updating the Credit Application

When a customer completes a credit application, the information provided is only accurate as of the date on which the form was completed. Thereafter, the actual circumstances of the customer will diverge from what it originally reported to the company. Over time, the credit department will be making credit decisions concerning that customer based primarily on the company's own payment history with it, supplemented by occasional credit reports purchased from a reporting agency. To improve the information available, consider requiring a replacement application from time to time. Here are several possible scenarios for requiring a new application:

- *Bounced check.* When a customer's check payment is returned, due to not sufficient funds.
- *Larger customers.* An annual requirement for a new application if the annual order volume exceeds $___.

- *Near threshold.* When a customer's order volume is consistently near the top end of the allowed credit limit.
- *No recent history.* When a customer has not placed any orders recently and then places a large order.
- *Predetermined time period.* When the customer's last credit application is at least ___ years old.

While it is useful to obtain new credit information, it is also annoying for customers to fill out the form again. To keep from bothering customers, do not require a replacement application if the amount of credit that the customer needs is quite low.

The Credit Rating

It is possible to individually judge the merits of each customer's ability to pay for a sale made on credit, based on such information as credit applications, financial statements, and payment history. However, doing so on an individual basis introduces some inconsistency into the granting of credit to all customers. It is entirely likely that a credit manager will grant more credit to a customer because he or she likes the customer, or less credit because their accounts payable person is annoying – hardly quantitative reasons, but all too common.

A better approach is to develop a standardized method for granting credit that is based on hard facts, such as customer payment history and liquidity. Doing so results in considerable consistency in how much credit is granted across the entire spectrum of customers, and should also reduce the incidence of bad debt losses. Such a system should ideally reject a request for credit when a customer is likely to default, as well as extend credit when a customer is not likely to default. Though the concept seems obvious, it can be quite difficult for a standardized system to differentiate between acceptable and unacceptable customers. A high-quality credit rating system does the best job of sorting through the credit applications of *marginal* customers; the applications of substantially better and worse customers can be more easily sorted through by even the more pedestrian credit rating systems.

Internal Credit Rating Systems

It is possible to develop an internal credit rating system, since the credit department has access to a large amount of information about customers, especially those that have been doing business with the company for a long time. However, a credit rating system will only be useful if a company has well over a thousand customers, since statistical analysis yields better results across large populations. Trying to develop a credit rating system based on the information from a smaller pool of customers will not yield an accurate credit scoring system.

An internal credit rating system should be based on any factors that a company finds to be important in determining the credit quality of customers in its specific industry. It is entirely possible that a credit determinant of ability to pay in one industry is a relatively minor one in another industry. Thus, the mix and weightings given to factors in the home improvement industry for contractor customers may differ wildly from those used by a sporting goods manufacturer for its retailer customers. Despite the broad potential range of variability in factors, the following are considered to be among the more reliable indicators of creditworthiness:

- *Bankruptcy.* There should not have been a recent bankruptcy filing, or the prospect of one.
- *Legal proceedings.* There should be no tax liens or other judgments against the customer.
- *Liquidity.* The customer's current assets greatly exceed its current liabilities, as measured by the current ratio or quick ratio.
- *Payment history.* The customer should have a track record of reliably paying on time.
- *Profitability.* The customer has a recent history of achieving a profit over the past few years, preferably close to the median profit level for the industry.
- *Stability.* The longer the customer has been in business, the better.
- *Third party credit score.* The credit score assigned to the customer by a credit scoring business should indicate that it is a reliable payer to *all* of its suppliers.

To construct an internal credit rating system, itemize the factors to be used in the system, and assign a range of scores to each of the factors that are either added to or subtracted from a customer's score. The following table illustrates the concept.

Point Assignment for Credit Scoring

Credit Scoring Factor	Excellent	Average	Neutral	Poor
Liquidity	+10	+5	-5	-10
Profitability	+15	+5	-5	-15
Payment history	+20	+5	0	-10
Stability	+5	0	-10	-20
Adverse judgments	0	0	0	-20
Third party credit score	+10	0	-5	-10
Bankruptcy	0	0	0	-100

The scores assigned in the preceding table can vary substantially, depending on the company's experience with how a particular factor appears to impact the ability of a customer to pay in a timely manner. For example, the credit manager may decide that payment history is the most important factor, and so assigns a large number of points to an excellent rating for that factor.

Also, note how some scores in the point assignment table are only activated if there is a negative result. Thus, there are only large negative scores related to bankruptcy or adverse judgments; a customer is not awarded points for the absence of these factors.

The point scoring system should be designed to keep a large cluster of customers from inhabiting the high and low ends of the scoring range. It is not useful when the assigned scores indicate that all customers should be granted maximum credit, or that none of them deserve credit, since this does not provide useful information.

The points assigned under a credit scoring system can be used as thresholds for a variety of actions by the credit department. For example, a score of 60 or more may allow for the automatic granting of credit, while a score between 40 and 50 calls for an escalated review, and scores between 30 and 40 indicate the need for a personal guarantee.

EXAMPLE

The credit manager of Kelvin Corporation is evaluating the credit application of a prospective new customer, which has submitted a complete set of audited financial statements. Further investigation reveals that the applicant has a 3:1 quick ratio, has been solidly profitable for the past five years, and has no adverse judgments against it. The business has been assigned an average credit score by a third party scoring firm. Based on this information, the credit manager assigns the following score to the applicant:

Factor	Issues	Score
Liquidity	High liquidity level	+10
Profitability	High historical profitability	+15
Stability	Five year history	+5
Adverse judgments	None detected	0
Third party credit score	Average ranking	0
	Score	+30

In essence, the ranking indicates that the applicant is an ideal prospective customer. According to Kelvin's credit policy, the applicant should be offered a $10,000 initial maximum credit, with re-evaluation to occur once a payment history has been compiled over the next six months. If the payment history is acceptable, the applicant can then be assigned an additional ten points, which will give it a total credit score of 40 and allow the credit manager to increase its maximum credit to $25,000.

A number of additional features can be applied to an internal credit scoring system that may enhance its usefulness. Consider the following features:

- Adjust credit scores based on the economic environment, where (for example) a contracting economy results in an automatic 5% reduction in all credit scores, thereby contracting the total amount of credit offered.
- Adjust the credit score based on the average or trending number of days past terms that a customer pays, either with the company or according to a third party credit report.

- Cap the amount of credit granted at a certain percentage of the reported net worth of the applicant.
- Cap the amount of credit granted at the amount of credit granted by anyone else to that customer, as stated on the third party credit report.
- Reduce the credit score of a customer located in a country that is perceived to have a high level of political risk.
- Reduce a credit score an increasing amount based on how long the applicant has been unable to report a profit.
- Reduce the number of points assigned to an applicant if its financial statements have not been audited, thereby reflecting the increased unreliability of the underlying information.

A company may conclude that having an internal credit rating system is a competitive advantage, since the in-house system may give a superior ability to grant credit to those customers whose credit fundamentals might lead competitors to reject their requests for credit. The result may be increased sales and profits, but only if the internal system continues to generate high-quality information. It is quite possible that the accuracy of the system will decline over time unless the company continues to compare actual results to what was indicated by the scoring system, and adjusts the system accordingly. If it appears too difficult to maintain an in-house scoring system, then an alternative is to use a third party credit rating system, as described in the following section.

Third Party Credit Ratings

A business may find that it has too few customers to develop a sufficient pool of information for its own in-house credit rating system. Also, it may not compile enough information about its customers to develop a rating system. If so, a common option is to subscribe to a third party credit rating service. Even a business that has an internal credit rating system may buy such a subscription in order to supplement its own system.

A credit rating organization, such as Experian or Dun & Bradstreet, collects information from many customers about their credit experiences with other entities, and also collects public information about liens, bankruptcies, and so forth, and aggregates this information into a credit report. These credit reports can be purchased with varying amounts of information, such as a credit rating, payment performance trend, legal filings, corporate officers, and much more.

The credit rating assigned to a business is based on the credit scoring methodology developed by the credit rating organization, which uses certain types of information and applies weightings that may differ from what a company would use if it were to develop its own credit scores. Nonetheless, these third party credit scores can provide a valuable view of how outside scoring analysts calculate credit scores.

> **Tip:** If a credit reporting subscription is purchased, be sure to include automatic updates of major changes in customer status, so that notifications of large credit downgrades or bankruptcies are received by e-mail as soon as possible.

The range of inputs that a credit rating agency may employ for the scoring of individuals is well beyond what a company could compile on its own. For example, the following table contains some of the inputs that are reportedly used to derive the FICO score that comprises a large part of the credit rating for an individual.

FICO Scoring Inputs

Age of non-mortgage balance information	Number of accounts with delinquency
Amount of recent installment loan information	Number of bank revolving accounts
Amount owed on accounts	Number of other revolving accounts
Amount owed on revolving accounts	Number of consumer finance accounts
Amount past due on accounts	Number of established accounts
Delinquency on accounts	Number of inquiries in last 12 months
Length of credit history	Number of revolving accounts
Length of revolving credit history	Proportion of balances to credit limits
Number of accounts currently paid	Serious delinquencies
Number of accounts opened in last 12 months	Time since delinquencies recorded
Number of accounts with balances	

In short, a credit rating organization has access to much more information than a business could possibly access on its own, and uses this information to construct comprehensive credit reports about most larger businesses currently in existence, as well as for individuals.

Use of Credit Ratings

Credit ratings are valuable tools, and should be a mandated part of the credit management function. The corporate credit policy should require that a credit rating be developed or purchased for every credit application where doing so is cost-effective. Nonetheless, management may sometimes override the use of credit ratings when it wants to make a sale or increase profits. For example, if the intent is to gain market share, one approach is to acquire higher-risk customers by granting credit that competitors are not willing to issue. Conversely, management can increase the profit percentage (not necessarily total profits) by contracting the use of credit and thereby avoiding bad debt losses.

When management intends to increase or decrease the use of credit, credit ratings should still be used. If credit is to be increased, then the credit manager simply authorizes the extension of credit to customers whose credit scores are further down the continuum of credit ratings, rather than granting extra credit on a spot basis. Conversely, if credit is to be contracted, the reduction occurs at the low end of the current range of approved credit ratings, leaving the credit to higher-scoring customers relatively untouched.

Credit Rating Errors

Credit ratings are developed from historical information, and so cannot be expected to perfectly predict the future. For example, a corporate customer with a sterling payment history may suddenly lose its warehouse due to flooding or an earthquake, and no longer be able to pay its bills. Or, an individual with a high credit rating may lose his job, and immediately begin delaying payments. And in general, an escalation or decline in general economic conditions will create a corresponding change in the proportion of bad debts experienced.

Another issue with credit ratings is the information upon which they are based. The information collected about a customer may not be perfect. It could be outdated or incorrect, or may contain fraudulent information (such as false financial statements). Also, key information may be missing, such as the existence of a loan. Consequently, credit ratings are only as accurate as the information upon which they are based.

For both of the preceding reasons, credit ratings will generate misleading results from time to time, which means that bad debts will be incurred. The built-in errors associated with credit rating systems will likely result in an average rate of bad debt losses that is relatively consistent over time, barring the effects of such major systemic changes as a recession.

Credit Documentation

In order to engage in the monitoring of customer credit on an ongoing basis, the credit department should collect the following information, which it uses to reach decisions regarding changes in the credit terms it offers to customers:

- *Credit application.* Every customer asking for more than a minimal amount of credit should be required to complete a credit application. This document details the legal form of the customer, its ownership, financial condition, trade references, and other information.
- *Trade references.* Most credit applications require that an applicant for credit supply the names of at least three trade references. The results of any conversations with these trade references should be included in the credit file.
- *Personal guarantees.* If a party has provided a personal guarantee to pay for the debts of a customer, store the signed copy of this document in the company safe, and a photocopy of it in the credit documentation.
- *Notes payable.* If a customer has agreed to a longer-term payment plan to pay off its debts to the company, store this document in the credit documentation.

- *Credit reports*. If the company purchases credit reports on its customers, keep all of them on file; doing so is useful for developing trend line information for each customer.
- *Balance sheet*. The balance sheet describes the financial condition of a business as of a specific date (which should be listed in the header of this document). The line items in a balance sheet may be excessively aggregated by the issuing customer, so insist on line items describing cash, accounts receivable, inventory, fixed assets, accounts payable, and debt.
- *Income statement*. The income statement describes the financial performance of a business over a specific time period (which should be listed in the header of this document).
- *Statement of cash flows*. The statement of cash flows describes the general types of cash inflows and outflows experienced during a reporting period (which should be listed in the header of this document).

The preceding credit documentation items should be accumulated into a formal credit file for each customer.

Indicators of Future Payment Delinquency

When conducting ongoing credit monitoring activities, look for several flags that can indicate future payment difficulties with a customer. These flags include the following:

- *Bankruptcy*. Once a customer declares bankruptcy, the odds of the seller being paid decline rapidly. Consequently, subscribe to a bankruptcy notification service, under which a credit reporting agency provides immediate notice of bankruptcy filings.
- *Change from proprietorship*. A customer may have originally been granted credit in part because the business was a sole proprietorship, which means that the owner is personally responsible for the debts of the business. If the customer later converts the structure of the business into some form of corporation, this means that the owner is no longer liable for the debts of the business. When this change happens, it may be necessary to reduce the amount of credit to reflect the reduced amount of assets that are now available to the company for collection purposes. A change in the form of legal organization can be detected on a credit report.
- *Credit report results*. It may be that a customer is paying within terms, but is paying everyone else late, perhaps because the company's business is more important to the customer. If so, a declining payment history on a credit report will reveal this issue, as reported by the other suppliers of the customer.
- *Days to pay*. The main indicator of future delinquency is simply a lengthening of the number of days that a customer takes to pay an invoice. The number of days to pay is most easily monitored with a report that states the trend

line of days to pay for each customer. However, since this report may be generated only once a month, there are other more immediate indicators. For example, a check payment may be rejected by the bank on the grounds that there are not sufficient funds in the bank account of the customer. Or, a customer may avoid paying the largest outstanding invoice while still paying a number of smaller invoices on time. Another possibility is that the number of deductions taken will suddenly rise.

- *Decline in financial indicators.* If there is a noticeable decline in the financial condition or results of a customer, the decline will eventually be felt in their accounts payable area, which will not have sufficient cash with which to make timely payments. Of course, it is only possible to notice such issues if the credit staff has arranged for the ongoing receipt of financial statements from its customers.

- *Failed payment promises.* Whenever a debtor states that a payment will be made as of a certain date and in a certain amount, and that payment fails to appear, this represents a significant indicator of severe cash flow difficulties by the debtor. Such an event should be a clear trigger to shut down all credit to a customer.

- *Missing credit application information.* When a customer fills out a credit application, every field on the form should be completed. When this is not the case, it is entirely possible that the customer is attempting to hide information from the credit staff. It is particularly important to delve into this missing information to identify why no information was provided.

- *Order decline.* If a customer is facing financial hardship or a decline in its core business, it should cut back on the volume of its orders to the company. If the credit staff is monitoring the trend of these orders, it should cut back on the amount of credit granted to be more in line with actual order volume.

- *Ownership changes.* Whenever the ownership of a business changes hands, this indicates that the payment history associated with that account becomes much less reliable, since it is now based on the payment habits of the new owner. In essence, a change in ownership could trigger a resetting of credit to that of a new business. This issue is particularly important for a smaller business, where a new owner is more likely to directly impose his or her payment practices on the accounts payable department. It can be difficult to spot a change in ownership. It may be noted on a credit report, or indicated when a collection person's call is routed to a new person at a customer.

- *Triggering events.* An event may occur that is considered critical to the operations of a customer, such as an armed insurrection in a country where it generates most of its sales, or an earthquake that destroys its facilities. The credit staff needs to monitor news reports to be aware of these events. While rare, they can have a major impact on the credit terms extended to a customer.

The occurrence of any one of these items should certainly trigger a more detailed review by the credit staff, while a cluster of them should be considered a major warning sign that the amount of credit granted should be reduced forthwith.

The real issue with delinquency indicators is formulating a system for bringing them to the attention of the credit staff and ensuring that some action is taken, as described in the next section.

Ongoing Credit Monitoring Actions

The credit staff should decide upon the frequency and type of monitoring that it wants to impose upon its customers, which will be driven by many of the factors described in the preceding section. The *frequency* and *type* of monitoring are two different issues, and can be modified at the individual customer level, based on the circumstances. For example, a new customer that has reported shaky financial results could warrant a full quarterly review, as well as a requirement to issue its financial statements to the company as part of these quarterly reviews, on the grounds that the seller is at substantial risk of loss. Conversely, a cursory annual review may be sufficient for a small but well-established customer with a long history of on-time payments, since the track record is excellent and the amount of receivables at risk is small. In addition, it may be necessary to conduct a review whenever new customer orders result in a customer exceeding its allowed credit limit. This issue is dealt with in more detail in the next section, Requests for Credit Increases.

In addition to formal credit reviews, the credit staff's other main form of credit monitoring activity is centered on the accounts receivable aging report. This is a standard report generated by any accounting system, which classifies the age of unpaid accounts receivable by time bucket (such as for invoices that are 0-30 days old, 31-60 days old, and so forth). The credit staff can skim through this report each day to determine which customer receivables are trending longer than usual before being paid, which can trigger a more active and thorough credit investigation.

An alternative to the accounts receivable aging report is to review the days sales outstanding (DSO) for each customer, tracked on a trend line. If the DSO suddenly trends or spikes upward, this is a strong indicator of customer payment problems that should trigger a credit review. The calculation of DSO is:

$$\frac{\text{Accounts receivable}}{\text{Total credit sales}} \times \text{Number of days}$$

For example, if the credit sales to a customer for the past quarter were $100,000 and the accounts receivable due from that customer were $40,000 at the end of the period, then its DSO would be:

$$\frac{\$40,000 \text{ Accounts receivable}}{\$100,000 \text{ Total credit sales}} \times 90 \text{ Days} = 36 \text{ Days sales outstanding}$$

There is an issue with calculating DSO information over too short a period, such as the last 30 days, since the measurement will likely contain receivables from a prior period that should not be compared to the total credit sales shown in the denominator of the equation. To avoid this comparability problem, consider using a DSO calculation period of no less than 90 days, calculated on a rolling basis for the past 90 days. Thus, one could calculate DSO on a weekly basis for each customer, for the 90 days immediately preceding each calculation date.

The main forms of credit monitoring for many credit departments stop at the use of scheduled credit reviews and DSO analysis. However, there are other types of monitoring available that come from a variety of sources within and outside of the company, all of which provide useful clues regarding the financial condition of customers. Consider using the following additional types and sources of information:

- *Credit report updates.* Subscribe to the credit report updating service of a credit reporting agency. The agency will issue updates whenever there is a significant change in the status of a customer, including a bankruptcy filing.
- *Credit uptake.* A customer typically operates at a level where it does not use all of the credit allowed to it by the credit department. The difference between the amount of credit used and available tends to be fairly steady, except for seasonal industries. When there is a sudden surge from the normal amount of credit taken to a level close to the maximum allowed, this is known as *credit uptake*. A company's computer system can spot these sudden increases and bring them to the attention of the credit department, which can contact the indicated customers to learn more about the reason for the ordering change.
- *Customer service conversations.* Customers may contact the company for a variety of reasons, some of which provide clues to their financial condition or willingness to pay for a specific invoice. For example, a call about an improper installation of equipment could result in a delayed payment by a customer. The customer service staff should record a summary of all such calls in a database, which the credit staff can peruse for clues regarding credit issues.
- *Discounts not taken.* A customer may have been in the habit of taking all early payment discounts offered by the company, and suddenly stops doing so, which can indicate cash flow problems. This is an extremely difficult item to detect, since accounting systems do not monitor it. A possible option is to develop a list of customers that have historically taken early payment discounts, and periodically compare that list to the most recent payments made by customers.
- *Exception payments.* A notable sign of impending cash flow trouble is when a customer pays smaller invoice amounts on time, but not the larger invoices. This issue is most easily discernible by the cash application staff, which can readily see that invoices are not being paid at the point of cash application. They should note these situations in an e-mail to the credit department.

This approach gives the credit staff faster notification of a problem than if they simply reviewed the accounts receivable aging report on a periodic basis and gradually became aware that certain invoices were not being paid.

- *Industry rumors.* The sales department is the best-networked group in the company, and so has the best information about any rumors in the industry concerning specific customers. When these rumors could impact customer credit, the information should be forwarded to the credit department. This type of information can be difficult to extract from the sales staff, so consider having the credit manager and sales manager meet on a scheduled basis to discuss and interpret this information.

- *Not sufficient funds checks.* Someone within the accounting department is responsible for reviewing all notifications from the bank at which the company deposits its checks. These notifications can include a notice that a customer check was rejected, due to insufficient funds in the customer's bank account. Whenever such a notice is received, the credit department should be notified at once, preferably with complete information about the specific check that was rejected.

- *Public filings.* If a customer is publicly-held, it must submit regular filings to the Securities and Exchange Commission (SEC). These filings contain the complete financial statements of the business on the Forms 10-K and 10-Q. In addition, Form 8-K filings contain descriptions of significant events impacting the filing company. The Form 8-K disclosures can be particularly relevant to the credit department, since they reflect the current circumstances of the filing entity. SEC filings are available for public viewing at the www.sec.gov website.

- *Site visits.* The credit department should schedule an ongoing series of site visits with those customers having the most credit with the company, or for those situations where other information indicates that there may be a problem. The credit staff can look for a number of physical indicators of financial difficulty, as well as establish relations with their counterparts that may create better access to credit information.

If the company has installed a comprehensive enterprise resources planning system, it may be possible to collect some of the preceding information from the system, since an ERP system collects every possible scrap of information. If such a system is not available, a separate arrangement will have to be made with each person providing information to send it to the credit department by whatever means is most efficient and foolproof.

Requests for Credit Increases

Customers continually ask for increases in the amount of credit granted to them. There are several ways to deal with these requests, depending upon the perceived duration of the need for credit, and the amount of additional credit requested. Several possible credit-granting scenarios are:

- *One-time small order increase.* A customer may request a small credit increase, perhaps to allow for the acceptance of one incremental order. If so, an option is to grant additional credit just for that order, and then drop the credit level back to its pre-existing level once the order has been paid for by the customer. This approach calls for a small amount of additional monitoring by the credit staff, to reduce the credit level at a later date.
- *Permanent small order increase.* A customer may request a relatively small and permanent increase in its level of credit. If so, this likely results from a gradual, trending increase in the order volume from that customer. This common occurrence calls for a modest review by a credit staff person with a minimal request for additional information by the customer, and probably does not call for an excessive amount of approval escalation within the department.
- *Large increase by old customer.* An existing customer with a lengthy payment history may ask for a large increase in credit. In this case, the credit staff should move the customer to a higher reporting level, such as quarterly financial statements, quarterly credit reports, and oversight by a senior credit employee. Also, the additional amount approved should be escalated to a high level within the organization, such as the treasurer.
- *Large request by new customer.* The riskiest credit request is a large one from a new customer with which the company has no experience. In this case, the level of investigation is similar to what a lender would impose on a prospective borrower, including financial statements for the past few years, a credit report, an on-site meeting, and approval by the credit manager.

Thus, the information requested and the amount of additional analysis and management oversight required will increase in stages, based on the type of credit request. For the largest credit requests from the newest customers, the sheer volume of information needed and analysis to be conducted will require a fair amount of time; this may present a problem when a customer wants a quick decision on a credit increase.

The Riskiest Customers

A prior section described a number of indicators of payment delinquency, which can be used for ongoing credit monitoring purposes. In addition, there are several types of businesses that are worthy of particularly detailed examination on an ongoing basis. These are:

- *New businesses.* Most new businesses fail within a few years. This is an established fact, so be aware that any new business requesting credit is several times more likely to default on its trade receivables than a more established business.
- *Distributors and retailers with newly-granted credit increases.* Whenever a large increase in credit is granted to a customer, the customer is presumably banking on a ramp-up in its own business in order to sell the goods that haven been sold to the customer. However, an increase in business by the distributor or retailer may call for a presumed increase in market share, or extra distribution or marketing efforts that will not be realized. If so, the customer will not sell the goods, and so cannot pay the company.
- *Transitional businesses.* Whenever a customer is transitioning out of one line of business and into another, it is essentially encountering the same conditions that an entirely new business must deal with. In these cases, the risk of default is high. Unfortunately, it can be quite difficult to ascertain when such a change is occurring, since a business may give the appearance of having been in operation for years, and give no indication that it is abandoning one line of business and shifting to another.

Whenever a customer falls into this "riskiest" category, the credit staff must monitor every possible indicator of their condition and performance on a frequent basis. This high level of hands-on monitoring requires a great deal of credit staff time, which brings up the issue of whether it is cost-effective to have such customers. In those cases where the company is not doing much business with a "riskiest" customer and there are few prospects for more revenue, it makes sense to shut down the relationship entirely. Only in cases where sales to such a customer are expected to increase, and the customer will eventually progress beyond the "riskiest" classification does it make sense to extend credit to this class of customer.

Summary

When a business has many customers and offers them sales on credit, the treasurer may find that proper management of the credit department has a major impact on company finances. If so, the following points may be of assistance in developing an efficient and effective credit function:

- Review and update the credit policy when conditions change, so that the policy supports the current credit environment in which a business operates.
- If the credit function is spread through several locations, it is of particular importance to propagate changes in the policy to these locations, so that credit issues are handled on a consistent basis throughout the organization.
- Enforce the use of a credit application for all credit sales above a threshold level. Bad debt losses tend to be much higher among those customers that avoided submitting a credit application.
- The creation of an adequate credit rating system can take years to develop, which means that credit decisions made in the meantime could be based on inaccurate scoring results. If necessary, consider bringing in experts to implement the rating system, thereby improving the quality of the scores and mitigating bad debt losses.

Chapter 13
Working Capital Management

Introduction

The central component of the cash forecast is working capital. This mix of short-term assets and liabilities can consume a startling amount of cash, is difficult to control, and is variable enough to cause a cash forecast to report wretchedly inaccurate results.

In this chapter, we work toward a greater understanding of working capital by addressing the individual components of working capital, the optimum amount of working capital that a business should require, the impacts of sales growth and decline on working capital, and the strategies pertaining to each component.

> **Related Podcast Episode:** Episode 211 of the Accounting Best Practices Podcast discusses working capital management. It is available at: **accounting-tools.com/podcasts** or **iTunes**

The Nature of Working Capital

Working capital is the difference between current assets and current liabilities. Current assets are those assets on an entity's balance sheet that are cash or a cash equivalent, or which can be converted into cash within one year. Examples of current assets are:

- *Cash*. Includes cash on hand and cash held in bank accounts.
- *Investments that can be easily liquidated*. Includes overnight and short-term investments, such as money market funds and certificates of deposit.
- *Prepaid expenses*. Includes any expenditures paid out in advance of their associated consumption, such as prepaid rent or insurance.
- *Accounts receivable*. Includes trade receivables, which are amounts owed by customers for goods or services sold to them on credit. This amount is based on the number of units sold, the price per unit, and the days required for customers to pay. If any one of these elements changes, then so too will the amount of accounts receivable.
- *Inventory*. Includes the raw materials used to build products, work-in-progress, and finished goods. This amount is based on the cost of goods and the amount of time that inventory is held prior to sale.

A current liability is an obligation that is payable within one year. The following are common examples of current liabilities:

- *Accounts payable.* These are the trade payables due to suppliers, usually as evidenced by supplier invoices. This amount is based on the number of units bought from suppliers, the price of those units, and the number of days of credit granted by suppliers. If any one of these elements changes, then so too will the amount of accounts payable.
- *Sales taxes payable.* This is the obligation of a business to remit sales taxes to the government that it charged to customers on behalf of the government.
- *Payroll taxes payable.* This is taxes withheld from employee pay, or matching taxes, or additional taxes related to employee compensation.
- *Income taxes payable.* This is income taxes owed to the government but not yet paid.
- *Interest payable.* This is interest owed to lenders but not yet paid.
- *Bank account overdrafts.* These are short-term advances made by the bank to offset any account overdrafts caused by issuing checks in excess of available funding.
- *Accrued expenses.* These are expenses not yet payable to a third party, but already incurred, such as wages payable.
- *Customer deposits.* These are payments made by customers in advance of the completion of their orders for goods or services.
- *Dividends declared.* These are dividends declared by the board of directors, but not yet paid to shareholders.
- *Short-term loans.* These are loans that are due on demand or within the next 12 months.
- *Current maturities of long-term debt.* This is that portion of long-term debt that is due within the next 12 months.

EXAMPLE

Milagro Corporation has the following current assets and liabilities on its most recent month-end balance sheet:

Account Name	Current Assets	Current Liabilities
Cash	$60,000	
Investments	100,000	
Accounts receivable	350,000	
Inventory	75,000	
Accounts payable		$110,000
Income taxes payable		15,000
Accrued expenses		20,000
Customer deposits		10,000
Dividends declared		30,000
Totals	$585,000	$185,000

The net of all current assets and current liabilities as of the reporting date is $400,000, which is the working capital of Milagro Corporation.

The Importance of Working Capital

Working capital can comprise a large part of the asset base of a business. Any well-managed business should maintain a close watch over its assets, which brings up the following points regarding the importance of working capital:

- *Asset minimization.* Any investment in assets absorbs cash, which is obtained either from profits or outside financing. If a business has a limited amount of cash or available financing, it is critical to run operations with the minimum amount of working capital.
- *Asset losses.* All elements of the asset portion of working capital are at risk of loss. Cash will lose its value due to inflation, receivables may not be paid by customers, and inventory may become obsolete or be damaged or stolen. Given these ongoing asset losses, the investment in working capital must be minimized.

We return to these points in the next section.

The Optimum Amount of Working Capital

The traditional view of working capital has been that current assets should be at least twice as large as current liabilities (this comparison is known as the current ratio), on the grounds that there should be enough assets available to pay for all current obligations of the business. However, this simplistic view might drive a business to extend large amounts of trade credit to its customers and build up a formidable reserve of inventory, which would absorb a massive amount of cash. It could also mean that a business is hiding large amounts of uncollectible receivables and obsolete inventory on its balance sheet.

A better way to arrive at the optimum amount of working capital is to tightly manage receivables and inventory at a level that appropriately supports sales to customers, with no excess investments. The result will likely be a larger cash reserve, which is still part of the working capital calculation, and which therefore might still result in a current ratio of 2:1 or higher. However, the outcome might also be lower; if so, this merely shows that a business can operate in an efficient manner with a relatively small amount of current assets.

Our view of what constitutes an optimum amount of working capital is admittedly vague, since it should vary depending on the characteristics of each individual business. The real question is why a 2:1 current ratio is considered the standard benchmark to be met. A business might comfortably meet the 2:1 standard, and yet a closer examination might reveal that most of its current assets are comprised of inventory, which can be exceedingly difficult to convert into cash. In this situation, the 2:1 ratio does not really indicate a high level of liquidity.

Rather than focusing on a particular ratio outcome, we prefer to focus on the fact that working capital does not generate any profits by being in existence, so it is not an income-generating asset. Instead, working capital is simply an amount of assets parked on the balance sheet, waiting to be converted into cash. From that viewpoint, the optimum amount of working capital is whatever level is reached as the result of tight control of the underlying assets and liabilities. That being said, there are ways to drive down working capital all the way to zero, as described in the next section.

Zero Working Capital

Under very specific conditions, it is possible to have zero working capital, which means that no funds at all need to be invested in working capital. The key goals in achieving zero working capital are:

- To force all customers to pay at the point of sale; and
- To build to order.

This scenario can be achieved in two situations in particular, which are:

- *Internet stores.* An on-line store can take credit card orders from customers and then place orders for these items from suppliers, and pay the suppliers with the funds from the credit cards. There is no investment in inventory. The main problem is that customers may have to wait a long time to receive whatever they have ordered, since these items are not bought by the Internet store until their orders have been placed.

- *Just-in-time custom production*. If a manufacturing business is configured to only produce custom goods to order, it can justifiably demand payment in advance. It then places orders with its core group of suppliers to deliver goods on a just-in-time basis to the production line. The inventory investment may only last for a few days, and the customers' advance payments are used to pay suppliers. There will be a delay of a few days for the production process, so the customer will need to wait a certain amount of time for delivery.

For competitive or structural reasons, few organizations can operate without a certain amount of receivables or inventory. Nonetheless, these examples show that a zero working capital investment can be achieved.

Another possibility for attaining zero working capital is when a business has so much purchasing power over its suppliers that it can unilaterally impose very long payment terms on them. If customers are paying the company on much shorter terms, then the differential is essentially a supplier loan that can be used to finance inventory. For example, a large grocery store or retail chain could impose severely long terms on its suppliers and collect cash from its customers at the point of sale, leaving plenty of cash to invest in inventory. Clearly, this situation only applies to organizations that are in a position to exert considerable pressure on their suppliers with impunity, which leaves this option open to few entities.

Working Capital for a Growing Business

When a business has experienced steady sales for a long time, management might not consider working capital to be an issue at all. The firm's receivables, inventory, and payables levels are probably fairly consistent over time. However, the situation is entirely different when sales are growing at a rapid rate. In this case, there is likely to be a certain amount of working capital that the business needs to invest in sales, so as sales increase, so too does the need to fund a proportionately increasing amount of working capital.

As a business expands over time, it is possible to use a ratio to estimate whether the amount of working capital now being used is appropriate. We do this by assuming that the historical ratio of working capital to sales represents a reasonable proportion, and then rolling this ratio forward to the current period to see how it compares to the current proportion. If the current proportion has declined, this represents a reduction in the amount of working capital needed to support sales, and vice versa. To derive the working capital roll forward measurement, follow these steps:

1. Calculate the percentage change in revenue from the baseline period to the current period
2. Multiply this percentage change by the working capital figure for the baseline period
3. Subtract the result from the working capital figure for the current period

The working capital roll forward formula is:

Current period working capital – (Baseline period ending working capital
× (1 + percent change in revenue from baseline period))

= Working capital roll forward

This measurement is most useful when a company is comparing results between periods that have not been modified by alterations to the business plan, such as changes in price points, expansions into new geographic regions, and so forth. Such changes may alter the amount of working capital that must be maintained, rendering a comparison to working capital in a prior period less applicable to the current circumstances.

EXAMPLE

Quest Adventure Gear has been expanding rapidly in its core market of rugged travel equipment. In the immediately preceding year, the company required $1,200,000 of working capital to support sales of $5,000,000. In the current year, sales increased by 20%, to $6,000,000, while working capital increased to $1,680,000. The working capital roll forward for the current year is calculated as follows:

$1,680,000 Current period working capital – ($1,200,000 Baseline working capital × 1.2)

= $240,000

The ratio reveals that Quest's working capital increased by $240,000 more than expected, based on a proportional comparison to the baseline period. Further investigation reveals that the sales manager granted longer payment terms to a large retailer in exchange for its agreement to sell the Quest line of products.

The preceding example illustrates a major issue with rapid increases in sales, which is that gaining market share frequently comes at the price of adding a disproportionate amount of working capital. In the example, sales increased at the expense of allowing longer payment terms to a new customer. As a business tries harder and harder to increase sales, it will likely find that the related working capital cost becomes greater for each additional tranche of sales. The concept is shown in the following chart, where management wants to increase sales at a certain pace, but finds that it can only do so by making decisions at certain points to invest in a greater amount of working capital. The result is not only the typical gradual increase in working capital that roughly matches sales, but also several points at which the working capital investment steps up to a higher level.

Working Capital Investments to Increase Sales

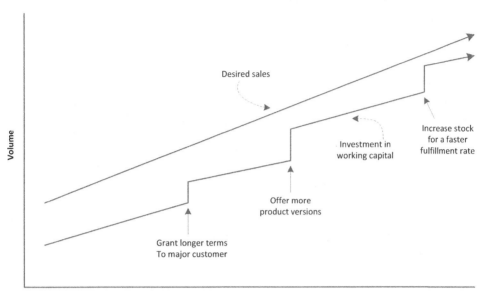

We have established that a large investment in working capital may be needed to fuel rapid sales growth. How is this growth to be funded? The main issue to consider when making this decision is whether the sales increase is expected to be permanent, or if it is a seasonal or one-time event, after which sales will return to a lower level. If sales are expected to be permanent, then funding should come from a long-term debt arrangement or the sale of stock, so that there is a firm source of funding to offset a long-term asset investment. Conversely, if the sales increase is expected to be short-term, then short-term financing solutions may be acceptable, such as a line of credit or receivables financing. The worst situation would be to fund a long-term increase in working capital with a high-cost short-term financing solution, such as receivables financing, since the lender will charge a high interest rate on what will eventually turn into quite a large loan.

In addition, there are two situations in which a business may be able to fund its own growth, which are:

- *High profits*. If a business is generating very high profits on each sale transaction, then the profits generated can fund the requisite working capital investment.
- *Zero working capital*. If an entity has arranged its operations so that there is no working capital investment or only quite a small one, then it can grow without needing to fund any additional working capital.

Many smaller organizations without access to lenders or investors have found that the lack of long-term funding availability to pay for working capital has turned out to be their greatest bottleneck in pursuing rapid sales growth. A common outcome is that they can only grow at a modest clip, plowing profits back into the business to pay for incremental increases in working capital. This results in a slow rate of increase in sales over a long period of time.

Working Capital for a Declining Business

The issues just noted for a business with increasing sales are exactly reversed when sales are declining. In this latter case, accounts receivable are being supported in ever-decreasing amounts, while inventory is not being replenished as rapidly as used to be the case. In these situations, there is a one-time increase in cash being spun off from working capital as receivable and inventory levels decrease.

This situation can result in an unexpected cash windfall for an organization that had not anticipated the results of a working capital liquidation, and especially when sales are in a steep decline. As long as management also reduces its outlays for all supporting administrative and other costs as sales decline, it should be possible to accumulate a large amount of cash. When planned for properly, this surge in cash can be used to fund new business activities, provide a reserve of cash, and/or a return of funds to investors.

Responsibility for Working Capital

The preceding discussion will hopefully have made it clear that a business needs to at least monitor its working capital level, if not actively manage it to keep funding requirements as low as possible. The trouble is that decisions impacting working capital are made every day, and usually not by those with the most knowledge of the pernicious effects of working capital. For example:

- The purchasing manager offers shorter payment terms to a supplier in exchange for a prioritized delivery
- The sales manager offers a major customer a generous early payment discount in exchange for a large order
- The production planner halts a production job midway through its processing, in order to make room for a higher-priority order
- The controller is trying to close the books, and so decides to delay issuing invoices to customers for a week

Each of these decisions might have been made for an excellent reason, but the net effect of each one is an increase in working capital. In addition, each of the decisions involved a different department. Given the dispersed nature of these decisions, it is evident that establishing control over working capital can be quite difficult. Several possibilities are:

- Create a committee that involves all of the affected departments, which monitors working capital levels and takes actions as needed

- Require training in working capital issues for all individuals who make decisions that can affect the working capital level
- Include expected working capital levels in the budget, and routinely report to management regarding how well the business is meeting the targeted levels

The Receivables Component of Working Capital

Accounts receivable may be the center of a great deal of attention, since any number of decisions and activities can alter the amount of receivables outstanding. Before we delve into these decisions and activities, it is useful to first consider the actual amount of cash invested in accounts receivable. When a sale on credit is recognized and recorded in the accounting system, it includes both the cost of the goods or services sold and the profit margin on the transaction. If there is a large profit margin associated with a sale, then the actual amount invested in the receivable could be relatively low. For example, a producer of high-fashion clothing may sell a large number of silk pajamas for $20,000. The cost of these goods is only 20% of the total sale price, or $4,000. In this transaction, the investment in accounts receivable is $4,000 and the associated profit is $16,000. Conversely, if a company sells commodity products in a competitive market, the margin on a sale may be only 5%, in which a sale of $20,000 would have a cost component of $19,000 and a profit of $1,000. In short, when we discuss the amount of funds invested in working capital in general, remember that this is not quite the case for accounts receivable.

A different way of looking at accounts receivable is the amount of money that will be released when a receivable is collected. From this perspective of potentially available funds, only the full amount of the receivable matters – the cost of goods or services related to the receivable is irrelevant.

Receivables Strategy

The use of receivables can be a key part of the strategy that a business employs to carve out a position for it within an industry. The typical progression of receivables usage is that the owners of a company have little excess cash available to invest in receivables, and so require up-front cash for their services. This approach will only attract a certain proportion of customers who are indifferent to such terms. Once the organization is on a more stable financial footing, it will be possible to gradually expand the use of credit, with the specific intent of attracting a new group of customers.

EXAMPLE

Henderson Industrial is a startup company that makes biodegradable milk jugs for dairies. It begins with little capital, and so is unable to offer credit terms to its customers. It is still able to generate $2,000,000 in sales because of its innovative product, on which it earns a 50% margin.

After a few years, the company has sufficient cash to begin offering credit, which it does at the industry-standard 30 day terms. This applies to all customers, including the existing customer base. The result is an expansion of sales into a new tranche of customers, resulting in total sales of $6,000,000. The credit manager maintains a close watch over customers, and limits sales to just those customers actually capable of paying on time. The result is receivables that are indeed collected in 30 days. This means that the company has made a cash investment of $246,575 in its receivables, which is calculated as follows:

$6,000,000 sales × (30/365 days) × 50% margin = $246,575 invested in credit

The sales manager conducts an investigation of potential customers, and concludes that the company can generate an additional $2,000,000 of sales if it increases credit terms to 40 days, thereby attracting an additional tranche of customers that needs the more generous terms. This means that the company will need a total cash investment of $438,356 in its receivables, which is calculated as follows:

$8,000,000 sales × (40/365 days) × 50% margin = $438,356 invested in credit

The management group needs to decide whether it wants to invest the additional amount of cash to increase its sales, or if the incremental increase in its working capital investment is too large.

A more aggressive form of receivables strategy is to offer longer-term sales financing, though this approach is normally only used when the goods being sold are fixed assets that can be designated as collateral on the financing agreements. In this situation, the seller might generate an unusually large receivable asset, which will require a large amount of funding to support. In many cases, the cash flows associated with a sales financing arrangement are so demanding that management elects to offload the financing arrangements to a third party lender, which pays the company immediately and bears the risk of customer nonpayment.

> **Tip:** If a third party lender is used for sales financing, this can introduce a lengthy delay into the sales process that is caused by credit checks and approvals. If sales financing is considered a key part of the sales proposition, then it may be necessary to keep the sales financing function in-house, which results in the faster closing of sale transactions.

There are a number of dangers associated with expanding credit terms to customers in order to garner market share, which are:

- *Competitor response.* If the result is a large-scale defection of customers from competitors, it is possible that competitors will match the new credit terms in order to win back their customers.
- *Quality of customer.* The type of customer that is attracted solely by long credit terms tends to be a more value-oriented customer that will skip to a competitor as soon as it is offered a better deal, so it is questionable whether these types of customers are desirable. These customers are also more likely to not pay, thereby decreasing the margin on this class of customer.
- *Cost of credit.* If new and longer credit terms are offered to all customers, rather than just to newer customers, the amount of working capital required to support longer terms can be substantial.
- *Precedent set.* Once credit terms have been extended, it can be difficult to return to the shorter industry-standard terms, since customers will have become accustomed to the new arrangement.

The main issue with using receivables terms as a strategic weapon is that this is not a unique advantage. Any competitor that wants to can also offer extended terms, which means that the comparative market shares in the industry will not change if everyone offers longer terms. Consequently, we do not recommend setting credit terms that are longer than the industry average – doing so only results in a larger investment in working capital.

Inventory Strategy

The management of inventory is usually considered to relate solely to immediate tactical issues, such as reducing inventory holding costs or reducing the overall working capital investment in inventory. However, there is more to inventory management than these goals. In the following sub-sections, we address several key strategies that center on the use (or non-use) of inventory, and how they can help a company compete. None of these strategies are easy to achieve, since they involve configuring many company processes to support the use (or non-use) of inventory in a particular way. Consequently, the management team should proceed with considerable deliberation when implementing one of these strategies, to ensure that the company can still operate effectively while not investing too much in its inventory asset.

Replenishment Strategy

A company can pursue a strategy of replenishing its inventory at a rate much faster than its competitors. This means that the total stock of inventory is being replaced by new inventory during a period when competitors are still offering older goods for sale. By doing so, a business can achieve the following advantages:

- *Investable cash.* The company can maintain the same order fulfillment rate as competitors, while investing far less money in inventory. The difference can be used elsewhere to gain a competitive advantage, such as by increasing spending on new product development, loosening credit to expand sales, or by investing in more efficient production equipment.
- *Broader product line.* The company can choose to match the total inventory investment of competitors, but because it is replenishing inventory much more quickly, the result is a broader product line from which customers can choose.
- *Faster product replacement.* Since inventory is being flushed out of the company much faster than for competitors, the company can choose to replace its product line at more frequent intervals. This is a particular advantage in fashion or trend-oriented businesses, where sales can spike and suddenly decline within very short periods of time. Also, faster product replacement allows the seller to lock up the best distributors, since distributors want to differentiate themselves by offering the latest product innovations.

EXAMPLE

Quest Adventure Gear has achieved an inventory turnover rate that is double the rate attained by its competitors. By doing so, Quest has reduced its investment in inventory by $5,000,000. The management team decides to use this advantage by creating a new product line, which will require $2,000,000 of development costs to create and $3,000,000 of an investment in inventory to support. Competitors cannot match this action, unless they raise $5,000,000 through an equity offering or obtain $5,000,000 of debt (for which interest payments must be made).

In addition to the advantages already noted, it is possible that the following ancillary benefits may also be gained from a fast replenishment strategy:

- *Reduced obsolescence cost.* If inventory is being flushed out of a company at an accelerated rate, it is possible that there will be a reduced amount of loss from product obsolescence. However, obsolescence can still occur, since a few products may only sell poorly, irrespective of the overall inventory turnover rate. Also, some raw materials may still become obsolete if they are not used up prior to the official termination of a product.
- *Increased prices.* If a company markets its accelerated replenishment strategy properly, customers will come to appreciate their ability to buy the freshest product concepts from the company. This can be a powerful brand-

ing tool that may allow the company to charge higher prices than competitors.

- *Reduced forecasting uncertainty.* If inventory is being replaced with great rapidity, this means that product demand only needs to be forecasted for a relatively short period of time. Since forecasting tends to be more accurate over the short-term, this means that a company is at much less risk of adopting a production schedule that mandates the manufacture of goods that will not be sold.

- *Better reseller penetration.* When the supplier can replenish the stocks of a retailer or distributor within a few days, this means that the retailer or distributor can keep less inventory on hand to guard against stockout conditions. The retailer or distributor therefore invests less cash in inventory, and so will be more likely to buy goods from the fast-replenishment supplier. Further, retailers and distributors can use the savings from reduced funding to grant easier credit to *their* customers, which in turn increases the orders they place with the supplier.

EXAMPLE

Quest Clothiers produces clothes designed for the adventure market, specifically focusing on women's products. Changes in this market are more rapid than for men's adventure clothes, with styling changes occurring in as little as three months. Quest has concentrated on increasing the replenishment speed of its inventory by forcing a key supplier to locate a facility a short distance away from Quest's headquarters. The result is an ability to issue new fashions in just six weeks, which is twice the speed of every other competitor. This triggers an immediate increase in market share, as competitors struggle to keep up with Quest's continuing product line changes.

Tip: Reduced forecasting uncertainty is particularly important when a company forecasts demand too low, since this equates to lost sales. Consequently, in industries where forecasted demand is especially prone to error, it can be especially important to pursue a rapid replenishment strategy with the specific target of shortening the forecasting period.

Fulfillment Strategy

A company may elect to be a full-service provider of goods to its customers. This means being the monolithic supplier of as many goods as possible. This approach can be comprehensive, such as being the sole supplier of maintenance, repair and operations (MRO) supplies. Alternatively, it can mean being the sole supplier of a particular category of goods, such as the supplier of all air filters to large industrial suppliers, no matter what type of filter is required.

The fulfillment strategy may call for a large investment in inventory, in order to ship most customer order line items on the same day of receipt. Alternatively, it may mean that the seller can improve upon the promised ship dates of its competitors, as may be the case when products are configured for a specific customer. This strategy also involves building relations with a financially sound and reliable group of suppliers, so that they can forward materials and goods to the company in an extremely reliable manner. The outcome of these actions is to present to customers a business that can comprehensively meet their needs on the shortest possible delivery terms, as reliably as possible. In exchange for pursuing this strategy, a company can expect the following outcomes:

- *Increased market share.* As customers realize the reliability of the company, they will allocate a greater percentage of their spend to the company, resulting in an ongoing increase in market share.
- *Reduced unit costs.* As market share expands, the company can increase its production volumes, which means that fixed costs are spread over more units, resulting in a decline in average costs and therefore increased profits.

However, this strategy is not without its risks. The company must carefully monitor its inventory levels, since it may be committing to maintain much larger stocks of inventory than might normally have been the case. Also, customers may ask the company to act as primary supplier for a whole range of products, which means that the company must have the managerial skill to coordinate the actions of a number of secondary suppliers.

Customization Strategy

Some customers want products that vary somewhat from the standard offerings that a seller provides. These customers may be more than willing to pay a premium for their non-standard demands, and will be especially willing to do so if the seller can provide customized goods within a short period of time. If a company can refine its order-handling and production systems to provide somewhat customized goods within a compressed time frame, this can be an excellent strategy. In addition to the pricing advantage, here are several other benefits of the inventory customization strategy:

- *Loyalty.* Few companies are willing to provide customized goods within a short time frame. Those that can do so garner high levels of customer loyalty, which translates into repeat business. Further, these customers may be so impressed with a company's service that they go out of their way to refer other potential customers – which reduces new customer acquisition costs for the organization.
- *Broader purchases.* A customer that has had a good experience with a customized product purchase is more likely to buy other, more standardized goods from the same seller. Thus, the use of customization can be used as a wedge to obtain all types of additional sales.

Further, customization does not have to be considered a niche strategy that only applies to small segments of a market. If a company can redefine its systems to handle modest amounts of customization for many orders, it can become the dominant player in an industry.

This strategy only applies to markets where customers value differentiated products. For example, a company could successfully pursue the customization of electric guitars or skis, but would be less successful in customizing cleaning products.

Startup Outsourcing Strategy

The founders of a company may choose to invest their limited funds in only a small number of key areas, such as product design and marketing, and outsource all other activities. Since the production and warehousing of goods can require a large amount of funding, these activities are more likely to be outsourced. If so, the startup company trades off a higher per-unit cost to a third party contract manufacturer in exchange for reduced funding requirements. There is also a risk that the manufacturer will learn so much about the company's products that it can eventually become a direct competitor. However, if the company does an adequate job of branding its products, this can be a lesser concern.

The startup outsourcing strategy does not always work for the entire life cycle of a company. As the business grows, management may realize that a large part of the company's profits are being handed to suppliers. Also, customer concerns over the quality of goods and/or the speed of product delivery may lead the company to take over control of its production and warehousing. Nonetheless, avoiding all contact with inventory can be a smart strategy for a small startup operation.

Payables Strategy

There is far less strategy involved in accounts payable than was the case for the accounts receivable and inventory components of working capital. There are usually only two approaches to payables, which are:

- *Defensive posture*. Suppliers are considered essential to the well-being of a business, so the only focus is on paying them exactly on time. There are minor ways to extend the payment term by a few days, but there is not a large impact on the total amount of funds obtained from payables.
- *Source of funds*. When a company controls a large distribution channel or customer base that suppliers cannot access in any other way, it can force egregiously long payment terms on the suppliers. By doing so, management achieves a strategy of forcing suppliers to pay for the funding requirements of the business. This option is only open to a few of the largest organizations, where suppliers have no power in the relationship.

Summary

The treasurer does not have direct control over working capital. Instead, responsibility for its various components is spread throughout the organization. However, the treasurer is the one person in an organization who is most directly impacted *by* working capital, so it pays to understand what comprises this net user of funds, and how it can be influenced. We have paid particular attention to the effects of different corporate strategies on working capital, so that the treasurer will understand how working capital requirements may change over time. In many cases, the selection of a particular strategy will result in a notable increase in working capital, which the treasurer must be able to anticipate and fund.

Chapter 14
Accounting for Treasury Transactions

Introduction

Treasury transactions involve many accounting entries, some of which result in the immediate recognition of gains and losses, while this recognition is delayed in other cases. In the following sections, we describe the accounting for investments, hedging, and insurance. The accounting for hedging is specifically designed to allow for the deferred recognition of gains and losses. Deferred recognition is also possible for investments, if the investments continue to be held. The accounting for insurance is relatively simple, being mostly concerned with when to recognize insurance payments and the receipt of claims.

Other Comprehensive Income

In the following sections, we will refer to the recordation of investment gains and losses and certain hedging results in other comprehensive income. What is other comprehensive income?

The intent behind the concept of comprehensive income is to report on all changes in the equity of a business, other than those involving the owners of the business. Not all of these transactions appear in the income statement, so comprehensive income is needed to provide a broader view. Comprehensive income is comprised of net income and other comprehensive income. Other comprehensive income is comprised of the following items that relate to treasury activities:

Foreign Currency Items

- Foreign currency translation adjustments
- Gains and losses on intra-company foreign currency transactions where settlement is not planned in the foreseeable future

Hedging Items

- Gains and losses on derivative instruments that are cash flow hedges
- Gains and losses on foreign currency translation adjustments that are net investment hedges in a foreign entity

Investment Items

- Unrealized holding gains and losses on available-for-sale securities

- Unrealized holding gains and losses resulting from the transfer of a debt security from the held-to-maturity classification to the available-for-sale classification
- Amounts recognized in other comprehensive income for debt securities classified as available-for-sale and held-to-maturity, if the impairment is not recognized in earnings
- Subsequent changes in the fair value of available-for-sale securities that had previously been written down as impaired

If the items initially stated in other comprehensive income are later displayed as part of net income (typically because the transactions have been settled), this is essentially a reclassification out of the other comprehensive income classification. For example, an unrealized gain on an investment is initially recorded within other comprehensive income and is then sold, at which point the gain is realized and shifted from other comprehensive income to net income. In short, there is a continual shifting of items from other comprehensive income to net income over time.

Items of comprehensive income must be reported in a financial statement for the period in which they are recognized. If this information is presented within a single continuous income statement, the presentation encompasses the following:

- Net income and its components
- Other comprehensive income and its components
- Total comprehensive income

EXAMPLE

Armadillo Industries presents the following statement of income and comprehensive income.

Armadillo Industries
Statement of Income and Comprehensive Income
For the Year Ended December 31, 20X2

Revenues	$250,000
Expenses	-200,000
Other gains and losses	10,000
Gain on sale of securities	5,000
Income from operations before tax	$65,000
Income tax expense	-20,000
Net income	$45,000
Other comprehensive income, net of tax	
Foreign currency translation adjustments	2,000
Unrealized holding gains arising during period	11,000
Other comprehensive income	13,000
Comprehensive income, net of tax	$58,000

In addition, the total of other comprehensive income for the reporting period must be stated in the balance sheet as a component of equity.

EXAMPLE

Armadillo Industries reports accumulated other comprehensive income within the equity section of its balance sheet as follows:

Equity:	
Common stock	$1,000,000
Paid-in capital	850,000
Retained earnings	4,200,000
Accumulated other comprehensive income	270,000
Total equity	$6,320,000

Investment Classifications

When an organization acquires a security, it must classify the investment into one of the following three categories:

Investment Classification

Investment Classification	Description	Applies To
Trading securities	This is a security acquired with the intent of selling it in the short-term for a profit.	Debt or equity securities
Held-to-maturity securities	This is a debt security acquired with the intent of holding it to maturity, and where the holder has the ability to do so. This determination should be based not only on intent, but also on a history of being able to do so. Do not classify convertible securities as held-to-maturity.	Debt securities
Available-for-sale securities	This is an investment in a security that is not classified as a trading security or a held-to-maturity security. It is not held strictly for short-term profits, not is it expected to be held to maturity (in the case of debt securities). Thus, it is an "everything else" classification for securities that cannot be assigned the "trading" or "held-to-maturity" classifications.	Debt or equity securities

Additional points regarding these three investment classifications are as follows:

Trading securities

- *Current asset status.* Since trading securities are expected to be sold in the near term, they are always classified in the balance sheet as current assets. If a security were to be classified as a long-term asset, this would imply that the asset is not a trading security.
- *Fair value requirement.* These securities must have readily determinable fair values. This requirement tends to limit the applicable securities to those registered for trading on an exchange or in the over-the-counter market. If an investment is in a mutual fund, fair value can be derived from the published fair value of the fund. Securities issued by privately-held entities can be quite difficult to value, and so cannot be considered trading securities, even if the intent of management is to sell them in the short-term for a profit. Fair value is especially difficult to obtain when there are restrictions on the stock of an investee, since the restrictions limit the ability of the investor to sell the shares.

- *Market price not available.* If no market price can be obtained for debt securities, it is allowable to instead use the present value of future cash flows related to the securities, as well as other valuation methods.
- *Trading intent.* The intent of management should be to sell these securities in the short-term for a profit, which can be defined as within the next three months. This short-term focus applies well to the activities of a treasury department that is continually seeking to invest a company's excess cash flows in low-risk investments, with the intent of selling the investments and returning the cash to the company to meet projected cash needs.

Held-to-maturity securities

- *Debt only.* As the title of this security implies, held-to-maturity securities must have maturity dates. Since equity securities do not have maturity dates, they cannot be classified as such.
- *Convertible securities.* A convertible debt security cannot be classified as held-to-maturity, since it is possible that the investor will be tempted to convert the security into the equity of the borrower, if the conversion feature is profitable. Also, the interest rate paid on such a security is generally lower than usual, because of the valuable conversion feature. It is too much to expect an investor to continue holding the security to maturity while earning an unusually low rate of return.
- *Intent of the holder.* Use of this classification depends heavily on the intentions of the holder. If there is a reasonable chance that the investor will sell off a debt security as part of its asset management activities, there is no real intent to hold to maturity, and so some other designation must be used. For example, do not use this classification if management is willing to sell a debt security under any of the following circumstances:
    - There are changes in market interest rates
    - There are changes in the prepayment risk associated with a debt security
    - The investor will have a need for liquidity
    - There are changes in the availability of alternative investments
    - There are changes in the available yield on alternative investments
    - There are changes in the sources of available funding, and the terms being offered
    - There are changes in the risk associated with foreign currency holdings
    - In response to a tax planning strategy
    - The need to meet regulatory capital requirements

EXAMPLE

The treasurer of Nefarious Industries has a large amount of excess funds available that spin off from the company's (admittedly) nefarious industries. The ownership of the organization is partially comprised of the sons and daughters of the founding family, who want frequent and large dividend distributions. To meet this requirement, the treasurer is constantly looking for higher-yielding debt instruments, and is willing to shift investments to obtain these higher yields. Since the intent is not necessarily to hold these securities to maturity, the investments must be accounted for under some other designation than held-to-maturity. The most likely alternative classification is the available-for-sale designation.

- *Reclassification policy*. If the investor has a policy of automatically shifting the classification of all held-to-maturity securities to a different classification on a certain date prior to maturity, this implies that the investor never intended to hold any securities to maturity. If so, the held-to-maturity classification should never be used.
- *Borrower deterioration*. It is acceptable to sell a held-to-maturity investment prior to its maturity date if there is an actual deterioration of the creditworthiness of the borrower. However, if the sale occurs prior to the actual deterioration of the creditworthiness of the borrower, this calls into question the intent of the investor to hold its other debt securities through to their maturity dates.
- *Substantial recovery*. The main intent behind having a held-to-maturity classification is that the investor will recover its entire investment on the maturity date, irrespective of interest rate fluctuations in the meantime. If the terms of the debt agreement make this recovery unlikely, use a different investment classification.
- *Sale prior to maturity date*. It is possible for an investor to sell a held-to-maturity security prior to its maturity date, without interfering with the designation. This can occur in either of the following situations:
  - The sale is so close to the maturity date that the interest rate risk is essentially eliminated as a factor in the determination of the price of the security; or
  - The sale occurs after the investor has already collected at least 85% of the outstanding principal.
- *Unforeseen circumstances*. If circumstances arise that are of an unusual and nonrecurring nature, which force a business to sell off its debt securities prior to their maturity dates, doing so does not call into question the intent of the investor's future ability to hold debt securities to maturity. These circumstances must be unusual for the investor, and could not have been reasonably anticipated. Situations in which these criteria are met should be rare. The following are all situations that can be considered unforeseen circumstances:

- o A change in the tax law that alters the tax-exempt status of the interest associated with a debt security
- o A business combination or spin-off that requires the investor to alter its held-to-maturity holdings to maintain its credit risk policy or interest rate risk position (but not if the asset liquidation is intended to fund an acquisition)
- o An increase in a regulator's capital requirements that force the investor to sell its held-to-maturity securities
- o A change in statutory requirements in regard to the permitted size of certain types of investments

- *Taint.* If the actions of an investor indicate that there is a material contradiction between its stated intent to hold debt securities to their maturity dates and actual holding activity, all of its securities designated as held-to-maturity must be re-classified as available-for-sale securities. The net effect of this change is that holding gains and losses in each subsequent reporting period must be reported as unrealized gains and losses in other comprehensive income.

The general thrust of these additional points for held-to-maturity securities is that the accounting standards are designed to make it quite difficult to use this classification. In most cases, an investor will find that it only uses the trading and available-for-sale classifications for its investments.

Available-for-sale securities

- *Current asset status.* Being an "in between" classification, it is entirely possible that available-for-sale securities will be classified within either current assets or long-term assets on the balance sheet. If the intent is to hold them for less than one year, they should be classified as current assets.

The Realized and Unrealized Gain or Loss

An important concept in the accounting for investments is whether a gain or loss has been realized. A realized gain is achieved by the sale of an investment, as is a realized loss. Conversely, an unrealized gain or loss is associated with a change in the fair value of an investment that is still owned by the investor.

EXAMPLE

Rapunzel Hair Products owns 500 shares of Tsunami Products common stock. The cost basis of these shares is $10,000, or $20 per share. At the end of the current period, the fair value of the shares has risen by $3, to $23. This translates to a gain of $1,500. Since Rapunzel continues to hold the shares, the gain is unrealized. In the following period, the fair value of the common stock is unchanged. Rapunzel sells the shares, resulting in a realized gain of $1,500.

There are other circumstances than the outright sale of an investment that are considered realized losses. When this happens, a realized loss is recognized in the income statement and the carrying amount of the investment is written down by a corresponding amount. For example, when there is a permanent loss on a held security, the entire amount of the loss is considered a realized loss, and is written off. A permanent loss is typically related to the bankruptcy or liquidity problems of an investee.

An unrealized gain or loss is not subject to immediate taxation. This gain or loss is only recognized for tax purposes when it is realized through the sale of the underlying security.

Purchase and Sale of Investments

There are a number of issues that an investor needs to understand that relate to the purchase or sale of investments. In this section, we examine the details of how to calculate a gain or loss on the sale of an investment, how to account for noncash acquisitions of securities, lump-sum purchases, and other topics related to the purchase and sale of investments.

The Gain or Loss Calculation

At the most basic level, an investor buys an investment and later sells it, hopefully earning a profit from these transactions. What is the accounting for the purchase and sale of an investment? The key points are:

- When buying an investment, the initial cost of the investment is considered to be the purchase price, *plus* any brokerage fees, service fees, and taxes paid.
- When selling an investment, the net proceeds are considered to be the selling price, *minus* any brokerage fees, service fees, and transfer taxes paid.

The difference between these two figures is the realized gain or loss on sale of an investment.

EXAMPLE

Quest Adventure Gear buys 1,000 shares of the common stock of Sharper Designs, at a price of $18.50 per share. Quest also incurs a $75 brokerage fee. Thus, the total cost of the investment is $18,575. The calculation is:

$$(1,000 \text{ Shares} \times \$18.50/\text{share}) + \$75 \text{ Brokerage fee}$$

One year later, Quest sells all 1,000 shares for $19.25, while also incurring another $75 brokerage fee and also paying $150 in transfer taxes. Thus, the total proceeds from the sale are $19,025. The calculation is:

$$(1,000 \text{ Shares} \times \$19.25/\text{share}) - \$75 \text{ Brokerage fee} - \$150 \text{ Transfer taxes}$$

Quest's capital gain on this investment transaction is $450, which is calculated as the net proceeds of $19,025, minus the adjusted cost basis of $18,575.

Noncash Acquisition of Securities

In some instances, a security may be acquired through some form of noncash consideration, such as trading land for a group of securities. In this situation, the acquired securities are to be recognized at the fair value of either the consideration paid or received, whichever is more clearly evident.

Assignment of Costs to Securities

What if an investor has a favored security, which it routinely purchases and later sells in a series of transactions? If so, there needs to be a cost layering system in place that assigns costs to different tranches of purchases. The cost associated with each tranche is then used to derive the adjusted cost basis of securities sold. The three allowable methods for associating investment costs with investment sales are:

- *Specific identification.* Costs are assigned to specific securities, which are used to offset the revenue generated by the sale of those securities at a later date.
- *FIFO.* The first securities acquired are assumed to be the first securities sold. This is the first-in, first-out concept.
- *Average cost.* The average cost of all securities acquired is used to derive the cost of securities when they are sold.

EXAMPLE

Tesla Power Company purchases 5,000 shares of the common stock of Nautilus Tours in three separate transactions, for which the details are:

Date	Number of Shares	Cost/each	Total Cost
April 4	1,000	$17.000	$17,000
April 15	1,500	18.250	27,375
April 29	2,500	18.400	46,000
	5,000	$18.075	$90,375

As indicated in the table, the average cost of these purchases was $18.075 per share. In May, Tesla's treasurer needs cash to fund operations, and so sells 2,000 shares of Nautilus. The adjusted cost basis of these 2,000 shares is $36,150, which is derived by multiplying the $18.075 average cost of the shares by the 2,000 shares sold.

What if Tesla had instead used the FIFO method to derive the cost of the 2,000 shares sold? If so, the cost calculation would have included the following layers of costs:

Date	Number of Shares	Cost/each	Total Cost
April 4	1,000	$17.000	$17,000
April 15	1,000	18.250	18,250
	2,000	$17.625	$35,250

The table indicates that using the FIFO method to derive cost results in a cost that is $900 lower than what was derived under the average cost method, since the more expensive tranche of shares purchased on April 29 is not included in the cost calculation.

Lump-Sum Purchases

There may be a situation in which an investor purchases several different securities in a single lump-sum transaction. If so, the costs of the securities are assigned based on their relative market values. The concept is illustrated in the following example.

EXAMPLE

Micron Metallic agrees to buy the entire securities portfolio of a competitor for $50,000. The portfolio is comprised of the following securities:

Security	Number of Units	Market Price	Extended Price	Proportions	Proportional Application
Common stock alpha	2,000	$15.25	$30,500	50.8%	$25,400
Preferred stock beta	500	15.00	7,500	12.5%	6,250
Bond Charlie	2,200	10.00	22,000	36.7%	18.350
	4,250		$60,000	100.0%	$50,000

As noted in the table, Micron's treasurer determines the relative market values of the various securities, and uses this calculation to assign costs that match the $50,000 total price paid.

The assignment of costs to securities based on their relative market values may not work if no market value can be obtained for some of the securities. If so, assign costs first to those securities that have an identifiable market value. The residual balance of the amount paid is assigned to the remaining securities.

EXAMPLE

Laid Back Corporation buys the portfolio of investments from a failing competitor for $80,000. This portfolio is comprised of two securities. The first security is common stock that is listed on a national stock exchange, and which has a current aggregate market price of $60,000. The second security is the restricted stock of a privately-held business for which there is no stock trading information. Since there is no reliable market value information for the second security, Laid Back's treasurer assigns $60,000 of cost to the first security, and the remaining $20,000 to the second security.

Restricted Stock

Ideally, one should measure restricted stock based on the fair value of the quoted price of an unrestricted security issued by the same entity that is identical to the restricted stock in all other respects, with an adjustment for the effect of the restriction.

Conversion of Securities

There are situations in which an investor may hold a convertible security, such as a convertible bond or convertible preferred stock. The conversion feature allows an investor to convert the security into the common stock of the issuer, using a pre-determined conversion ratio. This conversion feature is valuable to an investor, who is protected against a decline in his investment by the interest payments made on the security (if the security is convertible debt), while also retaining the upside potential of an increase in the price of the common stock into which the security can be converted. If the price of the issuing entity's common stock does not increase, the investor does not convert its holdings into common stock, and instead continues to receive interest payments.

Since the only reason to convert to the common stock of the issuer is to take advantage of a price increase in the common stock, there should always be a gain when this conversion occurs. The investor records the market value of the common stock that it receives from the conversion. The difference between the cost basis of the security given up and the market value of the replacement stock is recognized as a gain in the investor's income statement.

EXAMPLE

Hammer Industries owns 800 convertible bonds issued by Horton Corporation. The terms of the bonds state that they can be converted into ten shares of Horton's common stock, beginning five years after the issuance date of the bonds. Following the designated waiting period, Hammer's treasurer notes that the bonds have a market value of $800,000, while the amount of common stock into which the bonds could be converted has a market value of $845,000. The treasurer therefore converts of the bonds, resulting in the following transaction:

	Debit	Credit
Investments – Equity securities	845,000	
Investments – Convertible bonds		800,000
Gain on bond conversion		45,000

Sale of Securities

The basic transaction to record the sale of an investment is to debit the cash account and credit the investment account, thereby eliminating the investment from the balance sheet. There are two alternatives for how to deal with gains or losses associated with these investments, which are:

- *Realized gains and losses.* If an investment is classified as a trading security, any gains and losses associated with changes in its fair value have been recognized in earnings at the end of each reporting period, so there may be no gain or loss left to recognize. The only possible gain or loss will have arisen between the end of the last reporting period and the sale date.
- *Unrealized gains and losses.* If an investment is classified as available-for-sale, any unrealized holding gains and losses associated with changes in its fair value have been recognized in other comprehensive income. As of the sale date, shift these gains and losses from other comprehensive income to earnings.

Accounting for Dividends and Interest Income

Thus far, we have been solely concerned with the purchase and sale of investments. But what about the more mundane receipt of dividends and interest income from those investments? The accounting for these items is relatively simple. In both cases, it is recorded as a component of other income. This means it is not considered part of the revenue of the investor, but is instead recorded in a line item lower down in the income statement. The following example shows the flow of transactions required to account for these items.

EXAMPLE

Ninja Cutlery has purchased 2,000 shares of the common stock of Mulligan Imports. Mulligan's board of directors declares an annual dividend of $1.00 at its March board meeting, to be paid in May. Ninja's controller is informed of the dividend declaration, and records the following receivable in March:

	Debit	Credit
Dividends receivable	2,000	
Other income - dividends		2,000

Mulligan pays the dividend in May. Upon receipt of the cash, Ninja's controller records the following entry:

	Debit	Credit
Cash	2,000	
Dividends receivable		2,000

Ninja also bought $20,000 of the bonds of Spud Potato Farms at their face value. There is no discount or premium to be amortized. Spud pays 7% interest on these bonds at the end of each year. Upon receipt of the payment, Ninja's controller records the following transaction:

	Debit	Credit
Cash	1,400	
Other income - interest		1,400

Stock Dividends and Stock Splits

An issuer of equity securities may issue additional shares to its investors, which is called a stock dividend. Investors do not pay extra for these shares, so there is no need to record an accounting transaction. The only change from the perspective of the investor is that the cost basis per share has now declined, since the carrying amount of the investment is being spread over more shares.

EXAMPLE

Icelandic Cod owns 10,000 shares of Kelvin Corporation, for which the carrying amount on Icelandic's books is $124,000. At the end of the year, Kelvin's board of directors elects to issue a stock dividend to investors at a ratio of one additional share for every ten shares owned. This means that Icelandic receives an additional 1,000 shares of Kelvin. The issuance of the stock dividend alters Icelandic's cost basis in the stock as follows:

	Shares Held	Carrying Amount	Cost Basis per Share
Before stock dividend	10,000	$124,000	$12.40
After stock dividend	11,000	124,000	$11.27

An issuer may also conduct a stock split, where more than 20% to 25% of the shares outstanding prior to the issuance are issued to existing shareholders. Though the issuer is required to account for this transaction, the number of shares issued has no impact on the investor, which still has no accounting entry to make – there is just a reduction in the cost basis per share, as just noted for a stock dividend.

Noncash Dividends

What if an investor receives a dividend that is other than cash or additional shares of the issuer? If so, an asset is being received, so some valuation must be assigned to it. This valuation is recorded as the fair value of the asset received.

Ongoing Accounting for Investments

Additional accounting is needed for investments while they are being held by an investor. There may be holding gains or losses, as well as the possibility of impairment in the value of an investment. The type of accounting applied to an investment depends upon the type of security that an organization holds, as well as management's intent regarding how the security is to be disposed of. Given the variety of possible accounting treatments, we separately address the accounting for each investment scenario, and include examples related to each one.

When a business acquires debt or equity securities for investment purposes, it must be cognizant of how these investments are to be classified, since the classification drives the accounting treatment. The following table summarizes the initial and subsequent accounting for the three classifications of investments.

Investment Accounting Table

Investment Type	Initial Recordation	Subsequent Accounting
Trading securities	Initially record at the purchase cost of the securities	Measure at their fair value on the balance sheet, and include all unrealized holding gains and losses in earnings. Evidence of fair value can be obtained from the market prices at which these securities are selling on each measurement date.
Held-to-maturity securities	Initially record at the purchase cost of the securities	Measure all held-to-maturity debt securities at their amortized cost in the balance sheet. Thus, there is no adjustment to fair value. See the following Effective Interest Method sub-section for more information.
Available-for-sale securities	Initially record at the purchase cost of the securities	Measure available-for-sale securities at their fair value on the balance sheet, and include all unrealized holding gains and losses in other comprehensive income until realized (i.e., when the securities are sold). However, if these gains or losses are being offset with a fair value hedge, include the amounts in earnings.

For all three investment types, when an investment is sold (i.e., realized) recognize the resulting gain or loss in the income statement. A gain or loss resulting from a sale does not appear in other comprehensive income.

EXAMPLE

Armadillo Industries buys $150,000 of equity securities that it classifies as available-for-sale. After six months pass, the quoted market price of these securities declines to $130,000. Armadillo records the decline in value with the following entry:

	Debit	Credit
Loss on available-for-sale securities (recorded in other comprehensive income)	20,000	
Investments – Available-for-sale		20,000

Three months later, the securities have regained $6,000 of value, which results in the following entry:

	Debit	Credit
Investments – Available-for-sale	6,000	
Gain on available-for-sale securities (recorded in other comprehensive income)		6,000

Investment Transfers

The generally accepted accounting principles framework mandates that an investor periodically review the appropriateness of how each investment is classified, and then alter the classification (and related accounting) as necessary. Whenever there is a transfer between classifications, the investment is recorded at its fair value. If there is an unrealized holding gain or loss on the date of reclassification, use the following table to determine the appropriate accounting.

Holding Gains and Losses on Reclassified Investments

Event	Related Accounting
Transfer out of trading classification	All unrealized gains and losses have already been recognized in earnings; do not change
Transfer into trading classification	Recognize all unrealized gains and losses in earnings
Transfer into available-for-sale classification from held-to-maturity	Recognize all unrealized gains and losses in other comprehensive income
Transfer into held-to-maturity from available-for-sale classification	Retain all unrealized gains and losses in other comprehensive income, but amortize it over the remaining life of the security as a yield adjustment using the same method for amortizing premiums or discounts

EXAMPLE

Luminescence Corporation has $30,000 of common stock in its available-for-sale investment portfolio. Given the company's declining cash position, the treasurer concludes that the shares are more likely to be sold in the near future, and so decides that they should be reclassified as trading securities. At the time of this re-designation, the fair value of the shares is $27,500. The transfer into the trading classification is made at fair value, which results in the following entry:

	Debit	Credit
Investments – Trading securities	27,500	
Unrealized holding loss (charged to net income)	2,500	
Investments – Available-for-sale		30,000

The Effective Interest Method

Investors may be willing to pay more or less for a debt security than would be implied by the stated interest rate on the security. For example, if the stated interest rate is 6% but the market rate is 7%, an investor would only want to pay a reduced amount for the security, so that the interest paid on the investor's investment will equate to a seven percent rate of return. Similarly, if the stated interest rate is higher than the current market rate, an investor would be willing to pay extra for the security, so that the interest paid on the investment will still equate to the market rate of return. The first case results in a bond discount, while the second case results in a bond premium.

When there is a bond premium or discount, the effective interest method is used to amortize the premium or discount over the remaining term of the security. For example, if a company buys a debt security for $95,000 that has a face amount of $100,000 and which pays interest of $5,000, the actual interest it is earning on the investment is:

$$\$5,000 \div \$95,000 = 5.26\%$$

Under the effective interest method, the effective interest rate discounts the expected future cash inflows and outflows expected over the life of a security. In short, the interest income or expense recognized in a reporting period is the effective interest rate multiplied by the carrying amount of the security.

EXAMPLE

Muscle Designs Company, which makes weight lifting equipment for retail outlets, acquires a bond that has a stated principle amount of $1,000, which the issuer will pay off in three years. The bond has a coupon interest rate of 5%, which is paid at the end of each year. Muscle buys the bond for $950, which is a discount of $50 from the face amount of $1,000. Muscle classifies the investment as held-to-maturity, and records the following entry:

	Debit	Credit
Held-to-maturity investments	950	
Cash		950

Based on the payment of $950 to buy the bond, three interest payments of $50 each, and a principal payment of $1,000 upon maturity, Muscle derives an effective interest rate of 6.90%. Using this rate, Muscle's controller creates the following amortization table for the bond discount:

Amortization of Bond Discount

Year	(A) Beginning Amortized Cost	(B) Interest Payments	(C) Interest Income [A × 6.90%]	(D) Debt Discount Amortization [C − B]	Ending Amortized Cost [A + D]
1	$950	$50	$66	$16	$966
2	966	50	67	17	982
3	982	50	68	18	1,000

In effect, the table shows that the value of the bond has increased from $950 to $1,000 over the three-year period. Since the 6.90% effective interest rate is multiplied by the increasing value of the bond, the amount of interest income derived from the bond increases over time. Using the table, Muscle's controller records the following journal entries in each of the next three years:

Year 1:

	Debit	Credit
Cash	50	
Held-to-maturity investment	16	
Interest income		66

Year 2:

	Debit	Credit
Cash	50	
Held-to-maturity investment	17	
Interest income		67

Year 3:

	Debit	Credit
Cash	1,050	
Held-to-maturity investment		982
Interest income		68

In the company's general ledger, the investment asset balance would increase in each year, to reflect the increasing value of the bond. The reported year-end balances would be:

	Ending Bond Balance
Year 1	$966
Year 2	982
Year 3*	1,000

* Prior to redemption of the bond

The effective interest method is preferable to the straight-line method of charging off premiums and discounts on debt securities, because the effective method is considerably more accurate on a period-to-period basis. However, it is also more difficult to compute than the straight-line method, since the outcome will be different for every month, while the straight-line method charges off the same amount in every month. If the amortization calculation in the preceding example had instead used the straight-line method, the formula for every year would have been:

Discount amount ÷ Number of years remaining = Annual amortization

or,

$50 Discount amount ÷ 3 Years remaining = $16.67 Annual amortization

In cases where the amount of the discount or premium is immaterial, it is acceptable to instead use the straight-line method. By the end of the amortization period, the amounts amortized under the effective interest and straight-line methods will be the same.

In the preceding example, the bond was purchased at a discount. What if the bond had instead been purchased at a premium? We will re-run the calculation under the assumption that the investor paid $1,050 for the $1,000 bond. To amortize the value of the bond down to its $1,000 face value, the effective interest rate now becomes 3.23%. The resulting amortization table is:

Amortization of Bond Premium

Year	(A) Beginning Amortized Cost	(B) Interest Payments	(C) Interest Income [A × 3.23%]	(D) Debt Premium Amortization [B − C]	Ending Amortized Cost [A - D]
1	$1,050	$50	$34	$16	$1,034
2	1,034	50	33	17	1,017
3	1,017	50	33	17	1,000

In essence, the investor is willing to accept a lower effective interest rate that the stated rate on the bond, and so pays more than the face value of the bond to achieve a return of 3.23%. Since amortization is gradually reducing the amortized cost of the bond, the amount of interest income recognized also declines over time.

Impairment of Investments

If a security is classified as either available-for-sale or held-to-maturity and there is a decline in its market value below its amortized cost, determine whether the decline is other-than-temporary. This analysis must be performed in every reporting period. If market value is not readily determinable, evaluate if there have been any events or circumstances that might impact the fair value of an investment. Several indicators of other-than-temporary asset impairment are:

- A deterioration in the earnings performance or prospects of the issuer of a security
- An adverse change in the business environment of the issuer
- A bona fide offer from the issuer to repurchase the security for an amount less than the cost of the investment, or a completed auction for the same or a similar security, with the same result
- A downgrade in the credit rating of a security
- The presence of negative conditions in the industry or overall economy

Several rules regarding the determination of other-than-temporary impairment are:

Debt securities:

- *Impairment evaluation.* If the business plans to sell a debt security, an other-than-temporary impairment is assumed to have occurred. The same rule applies if it is more likely than not that the company will have to sell the security before its amortized cost basis has been recovered; this is based on a comparison of the present value of cash flows expected to be collected from the security to its amortized cost. This assessment includes an analysis of the value of any underlying collateral, expected defaults, remaining payment terms of the security in question, and similar factors.
- *Cost basis.* Once the impairment is recorded, this becomes the new amortized cost basis of the debt security, and cannot be adjusted upward if there is a significant recovery in the fair value of the security.
- *Interest income.* Once an impairment has been recorded for a debt security, account for the difference between its new amortized cost basis and the cash flows the investor expects to collect from it as interest income.

Equity securities:

- *Impairment timing.* If the business plans to sell an equity security and does not expect the fair value of the security to recover by the time of the sale, consider its impairment to be other-than-temporary when the decision to sell is made, not when the security is sold.
- *Loss calculation.* If an impairment loss on an equity security is considered to be other-than-temporary, recognize a loss in the amount of the difference between the cost and fair value of the security.
- *Cost basis.* Once the impairment is recorded, this becomes the new cost basis of the equity security, and cannot be adjusted upward if there is a subsequent recovery in the fair value of the security.

EXAMPLE

Armadillo Industries buys $250,000 of the equity securities of Currency Bank. A national liquidity crisis causes a downturn in Currency's business, so a major credit rating agency lowers its rating for the bank's securities. These events cause the quoted price of Armadillo's holdings to decline by $50,000. The treasurer of Armadillo believes that the liquidity crisis will end soon, resulting in a rebound of the fortunes of Currency Bank, and so authorizes the recordation of the $50,000 valuation decline in other comprehensive income. The following entry records the transaction:

	Debit	Credit
Loss on available-for-sale securities (recorded in other comprehensive income)	50,000	
Investments – Available-for-sale		50,000

In the following year, the prognostication abilities of the treasurer are unfortunately not justified, as the liquidity crisis continues. Accordingly, the treasurer authorizes shifting the $50,000 loss from other comprehensive income to earnings.

What is a Derivative?

Derivatives are a key component of the hedging practices of a treasury department. What are derivatives? A *financial instrument* is a document that has monetary value or which establishes an obligation to pay. Examples of financial instruments are cash, foreign currencies, accounts receivable, loans, bonds, equity securities, and accounts payable. A *derivative* is a financial instrument that has the following characteristics:

- It is a financial instrument or a contract that requires either a small or no initial investment;
- There is at least one *notional amount* (the face value of a financial instrument, which is used to make calculations based on that amount) or payment provision;
- It can be settled *net*, which is a payment that reflects the net difference between the ending positions of the two parties; and
- Its value changes in relation to a change in an *underlying*, which is a variable, such as an interest rate, exchange rate, credit rating, or commodity price, that is used to determine the settlement of a derivative instrument. The value of a derivative can even change in conjunction with the weather.

Examples of derivatives include the following:

- *Call option.* An agreement that gives the holder the right, but not the obligation, to *buy* shares, bonds, commodities, or other assets at a predetermined price within a pre-defined time period.

233

- *Put option*. An agreement that gives the holder the right, but not the obligation, to *sell* shares, bonds, commodities, or other assets at a pre-determined price within a pre-defined time period.
- *Forward*. An agreement to buy or sell an asset at a pre-determined price as of a future date. This is a highly customizable derivative, which is not traded on an exchange.
- *Futures*. An agreement to buy or sell an asset at a pre-determined price as of a future date. This is a standardized agreement, so that they can be more easily traded on a futures exchange.
- *Swap*. An agreement to exchange one security for another, with the intent of altering the security terms to which each party individually is subjected.

In essence, a derivative constitutes a bet that something will increase or decrease. A derivative can be used in two ways. Either it is a tool for avoiding risk, or it is used to speculate. In the latter case, an entity accepts risk in order to possibly earn above-average profits. Speculation using derivatives can be extremely risky, since a large adverse movement in an underlying could trigger a massive liability for the holder of a derivative.

When entering into a derivative arrangement, neither party to the arrangement pays the entire value of the instrument up front. Instead, the net difference between the obligations of the two parties is tracked over time, with final settlement being based on the net difference between the final positions of the parties when the instrument is terminated. Also, there is no delivery or receipt of any non-financial item. This arrangement is referred to as *net settlement*.

By minimizing the need for an up-front investment, a business or individual can enter into a derivative arrangement at minimal cost. This makes the use of derivatives much more cost-effective than would be the case if they were paid for up front and in full.

The value of a derivative changes in concert with the variability of the underlying on which it is based. For example, if a derivative is tied to a benchmark interest rate and there is a minimal expectation that the interest rate will change during the life of the derivative, then the seller of the derivative bears little risk of having to pay out, and so will accept a low price for the derivative. Conversely, if there is an expectation of major changes in the underlying, the risk that the seller will have to pay out increases, so the seller will require a much higher price for the derivative.

It is possible for a derivative to not be a financial instrument. In this situation, the terms of the derivative must allow for the option to have a net settlement. Also, it cannot be part of the normal usage requirements of a business.

There may sometimes be uncertainty regarding whether a transaction is not a derivative. If not, the transaction might be a normal purchase or a normal sale. The characteristics of these transactions are:

- There is a probable physical settlement, such as the delivery of goods or services.

- There is documentation of the transaction, such as the basis for a decision that the contract will result in physical delivery.
- There is a clearly and closely related underlying.
- There are normal terms; that is, the terms of the contract are consistent with the terms of an organization's normal purchases and sales.

EXAMPLE

Winslow Refining enters into a contract to purchase crude oil at a pre-determined price on a future date. The intent is to process all of the acquired crude oil through the company's Houston refinery. Since this transaction is part of the normal usage requirements of the business, it is not a derivative instrument.

EXAMPLE

Just down the street from Winslow Refining is the headquarters of Burton Brothers Investments. Burton earns money by speculating on the price of crude oil. Burton enters into a futures contract to purchase 100,000 barrels of crude oil on August 10, and plans to net settle the contract on that date. Thus, Burton does not take delivery of the oil. By the end of June, the price of crude oil has increased by $2 per barrel, so Burton has (so far) earned a profit of $200,000 on the contract. Since this transaction is entirely speculative, the transaction is a derivative.

Hedge Accounting - General

The intent behind hedge accounting is to allow a business to record changes in the value of a hedging relationship in other comprehensive income (except for fair value hedges), rather than in earnings. This is done in order to protect the core earnings of a business from periodic variations in the value of its financial instruments before they have been liquidated. Once a financial instrument has been liquidated, any accumulated gains or losses stored in other comprehensive income are shifted into earnings.

The accounting for hedges involves matching a derivative instrument to a hedged item, and then recognizing gains and losses from both items in the same period. A derivative is always measured at its fair value. If the instrument is effective for a period of time, this may mean that incremental changes in its fair value are continually being recorded in the accounting records.

When a business uses a derivative as a hedge, it can elect to designate the derivative as belonging to one of the following three hedging classifications:

- *Fair value hedge*. The derivative is used to hedge the risk of changes in the fair value of an asset or liability, or of an unrecognized firm commitment.
- *Cash flow hedge*. The derivative is used to hedge variations in the cash flows associated with an asset or liability, or of a forecasted transaction.
- *Foreign currency hedge*. The derivative is used to hedge variations in the foreign currency exposure associated with a net investment in a foreign op-

eration, a forecasted transaction, an available-for-sale security, or an unrecognized firm commitment.

If a derivative instrument is designated as belonging within one of these classifications, the gains or losses associated with the hedge are matched to any gains or losses incurred by the asset or liability with which the derivative is paired. However, the hedging relationship must first qualify for hedge accounting. To do so, the relationship must meet all of the following criteria:

- *Designation.* The hedging relationship must be designated as such at its inception. The documentation of the relationship must include the following:
  - The hedging relationship
  - The risk management objective and strategy, which includes identification of the hedging instrument and the hedged item, the nature of the risk being hedged, and the method used to determine hedge effectiveness and ineffectiveness.
  - If there is a fair value hedge of a firm commitment, a method for recognizing in earnings the asset or liability that represents the gain or loss on the hedged commitment.
  - If there is a cash flow hedge of a forecasted transaction, the period when the forecasted transaction will occur, the nature of the asset or liability involved, either the amount of foreign exchange being hedged or the number of items encompassed by the transaction, and the current price of the forecasted transaction.
- *Eligibility (hedged item).* Only certain types of assets and liabilities can qualify for special accounting as a hedging relationship.
- *Eligibility (hedging item).* Designate either all or a portion of the hedging instrument as such. Also, several derivative instruments can be jointly designated as the hedging instrument.
- *Effectiveness.* There is an expectation that the pairing will result in a highly effective hedge that offsets prospective changes in the cash flows or fair value associated with the hedged risk. A highly effective hedge is one in which the change in fair value or cash flows of the hedge falls between 80% and 125% of the opposing change in the fair value or cash flows of the financial instrument that is being hedged. Over the life of a hedging relationship, the effectiveness of the pairing must be examined at least quarterly. A prospective analysis should also be made to estimate whether the relationship will be highly effective in future periods, typically using a probability-weighted analysis of changes in fair value or cash flows. If the relationship is no longer highly effective through the date of this assessment, then the pairing no longer qualifies for hedge accounting.

If a hedging relationship is not fully documented or is never documented at all, then all subsequent changes in fair value associated with these instruments must be immediately recorded as gains or losses in earnings.

Even if a hedge is considered to be effective, it is quite possible that some portion of the risk inherent in an underlying transaction will not be covered by a hedge. In this situation, gains and losses on the unhedged portion of a hedged pairing should be recorded in earnings.

EXAMPLE

Suture Corporation pays $1 million for an investment that is denominated in pounds. Suture's treasurer enters into a hedging transaction that is also denominated in pounds, and which is designed to be a hedge of the investment. One year later, Suture experiences a loss of $12,000 on the investment and a $9,000 gain on the hedging instrument. The full $9,000 gain on the hedging instrument is considered effective, so only the difference between the investment and its hedge - $3,000 – is recorded as a loss in earnings.

There may be cases in which a hedging instrument is being employed, where the third party is actually another entity under the umbrella of a parent company. In this case, risk is not being offloaded to a third party. Consequently, such a hedging instrument is not considered to be a hedge for the purposes of hedge accounting.

Hedge Accounting – Fair Value Hedges

The fair value of an asset or liability could change, which may affect the profits of a business. A fair value hedge is designed to hedge against this exposure to changes in fair value that are caused by a specific risk. It is possible to only hedge the risks associated with a portion of an asset or liability, as long as the effectiveness of the related hedge can be measured.

When a hedging relationship has been established for a fair value hedge, continually re-measure the fair value of the hedge and the item with which it is paired. The accounting for this re-measurement is as follows:

- *Hedging item.* Record a gain or loss in earnings for the change in fair value of the hedging instrument.
- *Hedged item.* Record a gain or loss in earnings for the change in fair value of the hedged item that can be attributed to the risk for which the hedge pairing was established. This also means that the carrying amount of the hedged item must be adjusted to reflect its change in fair value.

If the hedging relationship is fully effective, either the gain on the hedging instrument will exactly offset the loss on the hedged item that is associated with the hedged risk, or vice versa. The net result of a fully effective hedge is no change in earnings. If there is a net gain or loss appearing in earnings, it is due to hedge ineffectiveness, where the hedging relationship does not perfectly offset fair value changes in the hedged item.

EXAMPLE

Prickly Corporation buys ten bonds having an aggregate face value of $10,000. The bonds pay a 6% interest rate, which matches the current market rate. Prickly records the acquisition as an available-for-sale investment.

Prickly's treasurer reviews the investment, and concludes that an increase in the market rate of interest will reduce the value of the bonds. To hedge this risk, the treasurer enters into an interest rate swap whereby Prickly swaps the fixed 6% interest payments it is receiving from the bond issuer for payments from a third party that are based on a floating interest rate. The treasurer documents the interest rate swap as a hedge of the ten bonds.

Over the following months, the applicable market interest rate does indeed increase, which reduces the value of the bonds by an aggregate amount of $800. However, the interest rate swap yields an offsetting $800 gain, since the variable interest rate payments being received have increased to match the change in the market rate of interest. Prickly first records the following entry to document the loss in value of the bonds:

	Debit	Credit
Hedging loss	800	
Available-for-sale investment (asset)		800

Prickly also records the following entry to document the increased value of the interest rate swap:

	Debit	Credit
Swap asset (asset)	800	
Hedging gain		800

There is no net gain or loss arising from the increase in the market rate of interest, since the loss on the investment is exactly offset by the gain on the hedging instrument. This means the hedge pairing has been 100% effective.

Fair value hedge accounting should be terminated at once if any of the following situations arises:

- The hedging arrangement is no longer effective
- The hedging instrument expires or is sold or terminated
- The organization revokes the hedging designation

As noted in the preceding example, changes in the fair value of the hedged item are being used to adjust its carrying amount over time. Once the item is eventually disposed of, the adjusted carrying amount of the asset is recorded as the cost of the asset sold.

EXAMPLE

The treasurer of Prickly Corporation needs cash for operational requirements, and elects to sell the ten bonds that the company had acquired in the preceding example. In that example, the carrying amount of the bonds had been written down by $800 to reflect an increase in the market interest rate. The bonds are then sold for $9,200, resulting in the following entry:

	Debit	Credit
Cash	9,200	
Available-for-sale investment (asset)		9,200

Hedge Accounting – Cash Flow Hedges

There could be variations in the cash flows associated with an asset or liability or a forecasted transaction, which may affect the profits of a business. A cash flow hedge is designed to hedge against this exposure to changes in cash flows that are caused by a specific risk. It is possible to only hedge the risks associated with a portion of an asset, liability, or forecasted transaction, as long as the effectiveness of the related hedge can be measured. The accounting for a cash flow hedge is as follows:

- *Hedging item.* Recognize the effective portion of any gain or loss in other comprehensive income, and recognize the ineffective portion of any gain or loss in earnings.
- *Hedged item.* Initially recognize the effective portion of any gain or loss in other comprehensive income. Reclassify these gains or losses into earnings when the forecasted transaction affects earnings.

There are several additional special situations involving cash flow hedges that require different accounting transactions. The following scenarios reveal the more likely accounting variations:

1. *Exclusions from strategy.* If the documented risk management strategy does not include a certain component of the gains or losses experienced by the hedged item, recognize this excluded amount in earnings. Doing so reduces the aggregate amount of gains or losses in other comprehensive income. Next;
2. *Adjust other comprehensive income.* Reduce the amount of accumulated other comprehensive income related to a hedging relationship to the lesser of:

- The cumulative gain or loss on the derivative from the date when the hedge began, less any gains or losses already reclassified into earnings; or
- The cumulative gain or loss on the derivative that will be needed to offset the cumulative change in expected future cash flows on the hedged transaction from the date when the hedge began, less any gains or losses already reclassified into earnings.

3. *Further gain or loss recognition.* Recognize in earnings any remaining gain or loss on the hedging derivative, or to revise the accumulated other comprehensive income amount to match the balance derived in step 2.
4. *Foreign currency adjustments.* If a foreign currency position is being hedged, and hedge effectiveness is based on the total changes in the cash flow of an option, then reclassify from other comprehensive income to earnings an amount sufficient to adjust earnings for the amortization of the option cost.

A key issue with cash flow hedges is when to recognize gains or losses in earnings when the hedging transaction relates to a forecasted transaction. These gains or losses should be reclassified from other comprehensive income to earnings when the hedged transaction affects earnings.

EXAMPLE

Suture Corporation has acquired equipment from a company in the United Kingdom, which Suture must pay for in 60 days in the amount of £150,000. Suture's functional currency is the U.S. Dollar. At the time of the purchase, Suture could settle this obligation for $240,000, based on the exchange rate then in effect.

To hedge against the risk of an unfavorable change in exchange rates during the intervening 60 days, Suture enters into a forward contract with its bank to buy £150,000 in 60 days, at the current exchange rate. Suture's treasurer designates the forward contract as a hedge of its exposure to adverse changes in the dollar to pounds exchange rate.

At the end of the next month, the pound has increased in value against the dollar, so that it would now require $242,000 to settle the obligation. Luckily, the value of the forward contract has also increased by $2,000, which results in the following entry:

	Debit	Credit
Forward asset (asset)	2,000	
Other comprehensive income		2,000

The exchange rate remains the same for the following month, after which the treasurer settles the forward contract and the controller records the following entry:

	Debit	Credit
Cash (asset)	2,000	
Forward asset (asset)		2,000

The payables staff then pays the $242,000 obligation to the United Kingdom supplier, as noted in the following entry. The transaction also includes a $2,000 reduction of the purchase price, which represents the deferred gain on the forward contract.

	Debit	Credit
Fixed assets – Equipment (asset)	240,000	
Other comprehensive income	2,000	
Cash (asset)		242,000

The net result of this hedging transaction is that Suture has used a hedging instrument to offset the risk of an adverse change in the applicable exchange rate, and so is able to pay for the equipment at the original purchase price.

EXAMPLE

Suture Corporation borrows $10 million on January 1, to be repaid with a balloon payment of $10 million on December 31 of the same year. The interest rate on the loan is LIBOR plus 2.0%, and is to be paid semi-annually. LIBOR on January 1 is 4.50%, so the initial interest rate on the loan is 6.50%. The treasurer of Suture is concerned that interest rates will increase during the borrowing period, and so enters into an interest rate swap with 3rd National Bank on the same day. Under the terms of the swap, Suture pays a fixed interest rate of 6.80% semi-annually for one year, while 3rd National takes over the variable interest payments of Suture. The notional amount of the swap arrangement is $10 million. Suture's cost of capital is 7%.

The swap arrangement qualifies as a cash flow hedge.

On June 30, the interest paid for the first six months of the loan is based on the initial 6.50% interest rate, so Suture records the following entry for a half-year of interest at 6.50% for a $10 million loan:

	Debit	Credit
Interest expense	325,000	
Cash (asset)		325,000

In addition, Suture also pays the net difference in the swapped interest rates of 0.3% on the notional contract amount of $10 million for the same six-month period. The entry is:

	Debit	Credit
Interest expense	15,000	
Cash (asset)		15,000

On June 30, the reference LIBOR rate adjusts upward to 5.50%, which means that the interest rate on Suture's loan will now be 7.50% for the remaining six months of the loan period. This also means that Suture will be paid the 0.7% difference between the new 7.50% variable interest rate and the 6.80% fixed-rate amount stated in the swap agreement, with this payment being made by 3rd National on the next (and final) payment date, which is December 31. The amount of this payment will be $35,000; when discounted to its present value at Suture's 7% cost of capital for six months, the amount is approximately $33,775. The entry to record this future payment on June 30 is:

	Debit	Credit
Swap contract	33,775	
Other comprehensive income		33,775

On the loan termination date of December 31, Suture makes the following interest expense payment to the lender, based on the 7.50% interest rate that applied to the preceding six-month period:

	Debit	Credit
Interest expense	375,000	
Cash (asset)		375,000

In addition, Suture reverses its accrual of the present value of the swap contract that it recorded on June 30, and replaces it with a recordation of the cash received from 3rd National in settlement of the swap contract. As calculated earlier, the amount of this payment is $35,000.

	Debit	Credit
Other comprehensive income	33,775	
Swap contract		33,775
Cash (asset)	35,000	
Interest expense		35,000

The net undiscounted effect of the interest rate swap is a net decline in Suture's interest expense of $20,000 over the full year covered by the loan, which represents a net decline of 0.2% in the interest rate paid.

Cash flow hedge accounting should be terminated at once if any of the following situations arises:

- The hedging arrangement is no longer effective
- The hedging instrument expires or is terminated
- The organization revokes the hedging designation

If it is probable that the hedged forecasted transaction will not occur within the originally-stated time period or within two months after this period, shift the derivative's gain or loss from accumulated other comprehensive income to earnings.

Accounting for Insurance

The accounting for insurance is relatively easy. In the following two sub-sections, we note the accounting for insurance payments (cash outflows) and claims receipts (cash inflows).

Insurance Payments

When a premium is paid within the period being covered by the insurer, the amount paid is charged directly to expense in that period, reflecting the immediate consumption of the insurance. If a premium is paid that covers multiple future periods, it is first recorded as a short-term asset in the prepaid expenses asset account. As each successive period in the coverage period is reached, the insured entity charges a proportionate amount of the insurance asset to expense, leaving a progressively smaller residual amount in the prepaid expenses asset account.

EXAMPLE

Radiosonde Balloons spends $12,000 in advance for liability insurance coverage for the next twelve months. The company records this expenditure in the prepaid expenses account as a current asset. This is considered unexpired insurance. In each of the next 12 successive months, the business charges $1,000 of this prepaid asset to expense, thereby equably spreading the expense recognition over the coverage period.

If an insurance premium relates to a production operation, such as the property coverage for a factory building, this expense can be included in an overhead cost pool and then allocated to the units produced in each period. Doing so means that some of the insurance expense will be included in ending inventory and some will be assigned to the units sold during the period, so that the expense appears in the cost of goods sold.

Claims Receipts

When a business suffers a loss that is covered by an insurance policy, it recognizes a gain in the amount of the insurance proceeds received. The most reasonable approach to recording these proceeds is to wait until they have been received by the company. By doing so, there is no risk of recording a gain related to a payment that is never received.

An alternative is to record the gain as soon as the payment is probable and the amount of the payment can be determined; however, this constitutes a form of accrued revenue, and so is discouraged unless there is a high degree of certainty regarding the payment. If the gain is recorded prior to cash receipt, the offsetting debit to the gain is a receivable for expected insurance recoveries.

A gain from insurance proceeds should be recorded in a separate account if the amount is material, thereby clearly labeling the gain as being non-operational in nature. For example, the title of such an account could be "Gain from Insurance Claims."

Though a gain is being recorded, the likely total outcome of an insurance claim is a net loss, since the amount of such a claim is offset against the actual loss incurred, net of an insurance deductible.

Summary

The accounting for and disclosure of the three types of investments clearly differ, and so it would initially appear that a considerable amount of detailed investment monitoring is required to ensure that the related accounting will be correct. However, the situation can be made considerably less complex as long as the treasury group minimizes the need to transfer investments between classifications and develops a clear procedure for the treatment of each class of investment. The situation can be further clarified by restricting all investments to just one or two of the three allowed classifications (such as not using the held-to-maturity classification). Following these rules can result in greatly simplified accounting for debt and equity investments.

The accounting for hedges is among the most complex in all of accounting, especially for outlier situations where the circumstances must be closely examined to ensure that the proper accounting rules are followed. In many instances, and especially when dealing with a new transaction, it can make sense to consult with the company's auditors regarding the proper accounting to use.

The payoff for this high level of accounting complexity is a delay in the recognition of gains or losses in earnings. If management is not concerned about more immediate recognition, or if the gains or losses are minor, it may make sense to ignore the multitude of compliance issues associated with hedge accounting. Instead, simply create hedges as needed and record gains or losses on foreign exchange holdings and hedges at once, without worrying about the proper documentation of each hedging relationship and having to repeatedly measure hedge effectiveness.

Chapter 15
Treasury Management Systems

Introduction

A large part of the treasury department's time is taken up by a specific set of transactions, which include determining the daily cash position, adjusting the investment portfolio, altering the company's debt position, and taking action to mitigate the company's risk positions. These activities can be tracked on a spreadsheet, but doing so is time-consuming and subject to error. The information derived from these spreadsheets is then manually recorded in the general ledger. The recordation of this information is also slow and subject to error. A reasonable solution to these issues is to acquire a treasury management system (TMS). In this chapter, we discuss the components of a TMS, its advantages and disadvantages, and several related topics.

Components of a Treasury Management System

A treasury management system is a software package that incorporates a number of data feeds into a workstation that seamlessly aggregates a large amount of information into one place. As an example of how a TMS functions, an investment transaction entered into the system can generate a complete set of accounting journal entries, as well as an update to the cash forecast that reflects use of the cash and its eventual return upon maturity of the investment, plus create an electronic payment transaction to transfer the funds to the investee. A similarly comprehensive set of actions can be taken for a number of other transactions, including debt positions and foreign exchange hedges. The functional areas in which a TMS can aggregate information and provide enhanced usability include:

- Accounting
- Cash forecasting
- Cash pooling
- Foreign exchange deal making and confirmation processing
- Funds transfers
- Hedge deal making and confirmation processing
- Intercompany transaction settlements
- Investment management
- Risk management and scenario modeling

A TMS is prepackaged with a small number of standard reports. These reports will probably not fulfill all of a company's reporting requirements, so additional custom reports must be constructed. To fulfill this need, a TMS should have a report writing module that allows users to create their own customized reports. A report writing module allows users to create a report format, which the module automatically populates with information from the TMS database. Ideally, the system should also allow for the automatic creation and e-mail distribution of those reports deemed most useful to employees.

These areas of TMS functionality are usually combined into separate modules, which can be purchased or subscribed to individually. A treasurer may choose to obtain one or a few modules initially, which has the advantage of reducing the up-front purchase, conversion, and training cost of the system. The department can thereby pay for those modules it needs the most, and gradually expand the number of modules to obtain a full suite of capabilities. The only problem with this incremental rollout is that some module functionality may be lost if an acquired module depends on information that is entered into a module that has not yet been purchased.

Advantages of a Treasury Management System

A TMS system is an appealing solution for many larger organizations. In general, it can be used to automate many of the more clerical tasks and reduce transaction error rates. More specifically, a treasury workstation can take over or assist with the following functions:

- *Accounting.* Record the accounting transactions associated with treasury activities in the accounting system. The system creates a complete audit trail of all transactions.
- *Bank reconciliation.* Import the bank's record of transactions associated with the company, and reconcile them to the company's record of the same transactions.
- *Control.* Set investment position limits, and reconcile orders with settlements.
- *Exposure.* Identify and monitor any financial exposures to which the business is subjected.
- *Forecasting.* Assemble information from multiple sources to create a cash forecast.
- *Foreign exchange.* Monitor the company's positions in foreign currency holdings.
- *Investments.* Monitor and report on all types of investments, such as holdings in money market instruments, mutual funds, equities, and warrants. The system warns of upcoming maturities.
- *Payments.* Process outbound wire transfer payments.
- *What if analysis.* Estimate the company's exposure to a variety of scenarios, such as changes in the yield curve.

When these features are properly deployed, a treasury department can reduce costs in the following areas:

- *Cash use*. With better information about cash positions and cash usage needs, the treasury staff may be able to invest more idle cash.
- *Improper hedging*. It may be possible to determine which historical losses could have been avoided if a TMS had been available, and model what the savings would have been.
- *Staff efficiency*. All data entry tasks are eliminated with a TMS, which may lead to a reduction of the treasury staff.
- *Transaction costs*. If the department can initiate its own trades, this means it can avoid the third-party costs that it had been incurring to have trades completed on its behalf.
- *Yields*. If there is an expectation that the company will use a TMS to forecast further into the future, this may allow for the use of longer-term investments that have higher yields. If so, the incremental increase in return on investment can be estimated.

While it is not possible to precisely quantify the exact benefits of a TMS from each of the preceding items, it should be possible to develop a range within which benefits can be expected. If so, the treasurer can assign probabilities to the likelihood of attaining certain benefits, which can be used in a cost-benefit analysis.

Disadvantages of a Treasury Management System

The main disadvantage of a TMS system is cost. Even a minimum TMS software configuration will cost at least $30,000, while a fully-configured system may cost ten times as much. When evaluating whether to purchase a TMS system, consider that the cost of the software may comprise only a fraction of the total cost of the system. The following costs must also be included in the evaluation:

- *Hardware*. This is not only the computer hardware on which the software is located, but also any additional backup power systems, data backup devices, and security systems.
- *Training*. A TMS system is highly specialized, and so requires in-depth training for every user. Consider not only the initial training cost, but also the training required for any software updates, as well as for new employees.
- *Interfaces*. It is extremely likely that custom interfaces must be designed between the TMS software and the company's accounting system. Consider the cost of updating these interfaces whenever there are updates to the accounting software.
- *Price increases*. There may be statements in the contract that the vendor is allowed to enforce certain annual price increases.

- *Staff.* It is possible that some treasury employees will be uncomfortable with the complexity of the new system, and may have to be replaced. This may result in termination, hiring, and additional training costs.
- *Support fees.* The TMS provider will charge a hefty annual support fee, probably in the range of 15% to 18% of the initial purchase cost of the software.
- *Report customization.* If the report writer is difficult to use, the treasurer may hire an outsider to develop and maintain custom reports for the department.
- *Procedures and controls.* The internal and external auditors may require that the department spend time formalizing procedures for and controls over the use of the new system, which may also call for the participation of outside consultants.

Tip: The cost of a TMS can be reduced by shrinking the number of outside banks that a company deals with. Doing so reduces the number of custom interfaces that must be built and maintained.

Clearly, the treasurer must plan for substantial additional expenditures beyond the purchase of TMS software. Some of the larger consulting firms routinely estimate that all other implementation costs besides purchased software should sum to about five times the cost of the software. It would be reasonable to apply this estimate to TMS software.

Tip: Periodically review the usage levels of the various TMS modules, and consider cancelling any that are not being used. Otherwise, the company will continue to pay annual support fees on systems that it is not using.

Another concern is that the installation process can require a number of months before the company has linked the system to all of its banks and internal systems, and fully trained all users.

If a smaller entity were to make a large investment in a TMS, it might find that it has spent far more than it needs for its initial and presumably more limited TMS activities. If the organization does not continue to grow and increase in financial complexity, it is possible that most of the TMS will never be needed, and will represent a cost-*in*efficient solution.

Finally, there is a possibility that a TMS can be hacked, as is the case with any computer system. If so, an outside party might be able to access the system and use it to transfer company funds to untraceable offshore accounts. This risk can be mitigated through proper security measures.

Additional TMS Considerations

The unique circumstances of a business may call for the acquisition of a different flavor of TMS. Consider the following circumstances:

- *Small organization.* As noted earlier, the cost of a TMS can be prohibitively high. If so, a smaller organization could consider obtaining a TMS that is structured as a software-as-a-service (SaaS) configuration, where the system is accessed on-line. The provider maintains all hardware and provides software updates automatically, while also automatically backing up data for the user. This is a much lower-cost approach.
- *Multi-location.* The department's operations may be highly dispersed. If so, the SaaS solution just noted would be particularly effective, since there would be no need to maintain specialized systems at distant locations, with the attendant maintenance issues.
- *ERP system.* A company may already own an enterprise resources planning (ERP) system, which integrates all functional areas into a comprehensive package. If so, the ERP provider may offer some elements of a TMS within its system. Since these elements are fully integrated into the rest of the ERP modules, this is usually an obvious purchase for the treasurer.
- *Specialized needs.* The unique requirements of a business may only call for certain aspects of a TMS, such as account management or foreign exchange transactions. If so, software is available for just these functions. In the case of account management, the company's relationship bank may provide a perfectly adequate on-line system for free.
- *Customization.* The treasury group may have developed a customized manual process that they would like to duplicate in a TMS. If so, this may require customization of an existing commercial package. Such a conversion is not recommended, since it introduces an overlay to the commercial system that requires additional maintenance, may contain errors, and which may be broken when the next version of the commercial software is released.

Data Feeds

A larger treasury department will require access to a number of outside services that provide specialized cash management information. The most expensive services provide real-time information. When real-time information is not needed, a less expensive alternative is to obtain information feeds that are on a time-delayed basis, or which only provide end-of-day results.

One approach is to purchase subscriptions to each data feed. However, it is also possible to obtain interfaces to this information through a TMS, for which the company pays a single provider. Representative interfaces that these systems can include are:

- Reuters
- Bloomberg
- SWIFT
- A credit ratings feed

The treasury staff may occasionally want to conduct historical analyses that incorporate market data for the past few months or years. If so, much of it is available for free on the Internet. Historical information may also be included as part of the fee paid for a data feed.

Summary

A treasury management system can be a massive operational boon to a treasury department from the perspectives of efficiency, control, risk, and maximization of cash usage. However, it is quite expensive to install, and so may not be a cost-effective alternative for smaller companies. The SaaS alternative can allow a treasurer to gain access to a full-feature system without making a large up-front investment. At a minimum, consider revisiting the TMS decision at regular intervals, to see if the changing circumstances of the department will eventually make it a worthwhile investment.

Chapter 16
Treasury Controls

Introduction

Controls are needed to ensure that processes are completed as designed. A complete set of controls minimizes the risk of loss from fraud and error. Since large amounts of cash flow through the treasury department, it is essential to install controls to mitigate the risk of what might otherwise be crippling losses.

Treasury is responsible for a number of forecasting, hedging, investment, and fund raising activities. Since they are largely separate activities, we will deal with each one in a separate section. We address cash forecasting first, since the information provided by it is the foundation for the other activities noted later in the chapter. We also describe investing activities, hedging, obtaining debt, and selling stock. In each case, we describe a range of possible controls, the minimum set of allowable controls, and supporting policies.

Related Podcast Episode: Episode 170 of the Accounting Best Practices Podcast discusses treasury controls. It is available at: **accountingtools.com/podcasts** or **iTunes**

The Cash Forecasting Controls Environment

The treasury staff compiles a cash forecast, which it uses to estimate the cash requirements of the business for the upcoming period spanning the duration of its usual investment instruments and short-term debt. A comprehensive cash forecast can be an elaborate undertaking, since it requires inputs regarding the following cash-related issues:

- Expected cash receipts from customer billings (Source: Collections manager)
- Expected cash receipts from the sale of assets (Source: Controller)
- Expected cash receipts from gains on invested funds (Source: Treasury department)
- Expected cash outflow for payroll payments (Source: Payroll manager)
- Expected cash outflow for supplier payments (Source: Accounts payable manager)
- Expected cash outflow for interest expense (Source: Treasury department)
- Expected cash outflow for dividend payments (Source: Corporate secretary)
- Expected cash outflow for acquisitions (Source: Acquisitions department)
- Expected cash outflow for fixed asset purchases (Source: Controller)
- Expected cash outflow for tax payments (Source: Tax manager)

There are clearly many systems from which information must be drawn, which makes it difficult to consistently create an accurate forecast. The following controls are useful for improving the accuracy of the forecast:

- *Use a cash forecast checklist.* If the cash forecast is updated at fairly long intervals, or if responsibility for preparing it is shifted among several people, it is possible that some elements of the forecast will be inadvertently excluded from time to time. This risk can be mitigated by enforcing the use of a standard checklist of actions to take when constructing the forecast.
- *Verify the accuracy of cash forecasts.* It is impossible to have an investment strategy if the cash forecasting system is inaccurate. Consequently, the treasurer should routinely compare the actual cash position to what had been forecasted, and adjust the forecasting model accordingly.
- *Obtain additional cash forecast reviews.* If there is a great deal of investment reliance on the cash forecast, consider having several people review it. For example, the collections manager can provide the best estimates of cash receipts, while the accounts payable manager and payroll manager have the best insights into expected cash disbursements.
- *The corporate secretary warns the treasurer of approved dividends.* The board of directors must authorize dividends, so any such authorizations will be documented in the board minutes by the corporate secretary. The treasurer should be on the standard mailing list for board minutes, so that he or she will be made aware of any dividends that should be incorporated into the cash forecast.
- *The treasurer is informed of capital purchase plans.* The treasurer should be made aware of all changes to the capital budget, and in particular of all short-notice purchases of fixed assets, since these acquisitions can have a negative impact on the cash forecast.
- *The treasurer is informed of acquisition discussions.* An acquisition can be the largest use of cash that a company ever experiences, so the treasurer should be brought into all discussions regarding possible acquisitions and the amounts to be paid in cash. Reasonably probable acquisitions should be factored into the cash forecast.

The minimum controls likely to be needed for a cash forecasting system are:

- Use a cash forecast checklist
- Verify the accuracy of cash forecasts

These two controls are sufficient for the day-to-day maintenance of a cash forecast model that is well-established, and which experiences few unexpected changes over time. As the business environment becomes more volatile, the other controls should be added to maintain a high level of forecasting accuracy.

The cash forecast stands at the center of many decisions made by the treasury department, so it must be not only as accurate as possible, but also updated frequently enough to provide reliable forecasts to the treasury staff. The following policies address these issues:

- *A cash forecast shall be used as the basis for funds planning.* It is impossible to invest funds in longer-term investments without a reliable cash forecast. Otherwise, the treasurer is forced to invest solely in very short-term investments that usually carry lower interest rates. Conversely, there is great risk in placing funds in longer-term investments without the foreknowledge provided by a quality cash forecast.
- *A new cash forecast shall be issued on at least a [time period] basis.* The treasury staff should be required to issue cash forecasts with great regularity. This policy sets the minimum interval for issuing new forecasts.
- *The construction of the cash forecast shall be examined annually.* The spreadsheet used to construct a cash forecast may become outdated as a business changes, so there should be a mandatory examination of the spreadsheet itself, to see if it still generates an accurate forecast.

> **Tip:** The cash forecast should also be revised when the company is restructured, such as when there is a divestiture or acquisition.

The Funds Investment Control Environment

The treasurer uses the information in the cash forecast to estimate the amount of cash that can be invested, and the duration over which funds are invested. It is generally possible to obtain a higher rate of interest if a business is willing to invest for a longer duration, though there is a risk that the cash may be needed before the investment has matured.

The treasury staff recommends on an investment approval form the types of investments to which it would like to allocate funds during the cash forecasting period. If the treasurer approves the recommended investments, the staff invests the cash as planned.

Since a high-risk investment can potentially destroy the invested cash of a business, it is imperative that a strong set of controls be implemented to limit the types of investment vehicles used. Also, since investment activities involve shifting large amounts of cash outside of a business, there is some risk of fraud. The following controls address these and other issues:

- *Use standard investment guidelines.* The treasury staff should make all investments based on a standard investment policy that restricts them to certain types of investments. This reduces the chance of placing funds with an unduly risky or long-term investment vehicle.
- *Verify that the proposed investments do not exceed the period of the cash forecast.* It would be unwise to engage in any investment from which the company cannot extract itself within the term of its cash forecast. Otherwise, if cash flows decline after the latest forecasted date, the company might

have to borrow funds to meet its operating needs until such time as the investment reaches its maturity date.

- *Obtain interest rate quotes.* If the company invests its short-term funds through banks, have the treasury staff complete an interest rate quote sheet on which they formally document the interest rates quoted to the company by several banks.
- *Use a standard investment authorization form.* All proposed investments should be included on a standard form that includes a required authorization signature. This provides documentation that all investments made were properly authorized.

> **Tip:** If interest rate quotes were obtained, they should be attached to the investment authorization form as proof that the highest-return investment is being obtained within the standard investment guidelines.

- *Use workflow systems for treasury transactions.* If there is sufficient treasury volume to justify the cost, install a treasury management system that routes treasury transactions to the authorized parties for such transactions as authorizing or rolling over investments.
- *Obtain transaction receipts.* No matter what type of investment the treasury staff purchases, be sure to obtain a receipt for it, and staple the receipt to the original investment authorization form.
- *Match receipts to authorization form.* Someone not directly involved in investment activities should reconcile interest rate quotes to investment authorization forms and investment receipts, and report any unexplained variances to the treasurer.
- *Match interest rate quote to actual interest rate paid.* Someone should match the quoted interest rate to the amount actually paid by the bank, and bring variances to the attention of the treasurer.

> **Tip:** If a bank has a history of bidding one investment rate and paying a lower one, that bank should be removed from the company's approved list of banks.

- *Reconcile actual funds transfer transactions to authorized transactions.* Have a person not involved in funds transfers review all electronic funds transfers from the previous day, and see if any occurred that were not listed on the authorized funds transfer or investment form.

> **Tip:** This reconciliation should take place as soon as possible each morning for the previous day's transactions, while there may still be time to reverse the transactions (though only if they are ACH transactions – wire transfers are usually settled in minutes).

- *Update valuations.* Update the recorded valuations of all investments at the end of each reporting period. Otherwise, reported investment balances may be incorrect.
- *Reconcile recorded investment balances to amounts stated by third parties.* Someone not involved in the transfer of funds should reconcile the recorded amount of cash invested to the month-end statements provided by those third parties with whom the company has invested its funds.
- *Treasurer reviews and approves all treasury-related journal entries.* The treasurer should review the justification for every transaction related to cash transfers, investment valuations, the recognition of gains and losses, and so forth, and approves the related journal entries.
- *Treasurer reviews investment ending balances and disclosures.* The treasurer should review and approve the ending valuations of investments, as well as all associated disclosures and both recognized and unrecognized gains and losses.
- *Treasurer reviews and approves financial statement disclosures.* The treasurer should review and approve all treasury-related disclosures that are included in the financial statements.
- *Verify that actual investments comply with investment limitations.* If there is a policy defining the types of investments that the company is allowed to engage in, there should be a periodic comparison of actual investments to this policy, to ensure that the treasury staff is in compliance with the policy.

There are a large number of investment-related policies that are mostly intended to restrict the range of possible investments that the treasurer is allowed to engage in. Examples of what these policies could look like are:

- *Investments shall be restricted to [investment classification].* This policy is designed to keep the treasury staff from investing funds in investments that have inordinately high levels of risk or low levels of liquidity.
- *The maximum investment maturity shall be [months].* This policy is designed to keep a company's funds as liquid as possible. Even though this policy may keep the treasurer from investing in higher-return investments, liquidity is usually considered to be a significantly more important goal to pursue.
- *At least [days of working capital] shall be invested in completely liquid investments.* This is a sample of a policy designed to ensure that an adequate proportion of a company's likely cash requirements will be stored in immediately accessible investment funds.
- *Overnight investments shall only be made with a list of approved banks.* This policy keeps the treasury staff from investing funds in banks having less robust finances.

The preceding and rather hefty set of controls may all be used in a larger treasury department that handles large investments. In smaller organizations that only purchase short-term investments from a single bank, the following minimum set of controls may be sufficient:

- Use standard investment guidelines
- Obtain transaction receipts
- Reconcile recorded investment balances to accounts stated by third parties

This vastly reduced set of controls is only possible when the treasury department is so small that the treasurer is directly engaged in most transactions, and where most investments are extremely short-term and liquid. In this situation, there is less need for authorizations and reconciliations.

The following two policies are intended to restrict the number of people allowed to make investments, and to reduce the risk associated with the physical handling of securities:

- *The treasurer must authorize all investment transactions and funds transfers.* This policy is designed to introduce oversight into the transfer of what may be very large amounts of cash.
- *Securities shall be stored with an independent custodian.* Investment documents should be stored with an independent custodian, so there is never any risk that someone could steal securities. In practice, this is rarely an issue.

The Foreign Exchange Hedge Control Environment

If a company has a significant exposure to fluctuations in the value of its foreign exchange holdings, it may use hedging transactions to offset that exposure. If so, it is important to maintain a set of controls designed to ensure that this exposure is properly identified, and that hedges are correctly installed and monitored. The following controls and policies deal with these issues:

- *Match hedge transactions to authorized list.* Have the internal audit staff periodically review all hedging transactions to see if the persons who initiated them were authorized to do so. The auditors should use a treasurer-approved list of authorized employees as the basis for this analysis.
- *Review transactions prior to completion.* If a company has a history of entering into incorrect hedges, have an in-house hedging specialist review the details of all proposed hedges prior to finalization, to ensure that they are correct and meet the company's hedging objectives.
- *Confirm hedges.* Someone other than the initiator of a hedging transaction should confirm with the counterparty that the hedge is complete, and that both parties agree upon the terms of the hedge. This should involve the physical comparison of the deal terms as stated by both parties.

The following policy is designed to improve the level of control over foreign exchange transactions by centralizing them with a group of (presumably) experienced practitioners:

- *Foreign exchange trading operations shall be centralized at the parent company.* In a highly diverse business, this policy makes it easier to keep track of foreign exchange holdings and forecasted transactions, and to develop appropriate hedges for them.

There are cases where a treasurer may be tempted to enter into an over-the-counter hedging transaction with another party, rather than using an exchange. The following policy is designed to limit the number of these over-the-counter transactions:

- *Over-the-counter hedges must be approved in advance by the CFO.* There is a risk that the counterparty in an over-the-counter transaction will not fulfill its obligations under a hedge, resulting in a loss for the company. This policy is designed to limit the number of such transactions.

A policy that can be of use where there are large foreign exchange positions is a requirement to periodically stress-test a company's hedging strategy, as shown below:

- *The company's foreign exchange hedging strategy shall be stress-tested at least quarterly to determine losses under various hedging scenarios.* This policy mandates that the treasury staff periodically create a stress model that calculates the company's worst-case losses, based on its existing hedging strategy. The concept can be expanded further, to incorporate alternative hedging strategies and their projected results. The outcome of this analysis may be adjustments to the corporate hedging strategy to mitigate possible losses.

The following policy can be of use in providing specific guidance to the treasurer in regard to the amount of hedging that the department must engage in:

- *The benchmark hedge ratio shall be no less than __% for booked exposures and __% for forecasted exposures.* This policy sets specific hedging targets, which may be close to 100% for booked exposures and considerably less for forecasted exposures. The forecasted exposure target is lower, since it is difficult to estimate the amount of these more distant cash flows.

The Debt Procurement Control Environment

There are situations where there is so little cash on hand that the treasury staff is more concerned with obtaining debt than with investing excess funds. This may involve sending an authorization to the company's bank to draw down a line of credit, or arranging for a more formal long-term lending arrangement.

When there is a line of credit, the key control issues are that the treasurer be kept aware of the remaining available amount of unused debt, and that the amount of debt recorded on the company's books matches the amount recorded by the lender. These and other controls are as follows:

- *The treasurer approves line of credit drawdowns and repayments.* The treasurer should sign off on all changes in the company's line of credit.

> **Tip:** There should be a close linkage between maintenance of the cash forecast and expected debt changes, since these changes can have a major impact on the amount of cash available for investments.

- *Reconcile loan statement to the general ledger balance.* The treasury or accounting staff should reconcile any differences between the company's record of a loan balance and the loan balance indicated by the lender.
- *Compare collateral requirements.* The treasurer or corporate counsel should compare the terms of all debt agreements to see if the company has conflicting collateral requirements. It is entirely possible that more than one lender can claim the same assets as collateral. This is not a minor issue, since some lenders have been known to terminate loan agreements because of conflicting collateral obligations.
- *The board of directors approves new loans or bonds.* Board minutes signed by the company secretary should state that the board of directors has formally approved of the issuance of loans or sale of bonds.
- *Report debt levels and terms to the board of directors.* Periodically report to the board of directors the amount of all debt outstanding, interest rates being paid, how long before the agreements terminate, and the prospects for renewal. The board needs to know if there is a prospect for having a sudden cash shortfall caused by a called loan or debt nonrenewal, so do not treat this control lightly.

In the typical small-company environment where there are perhaps one or two long-term loans and a line of credit, only the following two controls need to be rigorously followed:

- The treasurer approves line of credit drawdowns and repayments
- Reconcile loan statement to the general ledger balance

The following policy is designed to reduce the cost of debt:

- *The company shall retire its debt and replace it with lower-cost debt whenever the market interest rate and the current debt terms make this feasible.* This requirement to reduce the cost of debt may appear cost-effective, but is realistically only useful when the terms of the existing debt agreement allow a company to retire its debt prior to the termination date.

The Stock Issuance Control Environment

Of all the fund raising activities that a company engages in, the issuance of stock requires the most in-depth range of controls. There are significant liabilities associated with the incorrect issuance of stock certificates, so *all* of the following controls should be followed; there is no recommended reduced set of controls:

- *Verify that there are sufficient authorized shares.* There must first be a sufficient number of authorized shares available to sell. It can require shareholder approval to increase the number of authorized shares, so this is not a minor matter.

> **Tip:** There should be sufficient authorized shares available for the proposed stock sale *after* including the conversion effects of all outstanding warrants and stock options.

- *The board of directors approves the sale of all stock.* Board minutes signed by the company secretary should state that the board of directors has formally approved of the sale of stock.
- *Obtain accredited investor letter.* If the company is selling unregistered stock, it should first obtain from all purchasing individuals a letter stating that they are accredited investors.
- *Issue stock through a stock transfer agent.* There should never be any blank company stock certificates held on-site. Instead, hire a stock transfer agent to issue shares to shareholders at the direction of the corporate secretary.
- *Use a formal letter of direction to issue stock.* The stock transfer agent should be instructed to only issue stock as per the direction of the corporate secretary, who must sign a letter of direction that states the specifics of each share certificate to be issued.

> **Tip:** The stock transfer agent should have a copy on file of the corporate secretary's signature, which it uses to validate all letters of direction received from the company.

- *Reconcile cash received to letters of direction.* The treasurer should verify that a letter of direction has been issued that corresponds to cash received from investors to purchase stock.
- *Reconcile shareholder list to letters of direction.* The treasurer should periodically request a shareholder list from the stock transfer agent, and match changes in it to copies of the letters of direction previously sent to authorize the issuance of stock.

> **Tip:** This control will not always work if some stock is registered with the Securities and Exchange Commission, for stockholders can then place their shares with a broker, whose name will appear in their place in the records of the stock transfer agent.

- *Audit shareholder list.* The internal audit staff should verify that the number of shares outstanding, as supplied by the stock transfer agent, matches the company's internal shareholder list.

The custody and tracking of stock certificates is an important area, since someone could fraudulently earn a large amount by gaining access to a company's stock certificates and then selling them. The following control addresses this problem.

- *Stock certificates shall be issued by a stock transfer agent.* This policy is designed to shift the custody of all blank stock certificates to a third party custodian.

A publicly-held company can get into trouble with the Securities and Exchange Commission (SEC) if it issues shares that have not first been registered with the SEC. The following policy guards against this issue:

- *All unregistered stock sold shall contain a restrictive legend.* This policy is designed to restrict the ability of the buyers of a company's unregistered stock to sell their shares until various regulations promulgated by the Securities and Exchange Commission have been met.

The SEC's rules related to stock issuances are numerous. To ensure that all securities solicitations will not run afoul of these rules, it is essential to enforce the following policy:

- *All securities solicitations must be approved by corporate counsel.* The designated securities law expert should examine all proposed issuances in advance, and approve them in writing. This policy is most easily enforced when the attorney is the only person allowed to issue documents to the SEC and investors.

Additional Treasury Controls – Fraud Related

There is a reasonable chance that fraud will occur in the treasury area, since it handles all of a company's cash. Accordingly, consider implementing the following controls to prevent or at least detect fraud:

- *Separation of duties.* The person who initiates a funds transfer cannot release or validate the transaction. This is a critical control, since someone could otherwise single-handedly shift large amounts of cash out of a business.

> **Tip:** If the treasury department is small, have the chief executive officer or chief financial officer release or validate the transfer of funds. This brings cash transfers to the attention of senior management.

- *Restrict use of authenticated computers.* A bank typically authenticates the security certificate associated with a particular computer, and then requires a company to initiate ACH and wiring instructions from that computer. If a third party can gain access to that computer, they can authorize funds transfers out of the company's bank account. This issue can be combatted by severely locking down use of the authenticated computer. This means that it is not used for web browsing or for e-mail downloads, or any other activities by which someone could insert keystroke logging software onto the computer, and then use the resulting information to hack into and use the computer from a remote location.

> **Tip:** While all computers should be protected with a firewall and antivirus software, this is especially important for the computer used to initiate wire transfers.

- *Use a clearing account.* Arrange with the bank to only allow wire transfers and ACH transactions from a designated clearing account. Then fund this account with only sufficient funds to cover all transactions. Thus, the clearing account requires that someone fraudulently move funds into the clearing account before they can send the cash outside of the company. The two-step nature of the transaction makes it more difficult to commit fraud.

Terminating Controls

The main focus of this chapter has been to present controls that should be installed within a treasury department. However, controls tend to slow down the flow of transactions within the department and result in extra costs, and so should only be used when there is a clear need for them. In addition, controls should only be retained for as long as the processes with which they are associated are unchanged. If a process is altered, the linked controls may no longer be needed, but are still retained because no one thought to remove them. The result is likely to be an excessive number of controls and a lower level of process efficiency than should be the case.

To avoid a burdensome number of controls, it is useful to periodically examine the current system of treasury controls and see if any should be removed. This can be done in the following ways:

- *Review at process change.* Whenever there is a change to a process, incorporate into the process flow analysis a review of all controls built into the process. Doing so may point out that specific controls can be eliminated, or replaced by other controls that are more cost-effective.

- *Review on scheduled date.* Even if there have been no process changes, conduct a comprehensive controls review on a scheduled date, such as once a year. This review may pick up on minor process changes that have been implemented but not formally noted. This approach also allows for consideration of new, more technologically-advanced controls that were not available in previous years.

Tip: Never review a control in isolation from the other controls in a process, since the entire set of controls may provide backup coverage for each other. Deleting one control may weaken a control issue elsewhere in the business process.

No matter which approach is used, it may also make sense to bring in a treasury controls specialist to review existing systems and recommend which controls can be terminated. By doing so, the company gains the benefit of someone who has seen a broad range of controls in many other companies, and who therefore has more experience upon which to base recommendations for changes. The report of this consultant can also be used as justification for changes to the system of controls.

If controls are to be terminated, be sure to discuss the changes thoroughly with the controller and chief financial officer, as well as the company's audit committee. These people may feel that a control should be retained, despite the dictates of efficiency, in order to provide some additional risk reduction. In addition, the termination of controls should be brought to the attention of the company's auditors, who may need to alter their audit procedures to account for the missing controls.

The termination of a control should not be a special event. Instead, it is an ongoing part of the alterations that a company makes as it changes its business processes.

Summary

The controls for several cash-related activities were described in this chapter – cash forecasting, investing funds, hedging, obtaining debt, and selling stock. All of these activities are based on the accuracy of the cash forecast, so it is imperative that there be a well-organized system in place for deriving the forecast, as well as a system for investigating variances between forecasted and actual results. Without an accurate cash forecasting system, the entire treasury management function is rendered far less effective.

In addition to cash forecasting issues, a company should pay particular attention to its controls over investments. It is possible for someone to fraudulently transfer all of a company's cash to a distant bank account from which there is no hope of recovery. Thus, even if the probability of such an event is low, the risk of loss is so massively high that it is mandatory to position controls to prevent this type of fraud.

Chapter 17
Treasury Measurements

Introduction

Treasury activities stand apart from the normal sales and production activities of a business, and so require a completely different set of measurements. This information can be used to gain insights into where and for how long cash is used within a company, how well cash flows can be predicted, the earnings generated on invested funds, the general level of liquidity and debt, and similar matters. This chapter includes a number of treasury metrics that can be of great use in monitoring these issues.

Treasury Metrics

At first glance, the treasury area might appear resistant to the use of any ongoing, standardized metrics to measure its performance. After all, we are merely finding sources of cash and then deploying the cash in the most profitable manner possible. In reality, there are a number of areas in which metrics can be employed. Consider the following conceptual areas for measurement:

- *Cash usage*. In what parts of the company is cash currently being used? The entire management team should be aware of which areas are using and providing cash, thereby engendering a discussion of how cash usage can be improved.
- *Cash forecasting*. It is critical to understand how well future projections of cash positions are matching actual outcomes, as well as how much lending capability the company has remaining on its borrowing base, in order to properly plan for the acquisition and use of cash.
- *Cash at work*. From an investment efficiency perspective, it is useful to be aware of those pockets of cash not being put to good use earning income for the business, as well as the extent of the returns on invested funds.
- *Liquidity and solvency*. When dealing with lenders and creditors, one should understand the company's ability to pay over the short term. This is essentially a comparison of obligations to projected available cash, and is described as the liquidity of a business. It is also useful to examine the same capability in relation to long-term obligations, which refers to the solvency of an entity – its ability to continue as a going concern.

In short, there are a number of areas in which metrics can provide valuable information for the treasury function. In the following sections, we discuss specific metrics that address all of the conceptual areas just noted.

Cash Conversion Cycle

The cash conversion cycle is the time period extending from the payment of cash for the production of goods, until cash is received from the sale of those goods to customers. The activities involved in the cash conversion cycle include the purchasing of raw materials or items to be resold, their storage, the production process, payments to employees related to the production process, and the sale of goods to customers. If a company only provides services, then the cash conversion cycle extends from the date of payments to employees to the receipt of cash from the sale of services to customers. The cash conversion cycle tends to be much shorter for the provision of services.

It is important to know the duration of the cash conversion cycle, for this is the time period over which cash is invested in a business. If the conversion cycle can be shortened, then cash can be permanently extracted from the business and made available for other purposes. The steps in the cash conversion cycle that can potentially be compressed include:

- The placement of orders for goods with suppliers
- The time required for goods to be delivered to the company
- The time required to inspect and log in received goods
- The inventory holding period
- The duration of the production process
- The time required to prepare goods for shipment
- The delay incorporated into payment terms with customers
- The time required to collect overdue accounts receivable

To calculate the amount of the cash conversion cycle, add together the days of sales in accounts receivable and the days of sales in inventory, and subtract the days of payables outstanding. For example, a company has 60 days of sales in accounts receivable, 80 days of sales in inventory, and 30 days of payables outstanding. Its cash conversion cycle is therefore:

60 Days receivables + 80 Days inventory – 30 Days payables

= 110 Days cash conversion cycle

The calculations for days of sales in accounts receivable, days of sales in inventory, and days payables outstanding are explained in the next three sub-sections.

Days Sales in Accounts Receivable

Days sales in accounts receivable is the number of days that a customer invoice is outstanding before it is collected. The measurement is usually applied to the entire set of invoices that a company has outstanding at any point in time, rather than to a single invoice. The point of the measurement is to determine the effectiveness of a company's credit and collection efforts in allowing credit to reputable customers, as well as its ability to collect from them. When measured at the individual customer level, it can indicate when a customer is having cash flow troubles, since the customer will attempt to stretch out the amount of time before it pays invoices.

There is not an absolute number of accounts receivable days that represents excellent or poor accounts receivable management, since the figure varies considerably by industry and the underlying payment terms. Generally, a figure of 25% more than the standard terms allowed may represent an opportunity for improvement. Conversely, an accounts receivable days figure that is very close to the payment terms granted to a customer probably indicates that a company's credit policy is too tight.

The formula for accounts receivable days is:

$$(\text{Accounts receivable} \div \text{Annual revenue}) \times \text{Number of days in the year}$$

For example, if a company has an average accounts receivable balance of $200,000 and annual sales of $1,200,000, then its accounts receivable days figure is:

$$(\$200,000 \text{ Accounts receivable} \div \$1,200,000 \text{ Annual revenue}) \times 365 \text{ Days}$$

$$= 60.8 \text{ Accounts receivable days}$$

The calculation indicates that the company requires 60.8 days to collect a typical invoice.

An effective way to use the accounts receivable days measurement is to track it on a trend line, month by month. Doing so shows any changes in the ability of the company to collect from its customers. If a business is highly seasonal, a variation is to compare the measurement to the same metric for the same month in the preceding year; this provides a more reasonable basis for comparison.

No matter how this measurement is used, remember that it is usually compiled from a large number of outstanding invoices, and so provides no insights into the collectability of a specific invoice. Thus, it should be supplemented with an ongoing examination of the aged accounts receivable report and the notes of the collection staff.

Days Sales in Inventory

Days sales in inventory (DSI) is a way to measure the average amount of time that it takes for a company to convert its inventory into sales. A relatively small number of days sales in inventory indicates that a company is more efficient in selling off its inventory, while a large number indicates that a company may have invested too much in inventory, and may even have obsolete inventory on hand.

To calculate days sales in inventory, divide the average inventory for the year by the cost of goods sold for the same period, and then multiply by 365. For example, if a company has average inventory of $1.5 million and an annual cost of goods sold of $6 million, then its days sales in inventory is calculated as:

$$(\$1.5 \text{ million inventory} \div \$6 \text{ million cost of goods sold}) \times 365 \text{ days}$$

$$= 91.3 \text{ days sales in inventory}$$

The days sales in inventory figure can be misleading, for the following reasons:

- A company could post financial results that indicate a low DSI, but only because it has sold off a large amount of inventory at a discount, or has written off some inventory as obsolete. An indicator of these actions is when profits decline at the same time that the number of days sales in inventory declines.
- A company could change its method for calculating the cost of goods sold, such as by capitalizing more or fewer expenses into overhead. If this calculation method varies significantly from the method the company used in the past, it can lead to a sudden alteration in the results of the measurement.
- The person creating the metrics might use the amount of ending inventory in the numerator, rather than the average inventory figure for the entire measurement period. If the ending inventory figure varies significantly from the average inventory figure, this can result in a sharp change in the measurement.
- A company may switch to contract manufacturing, where a supplier produces and holds goods on behalf of the company. Depending upon the arrangement, the company may have no inventory to report at all, which renders the DSI measurement useless.

Days Payables Outstanding

The accounts payable days formula measures the number of days that a company takes to pay its suppliers. If the number of days increases from one period to the next, this indicates that the company is paying its suppliers more slowly. A change in the number of payable days can also indicate altered payment terms with suppliers, though this rarely has more than a slight impact on the total number of days. If a company is paying its suppliers very quickly, it may mean that the suppliers are demanding short payment terms.

To calculate days payables outstanding, summarize all purchases from suppliers during the measurement period, and divide by the average amount of accounts payable during that period. The formula is:

$$\frac{\text{Total supplier purchases}}{(\text{Beginning accounts payable} + \text{Ending accounts payable}) \div 2}$$

This formula reveals the total accounts payable turnover. Then divide the resulting turnover figure into 365 days to arrive at the number of accounts payable days.

The formula can be modified to exclude cash payments to suppliers, since the numerator should include only purchases on credit from suppliers. However, the amount of up-front cash payments to suppliers is normally so small that this modification is not necessary.

As an example, a treasurer wants to determine his company's accounts payable days for the past year. In the beginning of this period, the beginning accounts payable balance was $800,000, and the ending balance was $884,000. Purchases for the last 12 months were $7,500,000. Based on this information, the treasurer calculates the accounts payable turnover as:

$$\frac{\$7,500,000 \text{ Purchases}}{(\$800,000 \text{ Beginning payables} + \$884,000 \text{ Ending payables}) \div 2}$$

$$= \$7,500,000 \text{ Purchases} \div \$842,000 \text{ Average accounts payable}$$

$$= 8.9 \text{ Accounts payable turnover}$$

Thus, the company's accounts payable is turning over at a rate of 8.9 times per year. To calculate the turnover in days, the treasurer divides the 8.9 turns into 365 days, which yields:

$$365 \text{ Days} \div 8.9 \text{ Turns} = 41 \text{ Days}$$

Companies sometimes measure accounts payable days by only using the cost of goods sold in the numerator. This is incorrect, since there may be a large amount of administrative expenses that should also be included. If a company only uses the cost of goods sold in the numerator, this creates an excessively small number of payable days.

Actual Cash Position versus Forecast

A cash forecast should be as accurate as possible. If there are any variations in actual cash flows from forecasted results, they should be investigated and the findings used to improve the forecasting model.

An excellent way to monitor cash forecast accuracy is to routinely compare the company's actual cash position, prior to financing activities, to the forecasted amount. The main point of this metric should be to note the size of the difference from the expected result. An unusually large variance, whether positive or negative, should be grounds for a review. Thus, the calculation should be on an absolute basis, rather than showing a negative or positive variance.

For example, a treasurer compares actual to forecasted results for the last six weeks, and obtains the following information:

Week	Actual Ending Cash	Forecasted Ending Cash	Variance	Absolute Variance	Percent Variance
1	$1,237,000	$952,000	-$285,000	$285,000	23%
2	1,080,000	1,274,000	194,000	194,000	18%
3	1,591,000	1,846,000	255,000	255,000	16%
4	826,000	727,000	-99,000	99,000	12%
5	739,000	658,000	-81,000	81,000	11%
6	2,803,000	3,083,000	280,000	280,000	10%

The actual versus forecast information in the table reveals that the treasury staff is rapidly improving its ability to accurately forecast cash flows.

Earnings on Invested Funds

In most situations, the treasurer does not want funds to be invested in high-yield securities, since there is usually a matching level of risk. Nonetheless, there may be cases where management is willing to put some cash at risk in an equity investment, which can generate equity gains or losses. Consequently, the following formula for earnings on invested funds includes market value changes:

$$\frac{\text{Interest income} + \text{Market value changes}}{\text{Average funds invested}}$$

Note that the calculation uses average funds invested, not the amount of cash invested as of the end of a reporting period. The amount of cash invested can change substantially by day, so the average investment figure in the denominator should be based on an average of the invested balance in every business day of a reporting period.

For example, a treasurer is authorized to invest in both short-term debt instruments and stocks. As a result, the business earns $45,000 in interest income and $15,000 from an increase in the market value of its equity holdings. During the measurement period, the company had average investments of $3,000,000. The company's earnings on invested funds is calculated as:

$$\frac{\$45,000 \text{ Interest income} + \$15,000 \text{ Market value changes}}{\$3,000,000 \text{ Average funds invested}}$$

$$= 2.0\% \text{ Earnings on invested funds}$$

In many organizations, a much higher premium is placed on risk avoidance than on investment earnings, so it is fairly common to downplay this metric. If it is used, the board of directors should confine the treasury department to specific types of conservative investment choices, so there is no temptation to earn outsized returns by making risky investments.

Ability to Pay Measurements

When estimating the correct amount of debt burden to maintain, it is useful to measure the ability of a business to pay its fixed costs, which include interest expenses. The following four measurements can be employed, beginning with the narrowly-focused interest coverage ratio, and then expanding the focus of the measurement in the debt service coverage ratio to include principal, and to other fixed costs in the fixed charge coverage ratio. Also, the cash coverage ratio looks at the ability to pay from the perspective of available cash, rather than earnings as reported under the accrual basis of accounting.

Interest Coverage Ratio

The interest coverage ratio measures the ability of a company to pay the interest on its outstanding debt. A high interest coverage ratio indicates that a business can pay for its interest expense several times over, while a low ratio is a strong indicator that an organization may default on its loan payments.

It is useful to track the interest coverage ratio on a trend line, in order to spot situations where a company's results or debt burden are yielding a downward trend in the ratio. An investor would want to sell the equity holdings in a company showing such a downward trend, especially if the ratio drops below 1.5:1, since this indicates a likely problem with meeting debt obligations.

To calculate the interest coverage ratio, divide earnings before interest and taxes (EBIT) by the interest expense for the measurement period. The formula is:

$$\frac{\text{Earnings before interest and taxes}}{\text{Interest expense}}$$

EXAMPLE

Carpenter Holdings generates $5,000,000 of earnings before interest and taxes in its most recent reporting period. Its interest expense in that period is $2,500,000. Therefore, the company's interest coverage ratio is calculated as:

$$\frac{\$5,000,000 \text{ EBIT}}{\$2,500,000 \text{ Interest expense}}$$

$$= 2\text{:}1 \text{ Interest coverage ratio}$$

The ratio indicates that Carpenter's earnings should be sufficient to enable it to pay the interest expense.

A company may be accruing an interest expense that is not actually due for payment yet, so the ratio can indicate a debt default that will not really occur, or at least until such time as the interest is due for payment.

Debt Service Coverage Ratio

The debt service coverage ratio measures the ability of a revenue-producing property to generate sufficient cash to pay for the cost of all related mortgage payments. A positive debt service ratio indicates that a property's cash outflows can cover all offsetting loan payments, whereas a negative ratio indicates that the owner must contribute additional funds to pay for the annual loan payments. A very high debt service coverage ratio gives the property owner a substantial cushion to pay for unexpected or unplanned expenditures related to the property, or if market conditions result in a significant decline in future rental rates.

To calculate the ratio, divide the net annual operating income of the property by all annual loan payments for the same property, net of any tax savings generated by the interest expense. The formula is:

$$\frac{\text{Net annual operating income}}{\text{Total of annual loan payments net of tax effect}}$$

There may be no tax effect associated with debt, if a company has no taxable income. Otherwise, the tax effect is based on the income tax rate expected for the year.

EXAMPLE

A rental property generates $400,000 of cash flow per year, and the total annual loan payments of the property are $360,000. This yields a debt service ratio of 1.11, meaning that the property generates 11% more cash than the property owner needs to pay for the annual loan payments.

A negative debt service coverage ratio may result when a property is transitioning to new tenants, so that it is generating sufficient cash by the end of the measurement period, but was not doing so during the beginning or middle of the measurement period. Thus, the metric can yield inaccurate results during transition periods.

Fixed Charge Coverage Ratio

A business may incur so many fixed costs that its cash flow is mostly consumed by payments for these costs. The problem is particularly common when a company has incurred a large amount of debt, and must make ongoing interest payments. In this situation, use the fixed charge coverage ratio to determine the extent of the problem. If the resulting ratio is low, it is a strong indicator that any subsequent drop in the profits of a business may bring about its failure.

To calculate the fixed charge coverage ratio, combine earnings before interest and taxes with any lease expense, and then divide by the combined total of interest expense and lease expense. This ratio is intended to show estimated future results, so it is acceptable to drop from the calculation any expenses that are about to expire. The formula is:

$$\frac{\text{Earnings before interest and taxes} + \text{Lease expense}}{\text{Interest expense} + \text{Lease expense}}$$

EXAMPLE

Luminescence Corporation recorded earnings before interest and taxes of $800,000 in the preceding year. The company also recorded $200,000 of lease expense and $50,000 of interest expense. Based on this information, its fixed charge coverage is:

$$\frac{\$800,000 \text{ EBIT} + \$200,000 \text{ Lease expense}}{\$50,000 \text{ Interest expense} + \$200,000 \text{ Lease expense}}$$

$$= 4{:}1 \text{ Fixed charge coverage ratio}$$

Cash Coverage Ratio

The cash coverage ratio is useful for determining the amount of cash available to pay for interest, and is expressed as a ratio of the cash available to the amount of interest to be paid. This is a useful ratio when the entity evaluating a company is a prospective lender. The ratio should be substantially greater than 1:1. To calculate this ratio, take the earnings before interest and taxes (EBIT) from the income statement, add back to it all non-cash expenses included in EBIT (such as depreciation and amortization), and divide by the interest expense. The formula is:

$$\frac{\text{Earnings before interest and taxes} + \text{Non-cash expenses}}{\text{Interest expense}}$$

There may be a number of additional non-cash items to subtract in the numerator of the formula. For example, there may have been substantial charges in a period to increase reserves for sales allowances, product returns, bad debts, or inventory obsolescence. If these non-cash items are substantial, be sure to include them in the calculation. Also, the interest expense in the denominator should only include the actual interest expense to be paid – if there is a premium or discount to the amount being paid, it is not a cash payment, and so should not be included in the denominator.

EXAMPLE

The treasurer of Currency Bank is concerned that a borrower has recently taken on a great deal of debt to pay for a leveraged buyout, and wants to ensure that there is sufficient cash to pay for its new interest burden. The borrower is generating earnings before interest and taxes of $1,200,000 and it records annual depreciation of $800,000. The borrower is scheduled to pay $1,500,000 in interest expenses in the coming year. Based on this information, the borrower has the following cash coverage ratio:

$$\frac{\$1,200,000 \text{ EBIT} + \$800,000 \text{ Depreciation}}{\$1,500,000 \text{ Interest expense}}$$

$$= 1.33 \text{ Cash coverage ratio}$$

The calculation reveals that the borrower can pay for its interest expense, but has very little cash left for any other payments.

Debt to Equity Ratio

The debt to equity ratio of a business is closely monitored by the lenders and creditors of the company, since it can provide early warning that an organization is so overwhelmed by debt that it is unable to meet its payment obligations. This may also be triggered by a funding issue. For example, the owners of a business may not want to contribute any more cash to the company, so they acquire more debt to address the cash shortfall. Or, a company may use debt to buy back shares, thereby increasing the return on investment to the remaining shareholders.

Whatever the reason for debt usage, the outcome can be catastrophic, if corporate cash flows are not sufficient to make ongoing debt payments. This is a concern to lenders, whose loans may not be paid back. Suppliers are also concerned about the ratio for the same reason. A lender can protect its interests by imposing collateral requirements or restrictive covenants; suppliers usually offer credit with less restrictive terms, and so can suffer more if a company is unable to meet its payment obligations to them.

To calculate the debt to equity ratio, simply divide total debt by total equity. In this calculation, the debt figure should also include all lease obligations. The formula is:

$$\frac{\text{Long-term debt} + \text{Short-term debt} + \text{Leases}}{\text{Equity}}$$

EXAMPLE

An analyst is reviewing the credit application of New Centurion Corporation. The company reports a $500,000 line of credit, $1,700,000 in long-term debt, and a $200,000 operating lease. The company has $800,000 of equity. Based on this information, New Centurion's debt to equity ratio is:

$$\frac{\$500,000 \text{ Line of credit} + \$1,700,000 \text{ Debt} + \$200,000 \text{ Lease}}{\$800,000 \text{ Equity}}$$

$$= 3{:}1 \text{ Debt to equity ratio}$$

The debt to equity ratio exceeds the 2:1 ratio threshold above which the analyst is not allowed to grant credit. Consequently, New Centurion is kept on cash in advance payment terms.

Average Cost of Debt

A company that uses a large amount of debt financing may not be aware of the average cost of the debt load that it has incurred. If so, consider deriving the average cost of debt, which could lead to an investigation of the more expensive tranches of debt, and possibly their payoff or refinancing with less-expensive types of debt.

The calculation of the average cost of debt should encompass all types of debt, which includes the costs of bonds, bank loans, and capital leases. The calculation is:

$$\frac{\text{Annual cost of interest on loans, bonds, and capital leases}}{\text{Average amount of bonds, loans, and leases outstanding}}$$

It may be easier to calculate the average cost of debt on a monthly basis, rather than an annual basis, if the amount of debt varies considerably over the one-year measurement period.

There are several issues with the collection of information for the average cost of debt, which are:

- *Lease rate*. It can be difficult to determine the interest rate contained within a lease. If the amount of a lease is quite small, its inclusion in the average cost of debt may be immaterial, and so it can be excluded. Otherwise, contact the lessor to obtain the rate.
- *Bond rate*. The effective interest rate should be used as the interest rate for a bond, rather than the stated interest rate. When a bond is sold for an amount other than its face amount, this means the associated interest rate varies from the stated interest rate. For example, if a company sells a bond for $95,000 that has a face amount of $100,000 and which pays interest of $5,000, then the effective interest rate being paid is $5,000 ÷ $95,000, or 5.26%. Thus, if a company sells a bond at a discount from its face value, the effective inter-

est rate is *higher* than the stated interest rate. If the company sells a bond at a premium from its face value, the effective interest rate is *lower* than the stated interest rate.

- *Other expenses.* There may be several additional expenses associated with debt, such as an annual audit required by the lender, and an annual loan maintenance fee. If these expenses would not be incurred in the absence of the debt, include them in the interest cost of the debt.

The interest rate paid does not reveal a complete picture of the borrowing instruments employed by a business. There may be restrictive covenants or conversion clauses built into these instruments that are of more importance than the interest rates being paid. For example, a covenant not to pay dividends could be of concern to a family-held business, while a conversion clause could allow debt holders to convert their debt to equity at extremely favorable rates.

EXAMPLE

Puller Corporation, maker of plastic and wooden doorknobs, has acquired a large amount of debt while acquiring competitors that make other door fittings. The treasurer is concerned about the cost of this debt, and asks for a derivation of the average cost. The resulting report contains the following information:

	Annual Interest Cost	Principal Outstanding	Interest Rate	Other Features
Factory lease	$280,000	$2,300,000	12.1%	No early payment clause
Senior bank loan	1,200,000	15,000,000	8.0%	Balloon due in 24 months
Junior bank loan	975,000	6,500,000	15.0%	Risk of acceleration
Bonds	1,680,000	24,000,000	7.0%	Convertible into common stock
	$4,135,000	$47,800,000		

Based on the table, Puller's average cost of debt is:

$$\frac{\$4,135,000 \text{ Annual interest cost}}{\$47,800,000 \text{ Principal outstanding}}$$

$$= 8.65\%$$

Overall, the interest rate being paid by Puller is acceptable. However, the interest rate on the junior bank loan is quite high, since the lender is unlikely to have access to the company's assets in the event of a default. There are also covenants associated with this loan that Puller could breach, resulting in loan acceleration. Consequently, the junior bank loan is clearly the loan to be paid off or refinanced, if the opportunity to do so is available.

Borrowing Base Usage

If a company does not have large cash reserves, it must rely upon a line of credit to provide it with sufficient cash to keep the company operational. Lenders almost always insist upon using a company's accounts receivable and inventory as the collateral basis (or *borrowing base*) for a line of credit. The amount loaned to a company under a line of credit agreement cannot exceed the borrowing base. Consequently, a critical financing metric to follow is borrowing base usage. This is the amount of debt that has been loaned against the collateral provided by a company.

EXAMPLE

A business has $1,000,000 of accounts receivable and $600,000 of inventory on hand. Its lender will allow a line of credit that is based on 75% of all accounts receivable less than 90 days old, and 50% of inventory. $20,000 of the accounts receivable are more than 90 days old. This means that the applicable borrowing base for the company is:

Applicable Assets		Discount Rate		Allowable Borrowing Base
Accounts receivable of $980,000	×	75%	=	$735,000
Inventory of $600,000	×	50%	=	300,000
		Total	=	$1,035,000

The unused amount of the borrowing base is crucial, since it must be compared to any cash shortfalls projected in the cash forecast to see if a business has sufficient available and unused debt to offset negative cash positions.

Borrowing base usage requires continual analysis, since the amount of receivables and inventory to be used as collateral is constantly changing. This is a particular concern in seasonal businesses, since they tend to build inventory levels prior to the sales season, followed by a build in accounts receivable levels during the sales season, followed by a quiet period when assets are liquidated and debts are paid off. The continual changes in debt needs and asset levels make borrowing base usage perhaps the most important metric for the treasurer of a seasonal business.

Additional Treasury Measurements

Thus far, we have provided descriptions of those measurements that are most likely to be of value to the treasurer. There are additional measurements that could be of use, depending on the particular circumstances in which a treasurer is working. These additional suggested items are as follows:

- Average available balance
- Average number of bank accounts per operating unit

- Hedge ineffectiveness
- Ratio of electronic to check payments
- Ratio of electronic to check receipts
- Total operational cost per bank account
- Trapped cash by operating unit, region, or country

Summary

Many of the metrics noted in this chapter yield information that can be difficult to act upon, or which will result in changes only over a long period of time. In many cases, the treasurer's range of authority does not permit a direct role in altering the outcome of a measurement. Of more immediate use is borrowing base usage, since management must understand exactly how much cash is still available to be borrowed under a line of credit arrangement. An entity that has substantial debt obligations should also monitor the debt service coverage ratio, to see if there will be an issue with loan repayment. If so, the treasurer should pay particular attention to the maturity dates of loans and the status of projected cash flows, to see if the business can indeed repay its liabilities. If not, it will be necessary to roll over loans as far in advance as possible.

Glossary

A

Accounts payable. The obligations of a buyer to pay its suppliers for goods or services which the buyer acquired from them on credit terms.

Accounts receivable. Amounts due from customers who have purchased goods or services from the seller on credit terms.

Accredited investor. A high net worth entity or individual; this investor is allowed to acquire shares under a Regulation D stock offering.

B

Bad debt. An account receivable that cannot be collected.

Base currency. The first currency stated in a foreign exchange quote. This is the home currency used by a business seeking a foreign exchange quote.

Benchmark hedge ratio. The proportion of currency holdings that will be hedged.

Bid price. The price at which a foreign currency dealer agrees to buy a currency.

Borrowing base. The total amount of collateral against which a lender will lend funds to a business.

C

Call option. An agreement giving the buyer the right to buy an investment instrument at a certain price and within a certain time period.

Cash conversion cycle. The time period from when cash is expended for the production of goods, until cash is received from customers in payment of those goods.

Cash flow hedge. A transaction entered into with the intent of offsetting the variability of cash flows.

Cash sweeping. The practice of automatically transferring cash at the end of each business day from an account into an investment option that earns interest income.

Check. A written order by a payer to its bank, stating a sum to be paid to the payee named on the order.

Claims-made policy. An insurance policy that provides coverage for claims made during a specific date range.

Co-insurance. A penalty imposed on an insured party if it under-insures the value of property.

Collateral. An asset that a borrower or guarantor has pledged as security for a loan.

Counterparty. The other party that engages in a financial transaction. For example, if a company sells an asset, there is a counterparty that is buying the asset.

Covenants. Conditions related to company operations and practices that are imposed by lenders.

Credit application. A standard form sent to customers, on which they enter information needed by a company's credit department to determine the amount of credit to grant customers.

Credit insurance. A guarantee by a third party against non-payment of an invoice by a customer.

Credit limit. The maximum amount of credit extended to a customer.

Currency pair. A statement of the amount of a quote currency required to purchase one unit of base currency. Foreign exchange pricing is always stated in terms of currency pairs.

D

Death spiral PIPE. A private investment in public equity where continuing declines in the stock price obligate the issuer to issue more shares to PIPE investors, possibly resulting in a change in control of the issuer.

Debt security. A security that involves a creditor relationship with a borrower, such as bonds, commercial paper, and Treasury securities.

Deductible. An initial loss amount that must be absorbed by the insured party.

Dilution. A reduction in the value of shares, caused by an increase in the number of shares outstanding.

E

Earnings credit. The interest paid on the funds in a bank account, to be used to offset account fees.

Effective interest rate. The actual interest rate earned on an investment, which incorporates any discount or premium paid on the investment.

Endorsement. An attachment to a contract that either adds or restricts coverage.

Expiry date. The expiration date of a contract.

F

Fair value hedge. A transaction entered into with the intent of offsetting changes in the fair value of an asset or liability.

Factor. A financing entity that purchases receivables from other parties.

Float. The time period during which funds are in transition between the various stages in the payment process.

Functional currency. The currency that an entity uses in the majority of its business transactions.

H

Hedge. An investment intended to offset adverse price movements in an asset.

Hedge effectiveness. The extent to which a transaction designated as a hedge offsets changes in a previously identified fair value or cash flow.

Hedging. Actions taken to reduce the volatility of cash flows, earnings, and/or the value of investments.

Held-to-maturity security. A security having a fixed maturity, for which the holding entity has both the ability and the intention to hold it to maturity.

I

Indemnity. A payment by an insurer for the monetary value of a loss.

Insurance. A contractual arrangement in which an organization pays an insurance carrier in exchange for the assumption of risk by the carrier.

Inventory. Tangible items held for routine sale, or which are being produced for sale, or which are consumed in the production of goods for sale.

L

Laddering. The strategy of investing in a set of securities having different maturities.

Letter of credit. A guarantee by a bank that a payment will be made to a supplier on behalf of the bank's client.

Limit of insurance. The maximum amount that an insurer will pay.

Line of credit. A commitment from a lender to pay a company whenever it needs cash, up to a pre-set maximum level.

Liquidity. The ability of an entity to pay its liabilities in a timely manner.

London Interbank Offered Rate (LIBOR). An interest rate at which banks borrow funds from each other in the London interbank market. LIBOR is based on the deposit rate for loans between the most financially-secure banks.

Loss. An unexpected and unintentional drop in the value received by an entity that is caused by an occurrence that causes damage or injury.

N

Notional amount. The face amount used to calculate payments on a financial instrument, such as an option or interest rate swap.

Notional pooling. A mechanism for calculating interest on the combined balances of bank accounts that a corporate parent chooses to cluster together, without actually transferring any funds into a central investment account.

O

Operational hedge. The alignment of sales and purchases within a country to avoid foreign currency transactions.

P

PIPE. A private investment in public equity, where investors purchase restricted stock that is intended to be registered with the SEC.

Put option. An agreement giving the buyer the right to sell an investment instrument at a certain price and within a certain time period.

Q

Quote currency. The second currency stated in a foreign exchange quote. This is the currency being purchased.

R

Receipts and disbursements method. The use of specific cash expenditure and receipt information to derive a cash forecast.

Reference rate. An interest rate used as the basis for an interest rate swap, floating rate security, or forward rate agreement.

Risk. Uncertainty regarding a future outcome.

S

Seasoned equity offering. An issuance of securities where the securities have been previously issued.

Self-insurance. When claims are paid by the entity experiencing losses.

Settlement risk. The risk that the counterparty to a transaction will not pay.

Shelf registration. The registration of stock up to three years before sale of the stock.

Software as a service. A system where software and related data are hosted by the vendor, and accessed on-line by clients.

Spot price. The price at which a currency can currently be purchased.

Strike price. The price at which an option or other similar contract can be exercised.

Supply chain financing. Interposing a lender between a company and its suppliers, with the lender offering to pay suppliers early in exchange for a discount.

T

Target balance. A designated minimum amount of cash to keep on hand, to meet short-term cash requirements.

Trading security. A security that an entity intends to sell in the short term for a profit, which it expects will be generated by changes in the price of the security.

Transaction exposure. The risk of loss from a change in exchange rates during the course of a business transaction.

Translation exposure. The risk of a reported change in value of a company's assets and liabilities, if they are denominated in a foreign currency.

Treasury management system. A computer system that manages cash, investments, and debt tracking, while also providing some risk analysis functionality.

U

Unregistered stock. Shares in a company that cannot be traded without first being registered with the SEC or qualifying under an exemption.

W

Wire transfer. The direct transfer of funds from the payer's account at one bank to the payee's account at another bank.

Working capital. The amount of an entity's current assets minus its current liabilities.

Y

Yield curve. A line that plots the interest rates associated with an investment having different durations. A normal yield curve reveals a gradual increase in interest rates as maturity dates increase. An inverted yield curve reveals declining interest rates as maturity dates increase.

Z

Zero balance account. A bank account in which a zero balance is automatically maintained by only transferring sufficient funds into it to cover presented checks, and to transfer out funds that are not immediately needed.

Index

Made in the USA
Coppell, TX
24 September 2020